# FROMMER'S

## COMPREHENSIVE TRAVEL GUIDE

# BERMUDA '94 -'95

by Darwin Porter
Assisted by Danforth Prince

PRENTICE HALL TRAVEL

NEW YORK • LONDON • TORONTO • SYDNEY • TOKYO • SINGAPORE

**FROMMER BOOKS**

Published by Prentice Hall General Reference
A division of Simon & Schuster Inc.
15 Columbus Circle
New York, NY 10023

ISBN 0-671-79768-9
ISSN 1069-3572

Design by Robert Bull Design
Maps by Ortelius Design

**FROMMER'S EDITORIAL STAFF**
Editorial Director: Marilyn Wood
Editorial Manager/Senior Editor: Alice Fellows
Senior Editor: Lisa Renaud
Editors: Charlotte Allstrom, Thomas F. Hirsch, Peter Katucki, Sara Hinsey Raveret,
    Theodore Stavrou
Assistant Editors: Margaret Bowen, Christopher Hollander, Ian Wilker
Editorial Assistants: Gretchen Henderson, Bethany Jewett
Managing Editor: Leanne Coupe

**Special Sales**
Bulk purchases (10+ copies) of Frommer's Travel Guides are available to corporations at
special discounts. The Special Sales Department can produce custom editions to be used as
premiums and/or for sales promotion to suit individual needs. Existing editions can be
produced with custom cover imprints such as a corporate logo. For more information write
to: Special Sales, Prentice Hall Travel, 15 Columbus Circle, New York, New York 10023.

Manufactured in the United States of America

# CONTENTS

# LIST OF MAPS

## INVITATION TO THE READER

In researching this book, I have come across many fine establishments, the best of which I have included here. I am sure that you will also come across recommendable hotels, inns, restaurants, guesthouses, shops, and attractions. Please don't keep them to yourself. Share your experiences, especially if you want to comment on places that you found to have changed for the worse. You can address your letters to:

Darwin Porter
*Frommer's Bermuda '94-'95*
c/o Prentice Hall Travel
15 Columbus Circle
New York, NY 10023

## DISCLAIMERS

## SAFETY ADVISORY

Whenever you're traveling in an unfamiliar city or country, stay alert. Be aware of your immediate surroundings. Wear a moneybelt and keep a close eye on your possessions. Be particularly careful with cameras, purses, and wallets, all favorite targets of thieves and pickpockets.

# CHAPTER 1

# GETTING TO KNOW BERMUDA

Only about two hours from the southeastern coastline of the United States, another, quite different world comes into view as you approach it from the air. It is a world of breathtaking natural beauty, with lush green hills, crystalline blue waters, and pink-hued sandy beaches. It is also a world of striking incongruities, where the modern coexists in strange harmony with the traditional and even the antiquated. That world is the British crown colony of Bermuda, an island in the Atlantic Ocean about 570 miles ESE of Cape Hatteras, N.C.

In Hamilton, the capital, you'll see colorful horse-drawn carriages ambling through quiet, tree-lined streets, indifferent to the sleek foreign cars that pass by. You'll see "bobbies" and businessmen walking around in shorts and knee-high socks—normal attire in this semitropical island where the annual average temperature is 70°F. You'll even see judges still wearing their customary powdered wigs as they head to Sessions House (the Parliament Building), where the Supreme Court meets.

Such a happy blend of contrasts—evident also in the island's architecture, music, and cuisine—gives Bermuda its particular character and makes it a truly exciting place to visit. With its large luxury hotels, fashionable shops, and lively evening entertainment—as well as its fine beaches and picturesque sites—Bermuda is one of the world's most sophisticated and popular resorts.

# 1. GEOGRAPHY

## THE ARCHIPELAGO

"Bermuda" is actually a group of some 300 islands, islets, and coral rocks, clustered in a fishhook-shaped chain about 22 miles long and 2 miles wide at the broadest point.

# WHAT'S SPECIAL ABOUT BERMUDA

## Beaches

☐ Elbow Beach, Paget, which some say made Bermuda a vacation legend—it's tops for fun in the sun.

☐ Horseshoe Bay, Southampton, one-quarter mile of pink sands—this is the beach that often appears in those Sunday travel supplements.

☐ Warwick Long Bay, the pinkest of the pink sandy beaches, and also the sun strip containing the longest stretch of sands.

## Great Towns/Villages

☐ Hamilton, the colony's capital, in pretty pastels and whites and the center for shopping.

☐ St. George's, Bermuda's first capital, founded in 1612—a town filled with intriguing old sights.

## Ace Attractions

☐ Ireland Island, a cruise-ship dock and tourist village, site of the Royal Naval Dockyard and the Bermuda Maritime Museum.

☐ Bermuda Railway Trail, stretching along the old train right-of-way for 21 miles and crossing three islands that make up the Bermuda archipelago.

## Historic Buildings

☐ Fort St. Catherine, at St. George's—now a museum, it towers over the beach where the shipwrecked *Sea Venture* crew first landed in 1609.

☐ Verdmont, Smith's Parish, an 18th-century mansion built on land once owned by the founder of South Carolina.

☐ Fort Hamilton, a massive Victorian fortification overlooking the city of Hamilton and its harbor.

## Natural Spectacles

☐ Crystal Caves, Bailey's Bay, translucent formations of stalagmites and stalactites, including a crystal-clear lake.

☐ Leamington Caves, also at Bailey's Bay, with a grotto with crystal formations and underground lakes—first discovered in 1908.

## Events and Festivals

☐ Bermuda Festival, a six-week winter International Festival of the Performing Arts—drama, dance, jazz, classical and popular music, and a lot more.

☐ Bermuda College Weeks during the spring break, a ritual that draws some 10,000 students from the United States.

---

Together, they're known as the Bermudas and form a landmass of about 21 square miles. Only 20 or so of the islands are inhabited. The largest one, called the "mainland," is Great Bermuda; about 14 miles long, it's linked to the other major islands near it by a series of bridges and causeways. The capital of this archipelago, Hamilton, is situated on the mainland.

Bermuda lies far north of the Tropic of Cancer, which cuts through the Bahamian archipelago—about 775 miles SE of New York City, some 1,030 miles NE of Miami, and nearly 3,450 miles away from London. It has a pleasant climate year-round, with sunshine prevailing almost every day. The chief source of Bermuda's mild weather is the Gulf Stream, a broad belt of warm water formed by equatorial currents, whose northern reaches separate the Bermuda islands from North America and, with the prevailing northeast winds, temper the wintry blasts that sweep across the Atlantic from west and north.

Until the mid-17th century or so, the Bermudas were known to seafarers as the "Isles of Devils." They probably had contributed to the popular pre-Columbian belief that ships sailing too far west from Europe fell over the edge of the earth into a monster-filled pit. Many ships sailing too close to these remote and uninhabited islands came to grief on the treacherous reefs close to the surface of the turquoise Atlantic. Even Shakespeare was familiar with the reputation of the Isles of Devils, making "the still-vex't Bermoothes" the setting for *The Tempest*.

○ **"Bermuda" consists of some 300 islands, islets, and coral rocks.**

Bermuda is based on the upper parts of an extinct volcano, which may date back 100 million years. Through the millennia, wind and water have brought limestone deposits and formed the islands far from any continental landmass—the closest is Cape Hatteras.

The first recorded discovery of the islands was made by the Spanish in the early 1500s (see "History and Politics" below). The uncharted islands were a navigational menace to ships that followed the trade routes of the Atlantic, as Spanish vessels did on voyages from the New World. Bermuda's location is at a point where galleons from New Spain could easily run into trouble in stormy weather, and the eroded wreckage of many ships, scattered on the ocean floor amid reefs and shoals, bears mute testimony to such tragedies.

Combined, the islands form a landmass of some 20½ square miles. Great Bermuda, often called the mainland, is the largest island, about 14 miles long, and contains the capital city of Hamilton. The other islands bear such names as Somerset, Watford, Boaz, and Ireland in the west, and St. George's and St. David's in the east.

This chain of islands encloses the archipelago's major bodies of water, which include Castle Harbour, St. George's Harbour, Harrington Sound, and Great Sound. Most of the other, smaller islands, or islets, lie within these bodies of water.

## DIVISION INTO PARISHES

The islands of Bermuda are divided, for administrative purposes, into several parishes. They are:

**SANDYS PARISH** In the far-western part of the archipelago, Sandys Parish is centered around Somerset Village. This parish (pronounced Sands) takes in the islands of Ireland, Boaz, and Somerset and is named for Sir Edwin Sandys, a major shareholder of the 1610 Bermuda Company. Somerset Long Bay is the biggest and best public beach in Bermuda's west end.

## IMPRESSIONS

*You go to heaven if you want to—I'd rather stay here in Bermuda.*
—MARK TWAIN, IN LETTER TO ELIZABETH WALLACE, 1910

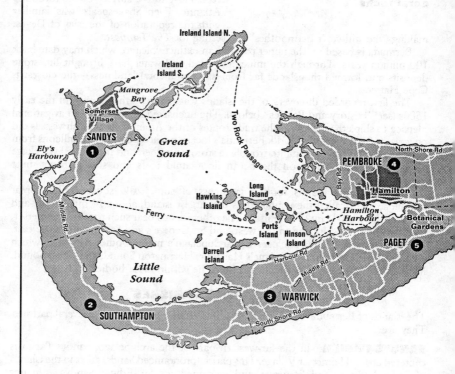

# BERMUDA

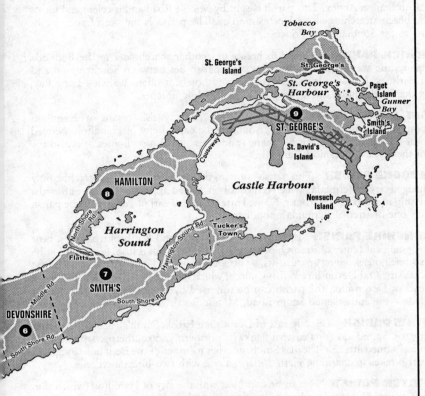

*Atlantic Ocean*

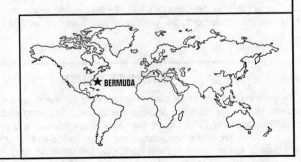

★ BERMUDA

**SOUTHAMPTON PARISH**   Going east, Southampton Parish (named for the third earl of Southampton) stretches from Riddells Bay to Tucker's Island, site of the U.S. Naval Air Station Annex. This parish is split by Middle Road and is celebrated for its public beach stretching along Horseshoe Bay. The parish is the site of such major resorts as the Southampton Princess.

**WARWICK PARISH**   Named in honor of another shareholder in the Bermuda Company, the second earl of Warwick, this parish lies between Southampton and Paget parishes. Known for its golf courses and hotels, it offers Warwick Long Bay, along the South Shore, one of Bermuda's best public beaches.

**PAGET PARISH**   East of Warwick Parish, Paget Parish begins at Hamilton Harbour in the east and lies directly south of the capital city of Hamilton. Named after the fourth Lord Paget, it has many residences and historic homes. It is also the site of the 36-acre Botanical Gardens.

**PEMBROKE PARISH**   This parish contains the capital city of Hamilton (the only full-fledged city in Bermuda), which is most often viewed as passengers arrive aboard a cruise ship in Hamilton Harbour. Named after the third earl of Pembroke, the parish shelters one-quarter of Bermuda's population.

**DEVONSHIRE PARISH**   Lying east of both Paget and Pembroke parishes, near the geographical center of the archipelago, Devonshire Parish is lush, green, and hilly. It has some housekeeping apartments, a cottage colony, and one of Bermuda's oldest churches, the Old Devonshire Parish Church, which dates from 1716. Named for the first earl of Devonshire, the parish can be traversed by three of the major roads of Bermuda—the aptly named South Road, Middle Road, and North Road.

**SMITH'S PARISH**   Directly east of Devonshire Parish, Smith's Parish opens onto Harrington Sound along its eastern flank. Its northern and southern coasts face the Atlantic. Named after Sir Thomas Smith, another member of the Bermuda Company, the parish takes in charming Flatts Village, along with two bird sanctuaries.

**HAMILTON PARISH**   Not to be confused with the city of Hamilton (which is in Pembroke Parish), Hamilton Parish lies directly north of Harrington Sound, opening onto the Atlantic. Named for the second marquis of Hamilton, the parish ropes itself around Harrington Sound, a saltwater lake stretching some six miles. On its eastern periphery, it opens onto Castle Harbour.

**ST. GEORGE'S PARISH**   In Bermuda's extreme eastern part, this historic parish is composed of several different islands, the largest of which are St. George's Island and St. David's Island. St. George's Island was the site of the *Sea Venture*'s wreck in 1609. Its major settlement, St. George's, was founded in 1612 and was once the

---

## IMPRESSIONS

*They be so terrible to all that ever touched on them, and such tempests, thunders, and other fearefull objects are seene and heard about them, that they be called commonly, the Devils Ilands, and are feared and avoyded of all sea travellers alive, above any other place in the world.*
—WILLIAM STRACHY, *A TRUE REPORTORY OF THE WRACKE AND REDEMPTION OF SIR THOMAS GATES* (1610), IN *PURCHAS HIS PILGRIMES* (1625)

capital of Bermuda. Filled with historic buildings, it contains St. Peter's Church, the oldest continuously used Protestant house of worship in the Western Hemisphere. The parish is flanked by Castle Harbour on the western and southern edges and bisected into two halves by St. George's Harbour. St. David's Island is linked to the rest of Bermuda by the Severn Bridge, which lies near the U.S. Naval Air Station and the country's international airport. The people who inhabit this most easterly part of Bermuda are longtime sailors and fishermen. St. George's Parish also includes Tucker's Town, founded in 1616 by Governor Daniel Tucker on the opposite shore of Castle Harbour.

# FLORA & FAUNA
## FLORA

Bermuda's temperate climate, frequent sunshine, and adequate moisture account for some of the most verdant gardens in the Atlantic. Coupled with its fertile soil are the effects of the Gulf Stream, which brings warm air currents to a climate that would otherwise be colder. Bermudian gardeners, in fact, pride themselves on the mixture of temperate-zone and subtropical plants that thrive on the island, despite the salty air.

Bermuda's once proud cedar forests succumbed to the effects of commercialization (many trees were felled for their copper-colored wood, used in boatbuilding) and a disastrous blight that struck in the late 1930s. The loss of the cedar forests is said to have removed valuable nesting sites for birds, as well as some of the island's most effective windbreaks.

Today, those native stands have been replaced on a large scale with casuarinas (Australian pines) and an array of deciduous and evergreen trees and shrubs (an estimated 500 species) imported from the far corners of the British Empire. Recent attempts at reforesting Bermuda with scale-resistant hybrids of the native cedar have proved moderately successful.

Even soils not noted for their clemency to plants manage to produce gratifying covers of foliage. Examples include the indigenous sea grape, which flourishes along the island's sandy coastlines, preferring sand and salt water to more arable soil, and the cassava plant, whose roots resemble the tubers of sweet potatoes. When ground into flour and soaked to remove a mild poison, these roots comprise the main ingredient for Bermuda's traditional Christmas pies. Also growing wild and abundant are prickly pears, aromatic fennel, yucca, and a spiked-leaf plant bearing, in season, a single white flower, known as a Spanish bayonet.

○ **Because of its mild climate and fertile soil, Bermuda supports a great variety of native and imported trees and plants.**

To the early colonial settlers Bermuda's only native palm, the palmetto, proved particularly useful. Its leaves were used to thatch colonial roofs. When crushed and fermented, the leaves provided a strong alcoholic drink called *bibby,* whose effects were condemned by the early Puritans. Its leaves were also fashioned into women's hats during a brief period in the 1600s, when they represented the height of fashion in London.

The banana, which flourishes today in Bermuda and constitutes one of its most dependable sources of fresh fruit, was introduced to the island in the early 1600s. Bermudian bananas, in fact, are said to have been the first ever brought back to London from the New World. They immediately created a sensation, leading to the cultivation of bananas in many other British colonies.

The plant that probably contributed most to the renown of Bermuda was the Bermuda onion (*Allium cepa*). Imported from England in 1616, and later grown from seed brought from the Spanish and Portuguese islands of Tenerife and Madeira, the Bermuda onion became so famous along the eastern coast of the United States that Bermudians themselves became known as "Onions." Sadly, however, during the 1930s Bermuda's flourishing export trade in onions declined because of high tariffs, increased competition from similar species grown in Texas, among other places, and the lack of arable land on the island.

Today, what you'll see decorating Bermuda's gently rolling landscapes are oleander, hibiscus, royal poinciana, poinsetta, bougainvillea, and dozens of other flowering shrubs and vines. Of the island's dozen or so species of morning glory, three are indigenous; they will quickly become rampant and overwhelm everything else in a garden.

Popular trees include pine, paw-paw (used in olden days for treating warts and fungal diseases of the skin), the indigenous olivewood bark, palm, casuarina, fiddlewood, the ubiquitous bay grape, and a luxuriant fruit tree known as loquat, which was introduced to the island by one of its governors in 1850. Indigenous flowers include the Bermudiana (sometimes known as the Bermuda iris), Darrell's fleabane (a member of the daisy family), and the maidenhair fern. Today, nearly all the important plants of the Bermudian islands are sheltered in the government's Botanical Gardens in Paget Parish.

## FAUNA

Because of the almost total lack of natural freshwater ponds and lakes, Bermuda's amphibians have adapted to seawater or to slightly brackish water. Amphibians include the tree frog (*Eleutherodactylus Johnstonei* and *Eleutherodactylus Gossei*), whose nighttime chirping is sometimes mistaken by newcomers for the song of birds. Small and camouflaged by the leafy matter of the forest floor, the tree frog may be spotted in the warm months between April and November.

More visible are Bermuda's giant toads, or road toads (*Bufo marinus*), which sometimes reach the size of an adult human's palm. Imported from Guyana in the 1870s in the hope of controlling the island's cockroach population, they search out the nighttime warmth of the asphalt roads, and are often crushed by cars in the process; they are especially prevalent after a soaking rain. The road toads are not venomous—and, contrary to legend, they do not cause warts.

Island reptiles include colonies of harmless lizards, often seen sunning themselves on rocks until the approach of humans or predators. The best-known species is the Bermuda rock lizard (*Eumeces longirostris*), also known as a skink, which is said to have been the only nonmarine, nonflying vertebrate in Bermuda before the arrival of European colonists. Imported reptiles include the Somerset lizard (*Anolis Roquet*), whose black-eye patches give it the look of a bashful bandit, and the Jamaican anole (*Anolis Grahami*), a form of color-changing chameleon.

Bermuda, partly because of its ample food sources, is home to abundant bird life, many species of which nest upon the island's terrain during annual migration patterns. Most of these birds arrive during the colder winter months, usually between Christmas and Eastertime. The island has recorded almost 40 different species of eastern warblers, which peacefully coexist alongside species of martin, doves, egrets, South American terns, herons, fork-tailed flycatchers, and even some species from as far away as the Arctic Circle. Two of the most visible imported species are the cardinal, probably introduced during the 1700s, and the kiskadee. Imported from Trinidad in 1957 to control lizards and flies, the kiskadee has instead wreaked havoc on the island's commercial fruit crops.

The once-abundant eastern bluebird has been greatly reduced in number since the depletion of the cedar trees, its preferred habitat. Another bird native to Bermuda is the gray and white petrel, known locally as a cahow, which lives for most of the year in burrows in the sands of the isolated eastern islands; the rest of the year it feeds at sea, floating for hours in the warm waters of the Gulf Stream. One of the most rarely sighted birds in the world, and once regarded as extinct, it is now protected by the Bermudian government.

Also native to Bermuda is the cliff-dwelling tropic bird, recognized by the elongated plumage of its white tail. Resembling a swallow, it is considered the island's harbinger of spring because of its annual appearance in March.

Although the gardens and golf courses of many of the country's hotels attract dozens of birds, some of the finest bird-watching sites are maintained either by the Bermuda Audubon Society or the National Trust. Isolated sites known for sheltering thousands of native and migrating birds include Paget Marsh, just south of Hamilton, the Walsingham Trust in Hamilton Parish, and Spittal Pond in Smith's Parish.

In the deep waters off the shores of Bermuda, photographers have recorded some of the finest game fish in the world, including blackfin tuna, marlin, swordfish, wahoo, dolphin, sailfish, and barracuda. Also prevalent are bonefish and pompano, both of which prefer sun-flooded shallow waters closer to shore. Any beachcomber is likely to come across hundreds of oval-shaped chitons (*Chiton tuberculatus*), a mollusk that adheres tenaciously to rocks within tidal flats (locally, this mollusk is known as "suck-rock").

○ **The single-celled marine animal foraminifer, with its perforated pink shell, accounts for Bermuda's miles of pale-pink beaches.**

Beware of the Portuguese man-o'-war (*Physalia physalis*), a floating colony of jellyfish whose stinging tentacles sometimes reach 50 feet in length. Washed up on Bermuda beaches, usually between March and July, it can sting even though it may appear dead. Give this dangerous and venomous marine creature a wide berth: severe stings may require hospitalization.

The most prevalent marine animal in Bermuda is responsible for the formation of the island's greatest tourist attraction, its miles of pale-pink sands. Much of the sand is composed of broken shells, pieces of coral, and the calcium carbonate remains of other marine invertebrates. The pinkest pieces are shards of crushed shell from a single-celled animal called foraminifer. Its vivid pink skeleton is pierced with holes, through which the animal extends its rootlike feet (pseudopodia), which cling to the underside of the island's reefs during the animal's brief life and are then washed ashore.

# 2. HISTORY & POLITICS

## HISTORY

### THE EARLY YEARS

The discovery of the Bermuda islands is attributed to the Spanish, probably the navigator Juan Bermúdez, sometime before 1511, for in that year a map was published in the *Legatio Babylonica* that included "La Bermuda" among

**DATELINE**

• c. 1511   Juan Bermúdez discovers Bermuda while sailing aboard the Spanish ship *La Garza*.

*(continues)*

## DATELINE

• **1609** The British ship *Sea Venture* is wrecked upon the reefs of Bermuda; all on board make it to shore safely and the settlement of Bermuda begins.

• **1612** The Virginia Company dispatches the *Plough* to Bermuda with 60 colonists on board. Richard Moore is appointed governor of Bermuda.

• **1620** The first Bermuda parliament session is held in St. Peter's Church, St. George's.

• **1684** The Bermuda Company's charter is taken over by the British crown. Sir Robert Robinson is appointed the crown's first governor of Bermuda.

• **1775** Gunpowder is stolen in St. George's and is shipped to the American colonies for use against the British.

• **1861** Bermuda becomes involved in the American Civil War when it runs supplies to the South to undermine the Union's blockade.

*(continues)*

the Atlantic islands. A little more than a century later, the British staked a claim and began colonization.

In 1609 the flagship of Admiral Sir George Somers, the *Sea Venture*, while en route to Jamestown, in Virginia, was wrecked on Bermuda's reefs. The dauntless crew built two pinnaces (small sailing ships) and headed on to the American colony, but three sailors hid out and remained on the island. They were the first settlers of Bermuda.

Just three years after the wreck of the *Sea Venture*, the Bermuda islands were included in the charter of the Virginia Company; 60 colonists were sent there from England, and St. George's Town was founded soon after.

Bermuda's status as a colony dates from 1620, when the first parliament sat (it is thus the oldest parliament in continuous existence in the British Empire, now Commonwealth). In 1684, Bermuda became a crown colony, under King Charles II. Sir Robert Robinson was appointed the crown's first governor.

Slavery became a part of life in Bermuda shortly after the official settlement. The majority of slaves were from Africa, but a few were Native Americans. Later, Scots imprisoned for fighting against Cromwell were transported to the islands, followed, in 1651, by Irish slaves. The lot of these bond servants, however, was not as cruel as that of plantation slaves in America and the West Indies. All slaves were freed by the British Emancipation Act of 1834.

## DEALINGS WITH AMERICA

Bermuda established close links with the American colonies. The islanders set up a thriving mercantile trade on the eastern seaboard, especially with Southern ports. The major commodity sold by Bermuda's merchant ships was salt from Turks Island.

During the American Revolution, trade with loyalist Bermuda was cut off by the rebellious colonies, despite the network of family connections and close friendships that bound them. The cutoff in trade proved a great hardship for the islanders, who, having chosen seafaring to farming, depended heavily on America for their supply of food. Many of them, now deprived of profitable trade routes, turned to privateering, piracy, and "wrecking" (salvaging goods from wrecked or foundered ships).

Britain's loss of its important American colonial ports led to a naval buildup in Bermuda. It was from there that ships and troops sailed in 1814 to burn Washington, D.C., and the White House.

Bermuda got a new lease on economic life during the American Civil War. The island was sympathetic to the Confederacy and, with approval of the British government, ran the blockade that the Union had placed on exports,

5

especially of cotton, by the Southern states. St. George's Harbour was a principal Atlantic base for the lucrative business of smuggling manufactured goods into Confederate ports and bringing out cotton and turpentine cargoes.

When the Confederacy fell, so did Bermuda's economy. Seeing no immediate source of money from the Atlantic, the islanders turned their attention to agriculture and found that the colony's fertile soil and salubrious climate produced excellent vegetables. Portuguese immigrants were brought in as farmers, and soon celery, potatoes, tomatoes, and especially onions were being shipped to the New York market (indeed, so brisk was the onion trade that Hamilton became known as "Onion Town").

During the Prohibition era, Bermudians again profited by developments in the United States as they engaged in the lucrative business of rum running. Although the distance from the islands to the mainland was too great to allow for quick crossings in small booze-laden boats, as could be done from the Bahamas and Cuba, Bermuda nevertheless accounted for a good part of the alcoholic beverages transported illegally to the United States before the repeal of Prohibition in 1933.

## WORLD WAR II ESPIONAGE

Bermuda played an important role in World War II. The story is dramatically told in *A Man Called Intrepid*, by William Stevenson, about the "secret war" with Nazi Germany.

Under the Hamilton Princess Hotel, a carefully trained staff worked to decode radio signals to and from German submarines and other vessels operating in the Atlantic, close to the United States and the islands offshore. Unknown to the Germans, the British early in the war had broken the Nazi code through use of a captured German coding machine called "Enigma." The British also intercepted and examined mail between Europe and the United States.

✪ **Bermuda was discovered by the Spanish sometime before 1511; the British landed a century later, in 1609.**

Bermuda served as a refueling stop for airplanes flying between the two continents. While pilots were being entertained at

## IMPRESSIONS

*Bermuda, despite her small size, her isolation and her position among evil reefs and evil Atlantic [hurricane] weather, was [once for imperial Britain] and is [now for superpower America] of considerable military importance.*
—SIMON WINCHESTER, *THE SUN NEVER SETS: TRAVELS TO THE REMAINING OUTPOSTS OF THE BRITISH EMPIRE* (1985)

the Yacht Club, the mail would be taken off the carriers and examined by experts. An innocent-appearing series of letters from Lisbon, for example, often had messages written in invisible ink. These letters were part of a vast German spy network. The British became skilled at opening sealed envelopes, examining their written contents, and then carefully resealing them.

These surreptitious letter readers were called "trappers." Many of them were young women without any previous experience in counterespionage work, yet some performed very well. As Stevenson writes, it was soon discovered that, "by some quirk in the law of averages, the girls who shone in this work had well-turned ankles." A medical officer involved with the project even reported it as "fairly certain that a girl with unshapely legs would make a bad trapper." So, amazingly, the word went out that women seeking recruitment as trappers would have to display their "gams," as the expression was then.

These women—and their colleagues, to be sure—in the course of their work discovered one of the methods by which the Germans were transmitting secret messages: They would shrink a whole page of regularly typed text down to the size of a tiny dot and then conceal the dot under an innocuously looking punctuation mark, such as a comma or period! The staff likened these messages with their secret-bearing dots to a plum duff, a popular English dessert. For these "punctuation dots [were] scattered through a letter like raisins in the suet puddings." The term "duff method" then came to be applied to the manner in which the Germans were sending military and other messages through the mail.

**✪ During World War II, Bermuda served as an Allied intelligence center in the Atlantic, tracking German spy activities.**

When the United States entered the war, it assigned agents of the Federal Bureau of Investigation to Bermuda. There, they joined the British in their intelligence operations.

## POSTWAR CHANGES

In 1953, British Prime Minister Winston Churchill chose Bermuda, which he had visited during the war, as the site for a conference with U.S. President Dwight D. Eisenhower and the premier of France. Several such high-level gatherings have followed in the decades since, the most recent, between British Prime Minister John Major and U.S. President George Bush, taking place in 1991.

Bermuda's increasing prominence led to changes in its relationship with Great Britain and the United States and also resulted in significant developments on the island itself. In 1957, after nearly two centuries of occupation, Britain withdrew its military forces, having decided to grant self-government to its oldest colony. The United States, however, under the Lend-Lease Agreement signed in 1941 and due to expire in 2040, continues to maintain a naval air station at Kindley Field, in St. George's Parish. Nearby, on Cooper's Island, the U.S. National Aeronautics and Space Administration operates a space-tracking system.

As Bermudians assumed greater control over their own affairs, they began to adopt significant social changes, but at a pace that did not satisfy some critics. Although racial segregation in hotels and restaurants ceased in 1959, it wasn't until 1971 that schools were integrated. Women received the right to vote in 1944, but the law still restricted suffrage only to property holders. However, this was rescinded in 1963, when voter registration became open to all citizens.

During the rocky road to self-government, there have been problems. Rioting broke out in 1968, so serious that British troops had to be called back to restore order. Then, in 1973, Sir Richard Sharples, the governor, was assassinated; in 1977 those believed to have been the assassins were themselves executed. These events, which occurred at a time when several of the islands in the region as well as in the Caribbean were experiencing domestic difficulties, proved to be the exception rather than the rule. For in the years since the situation in Bermuda has been marked largely by social and political calm, which everyone acknowledges is better for the island's economic well-being, as it encourages the industries on which Bermuda depends—tourism among them.

**✪ Bermuda became self-governing in 1957, when British forces withdrew from the island.**

In 1970, Bermuda was "expelled" from the sterling currency area, and Bermudians hitched their currency to the U.S. dollar.

The 1990s have brought talk about what role Bermuda will play in the future. Some advocate complete independence, from Britain, while others want to retain connections to the crown.

# POLITICS

Bermuda was accorded the right of self-government in 1968. It is therefore a self-governing dependency of Great Britain, with a governor appointed by the queen of England and representing Her Majesty's government in the areas of external affairs, defense, and internal security. The 12-member cabinet is headed by a premier. The elected legislature, referred to as the Legislative Council, consists of a 40-member House of Assembly and an 11-member Senate. Bermuda's oldest political party is the Progressive Labor Party, formed in 1963. In 1964 the United Bermuda Party was established and is the party currently in power. Bermuda's legal system is founded on common law. Judicial responsibility falls to the Supreme Court, headed by a chief justice. English law is the fundamental guide, and in court English customs prevail, as in the tradition of having judges don wigs and robes.

The nine parishes into which the island is divided are each managed by an advisory council. The capital, Hamilton, is located in Pembroke Parish.

## THE ECONOMY

Bermuda's political stability has proved beneficial to the economy, which relies heavily on tourism and foreign investment.

For much of the island's early history, the major industry was ship building, made possible by the abundant cedar forests. But when, in the second half of the 19th century, wooden ships gave way to steel ones, the island turned to tourism. Today, tourism, with annual revenues estimated at $450 million, is the leading industry. Approximately 550,000 tourists visit Bermuda each year. An estimated 86% arrive from the United States, 4% from Britain, and 7% from Canada. Bermuda enjoys a 42% repeat-visitor rate.

Because of favorable economic legislation incentives, several international companies are registered in Bermuda, representing the island's second-largest source of employment. More than 6,000 companies are registered—engaged mostly in investment holding, insurance, commercial trading, consultancy services, and shipping— but fewer than 275 companies are actually located on the island. There is no corporate or income tax.

The island's leading exported goods are pharmaceuticals, concentrates, essences, and beverages. Leading imports include foodstuffs, alcoholic beverages, clothing, furniture, fuel, electrical appliances, and motor vehicles. Bermuda's major trading partners are the United States, Canada, Great Britain, the Netherlands, and the Caribbean states.

## 3. BERMUDA'S FAMOUS PEOPLE

**Juan Bermúdez** (c. 1450–1519) Some Spanish historians credit this sea captain, commander of *La Garza* (the Heron), with the discovery of Bermuda sometime before 1511. Others more fancifully claim that Columbus sailed past the islands after discovering the Bahamas in 1492. Bermúdez, according to accounts, was said to have been taunted by "hostile birds."

**Governor Richard Moore** (also More; d. 1617) Moore launched the official colonization of Bermuda in 1612. He arrived with 60 settlers from England aboard the *Plough*. A former ship's carpenter, he became Bermuda's first official governor.

**Joseph Hayne Rainey** (1832–87) An African-American refugee during the American Civil War, Rainey settled in Bermuda, where he became a barber in St. George's. The Tucker House, a museum, has a memorial room honoring him. He returned to South Carolina sometime after the war. Rainey became the first member of his race to be elected a member of the U.S. House of Representatives during the Reconstruction days after the Civil War.

**Sir Richard Sharples** (1916–73) The governor of Bermuda, Sir Richard Sharples and his aide, Captain Hugh Sayers, made headlines around the world when they were assassinated at Government House on North Shore Road in Pembroke Parish. In 1977 those believed to have been the assassins were convicted and executed.

**Sir George Somers** (1554–1610) Admiral George Somers commanded the *Sea Venture*, which was shipwrecked off Bermuda's easternmost reefs. He was the first to explore and map the island on Bermuda. Upon his death, his heart was buried in Somers Gardens in St. George's.

**Edward Tucker** (1925–   ) Tucker became the most famous treasure retriever in the history of Bermuda. A local diver, he hit the jackpot in 1955 when he brought up a collection of gold bars and ornaments from the *San Antonio,* a Spanish vessel that had sunk in 1621. The treasure is on display at the Bermuda Maritime Museum. The prize piece of the exhibition—a gold cross mounted with seven emeralds—was stolen only moments before Queen Elizabeth II arrived in 1975 for a royal opening. It was replaced with a replica.

## 4. ART, ARCHITECTURE & LITERATURE

Perhaps more than any other island in the western Atlantic, Bermuda retains the strongest links to the artistic heritage of Great Britain. Nevertheless, its style in art and architecture, while recognizably British, displays the influence of the island's African-Caribbean and Portuguese settlers.

# ART

Bermuda's earliest artworks involved portraits painted by itinerant artists for the local gentry. The bulk of these were painted by the English-born Joseph Blackburn, whose brief visit to Bermuda in the mid-1700s resulted in requests from local landowners to have their portraits painted. Many of these hang today in the Tucker House Museum in St. George's. A handful of portraits from the same period were done by the American-born artist John Green.

○ **Many of Bermuda's historical artworks are landscape paintings made by British officers for military purposes.**

Also prized are a series of paintings, from the mid-19th century, depicting sailing ships. They're signed "Edward James," but the artist's real identity remains unknown.

During the 19th century also, the traditions of the English landscape painters, particularly the Romantics, came into vogue in Bermuda. Constable, with his lush and evocative landscapes, became the model for many.

Other than a few naïve artists, however, whose works showed great vitality but little sense of perspective, most of Bermuda's landscape paintings were executed by British military officers and their wives. Their body of work includes a charming blend of true-to-life landscapes with an occasionally stylized rendering of the picturesque or Romantic tradition then in vogue in England. Among the most famous of the uniformed artists was Lt. E. G. Hallewell, a member of the Royal Engineers, whose illustrations of the island's topography were used in the planning of naval installations.

Another celebrated landscapist was Thomas Driver, who arrived as a member of the Royal Engineers in 1814 and remained on the island until 1836. Trained to reproduce detailed landscape observations as a means of assisting military and naval strategists, he later adapted his style into a more elegant and evocative one. He soon abandoned the military and became a full-time painter of the scenes of Bermuda. Because of their attention to detail, Driver's works are frequently reproduced by scholars and art historians hoping to redefine the aesthetic and architectural accuracy of the island's earliest constructions.

Later in the 19th century, other artists spent laborious hours depicting the botany and floral life of Bermuda. Lady Lefroy, whose husband was governor of the island between 1871 and 1877, painted the trees, shrubs, fish, flowers, and animals of the island in much-imitated detail. Later, at scattered intervals of careers, such internationally known artists as Winslow Homer, Andrew Wyeth, George Ault, and French-born impressionist and cubist Albert Gleizes have all painted Bermuda scenes.

Among today's prominent Bermuda-born artists is Alfred Birdsey. His watercolors represent some of the most elegiac visual odes to Bermuda ever produced.

Birdsey's paintings, as well as the paintings of the other artists mentioned, may be viewed in galleries around the island. Protecting these works, however, so that they might continue to be exhibited in future, is a constant problem in Bermuda, because of the island's semitropical climate. As the administrator for a major art gallery explains, "Bermuda's climate is unquestionably the worst in the world for the toll it takes on works of art, with three elements—humidity, salt, and ultraviolet light all playing their part." The U.S. Navy uses Bermuda to test the durability of paint; if paint can stand up in Bermuda, it can stand up anywhere. The island's humidity can cause serious harm to a painting. It can be absorbed by the canvas, where you will see it later as mildew coming through the oils. Some very valuable prints have been totally destroyed. As a result, more and more galleries and exhibition rooms on the island have been air-conditioned.

In addition to painters, Bermuda also boasts several noted sculptors, among them Chelsey Trott, who produces cedarwood carvings, and Desmond Hale Fountain, who creates works in bronze. Fountain's life-size statues often show children in the act of reading or snoozing in the shade.

# ARCHITECTURE

The architecture of Bermuda is sometimes considered its only truly indigenous art form—a collection of idiosyncratic building techniques dictated by climate and the types of building supplies available on the island. Early settlers quickly recognized the virtues of the island's most visible building material, coral stone. A conglomerate of primeval sand packed beside crushed bits of coral and shells, this stone has been quarried for generations on Bermuda. Cut into oblong building blocks, it is strong but porous, rendering it unuseable in any climate where cycles of freezing and thawing would cause it to crack. Mortared together with imported cements, the blocks provide solid and durable foundations and walls.

Bermuda's colonial architects ingeniously found a way to deal with a serious problem on the island—the lack of an abundant supply of fresh water. During the construction of a house or any other sort of building, workers excavated a water tank (cistern) first, either as a separate underground cavity away from the house or as a foundation for the building. These cisterns served to collect rainwater funneled from rooftops via specially designed channels and gutters.

The design of these roof-to-cellar water conduits led to the development of what is considered Bermuda's most obvious architectural feature, the distinctive rooftops of its houses. Gently sloping, and invariably painted a dazzling white, they are constructed of quarried limestone slabs sawed into "slates" about an inch thick and between 12 and 18 inches square. Roofs are installed over a framework of cedarwood beams (or, more recently, pitch pine or pressure-treated wood beams), which are interconnected with a series of cedar lathes. The slates are joined

**❍ The moon gate, which graces many a Bermudian garden, is one of the island's distinctive architectural features.**

together with cement-based mortar in overlapping rows, then covered with a cement wash and one or several coats of whitewash or synthetic paint. This process corrects the porosity of the coral limestone slates, rendering them watertight. The result is a layered effect, as each course of limestone appears in high relief atop its neighbor. The angular, step-shaped geometry of Bermudian roofs have inspired watercolorists and painters to emphasize the rhythmically graceful shadows that trace the path of the sun every day across the rooflines.

Bermudian houses—unlike houses in the Caribbean, which they in many respects resemble—are designed without amply proportioned hanging eaves. Large eaves are desired because of the shade they afford, but smaller ones have proved to be structurally sounder during tropical storms. Wind gathers more lifting power from an overhanging eave than from any other part of a roofline, as validated by engineers' analyses of wind damage to buildings in southern Florida during Hurricane Andrew in 1992.

The interiors of Bermudian houses are usually graced with large windows, ample doors, and, in the older buildings, floors and moldings crafted from copper-colored planks of the almost extinct Bermuda cedar. Also common is a feature found in colonial buildings in Caribbean and other western Atlantic islands as well—tray ceilings, so named because of their resemblance to an inverted serving tray. Their shape allows them to follow the lines of the inside roof construction into what would otherwise have been unused space. The effect of these ceilings, whether sheathed in plaster or planking, gives Bermudian interiors unusual height and airiness even if the building has relatively low eaves.

No discussion of Bermudian architecture can fail to mention a garden feature that many visitors consider distinctive to Bermuda—the moon gate. A rounded span of coral blocks arranged in a circular arch above a wooden gate, the moon gate was introduced to Bermuda around 1920 by the duke of Westminster's landscape architect; the inspiration came from China and Japan.

# LITERATURE

Bermuda has long been a haven for writers. It has figured in many works of literature, beginning with Shakespeare's play *The Tempest*. Shakespeare had not visited the island himself but was inspired by accounts he had read or heard of it.

The Irish poet Thomas Moore (1779–1852), who did visit Bermuda for several months in 1804, was moved by its beauty to write:

> *Oh! could you view the scenery dear*
> *That now beneath my window lies.*

But for Americans it was Mark Twain who helped make Bermuda a popular tourist destination. He published his impressions in the *Atlantic Monthly* in 1877–78 and in his first book, *The Innocents Abroad*. So enamored did he become of the island that, as he wrote many years later to a correspondent, he would fain choose it over heaven.

Following in Twain's footsteps, Eugene O'Neill came to the island in 1924, and returned several times, at least through 1927, living at Spithead in Warwick. While here, he worked on *The Great God Brown, Lazarus Laughed,* and *Strange Interlude.*

During the 1930s, several eminent writers made their way to Bermuda, with fountain pen and paper (or portable typewriter), in search of idyllic surroundings and perhaps a little inspiration: Sinclair Lewis, who, however, spent all his time cycling around "this gorgeous island"; Hervey Allen, who proved more prolific, penning *Anthony Adverse,* his prodigious best-selling novel, at Felicity Hall in Somerset; and James Ramsey Ullman, who wrote *The White Tower* on the island.

**✪ Many famous writers have been drawn to Bermuda for rest and inspiration.**

Also among the literary visitors at this time was James Thurber, who during one of his several trips stayed long enough to finish *13 Clocks* at Lantana in Somerset.

Noël Coward came in 1956, to escape "the monstrously unjust tax situation in England." He was not, he said, "really mad about the place," yet he purchased

Spithead in Warwick, O'Neill's former home, and stayed some two years, working on *London Mornings,* his only ballet, and the musical *Sail Away.*

Other names can be added to the list of famous authors who visited Bermuda through the years: Rudyard Kipling, C. S. Forester, Hugh Walpole, Edna Ferber, Anita Loos, John O'Hara, E. B. White, Philip Wylie.

Bermuda itself has produced several writers, who, although not as internationally prominent, have nevertheless gained some recognition. Among them are William S. Zuill, a former director of the Bermuda National Trust, who wrote *The Story of Bermuda and Her People,* an excellent historical account of the island. Other writers are Nellie Musson, Frank Manning, Eva Hodgson, and Dale Butler, all of whom have written of the lives of African-Bermudians.

# 5. RELIGION & FOLKLORE

## RELIGION

About a third of Bermuda's population adheres to the Church of England, which has been historically dominant in the colony. Indeed, the division of Bermuda into nine parishes dates from 1618, when each parish was required by law to have its own Anglican church, to the exclusion of any other. That division still exists today, but more for administrative than religious purposes.

Religious tolerance is now guaranteed by law. There are some 10,000 Catholics, many of them from the Portuguese Azores. There are also many members of Protestant sects whose roots lie within what were originally slave churches, among them the African Methodist Episcopal Church. Established in 1816 by African-Americans, the sect was transported to Bermuda from Canada around 1870. Today the church has about 7,000 members.

Also found in Bermuda are Seventh-Day Adventists, Presbyterians, Baptists, Lutherans, and Mormons. Less prevalent are a handful of Jews, Muslims, Rastafarians, and Jehovah's Witnesses.

Bermuda today boasts more than 110 churches, an average of five per square mile. They range from the moss-encrusted parish churches established in the earliest days of the colony to modest structures with only a handful of members.

## FOLKLORE

Much of the folklore of Bermuda has its origins in the myths and legends of West Africa that the slaves brought to the island. Some of it, however, is, so to speak, homegrown.

Many tales are told about the fate of persons condemned for witchcraft during the 1600s. Anyone suspected of collusion with the devil was thrown into St. George's Harbour; whoever did not sink was adjudged guilty. Many women floated because of their skirts and petticoats; they were then fished out of the water and burned at the stake. The first woman to be found floating after her trial was Jeanne Gardiner, in 1651. Since her failure to plunge to the depths "proved" that she was a witch, the court ordered her removed from the water and hanged; she was then burned

○ **Much of the folklore of Bermuda has its origins in the myths and legends of West Africa.**

at the stake. Not only women, however, were tried for witchcraft; in 1652 a man was condemned to death for having cast a spell over his neighbor's turkeys. Justice in those Puritan times was stern, in Bermuda no less than in the American colonies.

Other kinds of tales abound, having to do with the island's maritime traditions. Many are ghost stories about colonial shipwrecks—stories about the tortured souls of sailors and passengers still roaming the coastlines of Bermuda on dark, stormy nights, searching for the wreckage of their sunken ships.

## THE BERMUDA TRIANGLE

The area known as the Bermuda Triangle encompasses a 1.5-million-square-mile expanse of open sea between Bermuda, Puerto Rico, and the southeastern shoreline of the United States. It is the source of the most famous—and certainly the most baffling—legend associated with Bermuda.

The legend of the Bermuda Triangle persists in many guises, some less credible than others, despite attempts by skeptics to dismiss them as fanciful tales. Can some of them be true? Here are three.

In 1881 a British-registered ship, the *Ellen Austin,* encountered an unnamed vessel in good condition sailing aimlessly without a crew. The *Austin*'s captain ordered a handful of his best seamen to board the mysterious vessel and sail it to Newfoundland. A few days later, the two ships encountered each other again on the high seas—but to everyone's alarm, the crewmen who had transferred from the *Austin* were nowhere to be found on the other ship!

Another often-told tale concerns the later disappearance of a merchant ship called *Marine Sulphur Queen.* It disappeared suddenly and without warning, and why no one could say. The weather was calm when the ship set sail from Bermuda, and apparently everything on board was fine, too, for no distress signal had been received from the crew. In looking for explanations, some have held that the ship probably had a weakened hull, which gave way, causing it to descend quickly to the bottom. Others attribute its loss to the mysterious forces that are behind all the Bermuda Triangle stories.

The most famous of all the Bermuda Triangle legends occurred in 1945. On December 5, five U.S. Navy bombers departed from Fort Lauderdale, Fla., on a routine mission. The weather was fine; no storm of any kind threatened. A while into the flight, however, the leader of the squadron suddenly radioed that they were lost—and then the radio went silent; all efforts by the ground to establish further communication proved fruitless. A rescue plane was quickly dispatched to search for the squadron—but it, too, disappeared. The Navy ordered a search, which lasted five days; but it found no evidence of a wreckage of any kind. To this day, the disappearance of the squadron and of the rescue plane remains a mystery as deep as the waters of the region.

○ **The Bermuda Triangle legend has its believers and debunkers, who will gladly tell you why.**

How do believers of the Bermuda Triangle myth explain these phenomena? Some contend that the area is a time warp to another universe; others, that the waters off Bermuda are the site of the lost kingdom of Atlantis, whose power sources still function deep beneath the surface of the waves. Still others believe that there exists a perpetual focusing of laser rays upon the region from outer space, or that under-water signaling devices are guiding invaders from other planets, who have chosen the site for the systematic collection of human beings for scientific observation and experimentation.

Some, drawing upon the Book of Revelations, are fully persuaded that the Bermuda Triangle is really one of the gates to Hell, the other lying midway between Japan and the Philippines, in the Devil's Sea.

No matter what your views on the Bermuda Triangle may be, you're bound to provoke an excited response by asking local residents their opinion of it. For no one is immune to the power of myths and legends, and on Bermuda almost everyone has an opinion of some kind about the biggest and most fascinating legend of all.

# 6. SOCIAL & CULTURAL LIFE

Bermuda's social life is imbued with British traditions. For Bermudians, inspired by an idealized image of Great Britain, seek to imitate everything English.

A profound sense of decorum is probably the most noticeable social feature on the island; it accounts for its somewhat formal dress code, which requires that even in ordinary social gatherings men should wear jackets and neckties and women should wear casually elegant clothes. Such attire is common during afternoon tea, a ritual observed as punctiliously on the manicured lawns of Pembroke Parish as in the finest hotels of London. Adherence to ritual is evident also during family events, such as weddings and funerals, when one is careful to do things precisely as they are done back in Britain, in accordance with the rites and traditions of the Church of England.

Politeness and formality are the norm, even on occasions when, confronted by life's petty problems, one would be more inclined, at least elsewhere, to raise one's voice in anger or exasperation. Such formality manifests itself physically in the islanders' attention to good grooming, as well as in the many charming, well-kept cottages and carefully tended gardens, which serve to enhance the natural setting of Bermuda and give it an unmistakable stamp of civilized orderliness. It even extends to a love of animals, which is here regarded as a peculiarly English virtue.

Cultural life in Bermuda attains a high point during the midwinter Bermuda Festival, held over a six- or seven-week period in January and February. The festival offers an opportunity to put on dramatic works from Britain, the United States, and Canada, as well as from other English-speaking Atlantic islands, with Bermudian and visiting theater troupes. Funding for such an event is provided both through the public sale of tickets and through private donations. An especially important feature of the festival is the volunteer efforts of many local residents, who administer to the transportation and hospitality-related needs of the festival's visiting artists.

○ **Politeness and formality characterize social life in Bermuda.**

Among the various works performed during the festival, a consistent favorite is, of course, Shakespeare's play *The Tempest*. Said to have been inspired by an account of the wreck of the *Sea Venture* in 1609, it is in its own way the oldest play in the English language with a direct link to Bermuda and its maritime traditions.

# THE PEOPLE

Some Bermudians can trace their ancestry back to the first settlers and some to successful privateers and to slaves. Today's 58,000 residents—mostly of African, British, and Portuguese derivation—have a high standard of living, with no personal income tax and virtually no unemployment. The population density, one of the highest in the world, is about 3,210 per square mile. About 61 percent of the population is black, and 39 percent is white. Many other minority groups are represented, the largest and most established being the Portuguese. The color bar, which continued even after slavery was abolished, has almost disappeared, and African-Bermudians have assumed a prominent place in the island's civic and government affairs. There is no illiteracy, and you won't see any slums or poverty.

As mentioned, the British influence is prevalent in Bermuda, what with predominantly English accents, police wearing helmets like those of London bobbies, and cars driving on the left. Schools also are run along the lines of the British system and provide a high standard of preparatory education. Children 5 to 16 years of age must attend school. The Bermuda College offers academic and technical studies and boasts a renowned hotel and catering program.

# CUSTOMS

**BERMUDA SHORTS** Bermuda shorts originated with the British Army in India. Later, when British troops were stationed in Bermuda, they were issued shorts as part of the military's tropical kit gear.

Bermuda shorts are now considered suitable attire for the Bermuda businessman and are worn with a blazer, collared shirt, tie, and knee socks. They should not be more than three inches above the knee and must have a three-inch hem.

**WEDDING-CAKE TRADITIONS** Custom dictates that Bermudians have two wedding cakes—a plain pound cake covered with gold leaf for the groom, and a tiered fruit cake covered with silver leaf and topped off with a mini–cedar tree for the bride. The tiny tree is planted on the day of the wedding to symbolize the hope that the marriage will grow and mature like the tree. The rest of the first tier of the bride's cake is frozen until the christening of the first child.

# MUSIC & DANCE

Modern Bermudian music is a mixture of native traditions and outside influences, chiefly from the islands to the south—Jamaica, Trinidad, and Puerto Rico—and from the United States and Britain. As elsewhere, American and British rock, modified by local rhythms, has proved the strongest and most lasting influence.

Yet, despite the popular new musical forms, Bermuda retains great pride in its original musical idioms. Gombey dancing, an art form whose roots lie deep within West Africa, is the island's premier folk art. Gombey dancers are almost always male; in accordance with tradition, men from the same family pass on the rhythms and dance techniques from generation to generation. Gombey is a combination of Africa's tribal heritage, mingled with the Native American and British colonial influences of the New World. Dancers outfit

○ **Gombey dancing, regarded as peculiarly Bermudian, derives from Africa and contains many local rituals and ceremonies.**

themselves in masquerade costumes, whose outlandish lines and glittering colors evoke the brilliant plumage of tropical birds. The most strenuous dances are usually presented during the Christmas season.

*Gombey* (spelled *goombay* in some other places, such as the Bahamas) signifies a specific type of African drum, as well as the Bantu word for "rhythm." These rhythms escalate into an ever faster and more hypnotic beat as the movements of the dancers become more and more uninhibited and the response of the spectators grows more and more fervent.

Although gombey dancing, with its local rituals and ceremonies, may be considered a major cultural contribution of Bermuda, it is not unique to the island. Variations of it may be found elsewhere in the western Atlantic, as well as in the Caribbean. Indeed, during its development, it was significantly influenced by some of these other versions. In colonial times, for example, when African-Caribbeans were transported to Bermuda as slaves or convicts to help build the British military installations on the island, they brought with them their own gombey traditions, which they mingled with those of Bermuda. What is unique about the Bermudian version of gombey, however, is its use of the British snare drum, played with wooden sticks, as accompaniment to the dancing.

Bermuda also has a surviving balladeer tradition. Although its exponents are fewer than they used to be, they continue to enjoy considerable popularity, among islanders and visitors alike. Reflecting the wry, self-deprecating humor that has always distinguished their compositions, they can strum on their guitar a song for any occasion. Many of their songs nowadays have to do with Bermuda's changing way of life. One of the foremost balladeers is Hubert Smith, whose original compositions have been part of the welcoming ceremonies for visiting notables from around the world.

In the past few years, calypso and reggae, the popular sounds of the Caribbean, have become famous in Bermuda. A more recent import is *soca,* a rock-influenced calypso, and *zouk,* which is a fusion of the various Caribbean rhythms, with French melodies thrown in.

## THEATER

In 1944 the Bermuda Musical and Dramatic Society was organized to bring a standard of culture to the island not seen before. Since that time, the organization has flourished, and it has brought a wide range of musical and theatrical productions to the island chain. Before its formation, many wealthy Bermudians visited New York for a theater "feast." Nowadays, the society presents about one production a month at its 100-seat theater in Hamilton.

# 7. SPORTS & RECREATION

Approximately 20 square miles of year-round action—that's what the outdoor sports enthusiast finds in and around Bermuda. A wide array of water sports is pursued here, with plenty of equipment, instructors, and facilities offered. You can go boating, windsurfing, sailing, waterskiing, or shore, reef, or deep-sea fishing on top of the water. The Bermuda-fitted dinghy is one of the world's most distinctive sailing crafts, carrying up to 1,000 square feet of sail—at only 14 feet 1 inch in length, this dinghy carries more sail for its size than any other craft.

If you prefer to disport yourself underwater, you have a choice of helmet diving, scuba diving, or snorkeling. Or you can just swim around, in the sea or in a pool. The pink fine-sand beaches of Bermuda are legendary.

Most of the large hotels have their own water-sports facilities and equipment for the use of hotel guests; these may also be available to guests of other hotels on request. Ask at your hotel.

Not a water buff? Then you may want to play tennis on one of the more than 90 courts in Bermuda. Or perhaps you'd like to golf on one of the eight fine courses, which support the claim that Bermuda has more golf per square mile than any island on earth. Pedal cycling, bowling, walking, and jogging are engaged in by many Bermudians and visitors alike.

If you'd rather be a viewer than a doer, you'll find a wide variety of spectator sports. These include such traditional British games as cricket, rugby, and soccer, plus lacrosse, field hockey, softball, cycle scrambling, and track-and-field events, among other pursuits.

For further information on the various sports and recreational activities to be found in Bermuda, see Chapter 8, "Sports & Recreation."

# 8. FOOD & DRINK

For years Bermuda was not considered an island of grand cuisine; food was too often bland, lacking in flavor. However, in the past 20 years there has been a remarkable change. Bermuda has shared the revived interest in fine cuisine that swept across America, beginning in the 1970s. Chefs seem better trained than ever, and many top-notch, albeit expensive, restaurants dot the archipelago, from Sandys Parish in the west to St. George's Parish in the east.

Italian food currently enjoys much vogue. The Chinese have also landed. And fast food is available, including Kentucky Fried Chicken.

In recent years, some Bermudians have shown an interest in their "roots," and many of the old-time dishes and recipes have been revived and published in books devoted to Bermudian cookery. (One of these books might make an interesting souvenir.)

Today, Bermuda imports most of its foodstuffs from the United States. Because of the high population density, much farmland has now given way to the construction of private homes. Nevertheless, private gardens are still cultivated, and at one Bermudian home I was amazed at the variety of vegetables grown on just a small plot of land. These plants included sorrel, from which a good-tasting soup was made, along with oyster plants and Jerusalem artichokes.

As related in any history of Bermuda, Admiral Sir George Somers and his 150 castaways arrived on the shores of Bermuda from their ill-fated *Sea Venture*. Within 30 minutes they set about fishing for food. They named the fish they caught "rockfish," and later wrote about how sweet and fat it was.

These early settlers also found wild hogs roaming the island. The swine were believed to have swum to shore when some ship or ships were wrecked off the coast of Bermuda. The settlers captured the boars and fed them cedarberries. Thus, when they didn't want to go fishing or the weather was too choppy, they could roast a pig.

# FOOD

## CUSTOMS

Perhaps the most delightful custom on Bermuda is the English ritual of afternoon tea. Many local homes preserve the custom. Hotels have also maintained the tradition, and visitors to Bermuda quickly take it up.

The typical afternoon tea is served in hotels daily from 3 to 4pm. Adding a modern touch, it is often served around a swimming pool, the guests partaking of the ritual in their bathing suits—a tolerated lapse from the code of formality that otherwise governs social functions on the island.

In its more formal observance, the tea is served at a well-laid table with silver, crisp white linen napery, and fine china, often imported from Britain. Finger sandwiches made with thinly sliced cucumber or watercress, or scones and strawberry jam, are usually served with the tea.

Again like the British, Bermudians enjoy a good sociable pub lunch. Several pubs are found in Hamilton and elsewhere on the island, especially St. George's. For further information, however, see Chapter 5, "Where to Dine in Bermuda." For the nonce suffice it to say that a pub lunch—consisting of a healthy serving of fish and chips or some other "pub grub," a pint or two of ale (preferably English), and much animated discussion about politics, sports, or the most recent royal visit—is an experience to be cherished, here as much as in any city or town in Britain.

**✪ Afternoon tea is an English tradition devoutly kept.**

In many resort hotels, guests are booked in high season (April through November) on the modified American plan (MAP) or half-board arrangement. To escape the routine of eating in the same dining room every night, some hotels offer a "dine around" program, allowing you to dine at other hotels either on your MAP plan or else at somewhat reduced prices. You should inquire about such arrangements when booking a room.

Most of the upmarket restaurants of Bermuda request that men wear a jacket and tie for dinner; some restaurants dispense with the tie but require a jacket. When making reservations, it is always wise to ask what the dress code is before showing up.

Perhaps the favorite meal of the typical Bermudian is Sunday brunch. Your hotel is likely to feature a big buffet at that time, or else you may take the opportunity to dine at some other establishment. "Casual but elegant" dress is preferred at most Sunday buffets.

Nearly all the major restaurants, except fast-food places, prefer that you make a reservation; many establishments require that you do so as far in advance as possible. Weekends in summer can be especially crowded. At certain popular restaurants, some travel-wise vacationers make their reservations even before coming to Bermuda.

The food of Bermuda is better than ever. When in doubt, however, order seafood. Nearly all meat is imported and may have arrived on the island considerably before you have.

## CUISINE

**SEAFOOD**   Around the coastline of Bermuda more species of both shore and ocean fish are found than in any other place—that is, if you can believe what any local fisherman is likely to tell you. The fish include grunt, angel fish, yellowtail, gray snapper, and the ubiquitous rockfish.

Rockfish is similar to the Bahamian grouper, and it appears on nearly every menu. It weighs anywhere from 15 to 135 pounds (or even more). Steamed, broiled, baked, fried, or grilled, rockfish is a challenge to any chef. There's even a dish known as "rockfish maw," which I understand only the most old-fashioned cooks—a handful still left on St. David's Island—know how to prepare. It's the maw, or stomach, of a rockfish that has been stuffed with a dressing of forcemeat and simmered slowly on the stove. You may want to try it, if you believe that dining is an adventure.

**✪ Rockfish, "guinea chick," and shark are popular seafood dishes.**

The most popular dish on the island is Bermuda fish chowder. Waiters usually pass around a bottle of sherry peppers and some black rum with which you lace your own soup. This adds a distinctive Bermudian flavor.

Shark is not as popular as it used to be. Many traditional dishes, though, are still made from shark, including hash. Old-timers use shark liver oil to tell the weather. It's said to be more reliable than the weatherperson. The oil is extracted at a specific time, then poured into a small bottle and left in the sun. If the oil lies still, then fair weather can be predicted; if, however, droplets form on the sides of the bottle, then foul weather can be expected.

The Bermuda lobster—or "guinea chick," as it is known locally—has been called a first cousin of the Maine lobster and is in season only from September to March. Its high price tag has led to overfishing, forcing the government to at times issue a ban on its harvesting. Lobster then is likely to be imported instead of caught in local waters.

You can occasionally still get a good conch stew in Bermuda at one of the local restaurants. Sea scallops, while still available, have become increasingly rare. Mussels are cherished in Bermuda. One of the most popular and most traditional mussel dishes is mussel pie Bermuda style.

**FRUITS & VEGETABLES**   In both restaurants and private homes Portuguese red-bean soup, the culinary contribution of the farmers brought to the island to till the land, precedes many a meal.

The Bermuda onion (once so common on the island that the people of Bermuda were called "onions") figures in a lot of Bermudian recipes, including onion pie. Bermuda-onion soup, an island favorite, is most often flavored with Outerbridge's Original Sherry Peppers.

Bermudians grow more potatoes than any other vegetable, chiefly the Pontiac red and the Kennebec white potato. At some homes in Bermuda, the traditional Sunday breakfast of codfish and banana cooked with potatoes is still served.

"Peas and plenty" is a Bermudian tradition. Black-eyed peas are cooked in onions and salt pork, to which rice is sometimes added. Dumplings or boiled sweet potatoes can also be added at the last minute. Another peas-and-rice dish, called Hoppin' John, is eaten either as a main dish or as a side dish with meat or poultry.

Bermudians and Bahamians share the tradition of Johnny Bread, or johnnycake, a simple pan-cooked cornmeal bread. Fishermen would make it over a fire in a box filled with sand to keep the flames from spreading to the craft itself.

The cassava, once very important in Bermuda, is now used chiefly at Christmas to make the traditional cassava pie. Another dish that has a festive holiday connection is sweet-potato pudding, traditionally eaten on Guy Fawkes Day.

Bermuda grows many fresh fruits, including strawberries, Surinam cherries, guavas, avocados, and, of course, bananas. Guavas are made into jelly, which in turn is often used to make the famous Bermuda syllabub, traditionally accompanied by johnny-cake.

## DRINKS

All the name-brand alcoholic beverages are sold in Bermuda, but prices on such a typical drink as a scotch and soda can run as high as $5. You have to watch where you drink or else you can run up some huge bar tabs.

**LOCAL FAVORITES** For some 300 years rum has been considered the national drink of Bermuda. Especially popular is Bacardi rum (they have a headquarters in Bermuda) and Demerara rum (also known as black rum). A rum swizzle is perhaps the most famous alcoholic drink in Bermuda.

An interesting drink is loquat liqueur, now exported. It can be made with loquats, rock candy, and gin, or more elaborately, with brandy instead of gin and the addition of such spices as cinnamon, nutmeg, cloves, and allspice.

Before bottled drinks, ginger beer—made with green ginger and lemons—was an island favorite.

# 9. RECOMMENDED BOOKS, FILMS & RECORDINGS

## BOOKS

The reader who is interested in finding out more about Bermuda can choose from an array of books, many dealing with some of the subjects covered in this chapter—the island's history, art and architecture, and flora and fauna. There are also several noteworthy general books with Bermuda either wholly or partly as their subject. An excellent work of fiction is also cited for being especially evocative of life in the island during the period that it covers.

Most of the books listed below have been printed in Bermuda. Thus, while they're readily available on the island, they may be hard to find in the United States and elsewhere.

### GENERAL

AHIAKPOR, JAMES C. W. *The Economic Consequences of Political Independence: The Case of Bermuda* (Frasier Institute, 1990).
KUSCHE, LARRY. *The Bermuda Triangle Mystery—Solved* (Harper, 1975).
ROBINSON, KENNETH E. *Heritage* (Macmillan Education and Berkeley Educational Society, 1979).
STEVENSON, WILLIAM. *A Man Called Intrepid* (Macmillan, 1976).

### HISTORY

IVES, VERNON A. (ed.). *The Rich Papers—Letters from Bermuda* (Bermuda National Trust and University of Toronto Press, 1984).

KENNEDY, JEAN DE CHANTAL. *Biography of a Colonial Town* (Bermuda Bookstores Publisher, 1961).

MCCALLAN, ERNEST A. *Life on Old St. David's* (Bermuda Historical Society, 1986).

PACKWOOD, CYRIL O. *Chained on the Rock: Slavery in Bermuda* (Baxters, 1975).

SMITH, JAMES E. *Slavery in Bermuda* (Vantage Press, 1976).

TUCKER, TERRY. *Bermuda's Story* (Bermuda Bookstores Publisher, 1959).

————. *Bermuda Today and Yesterday: 1503–1980s* (Baxters, 1983).

ZUILL, WILLIAM. *The Story of Bermuda and Her People* (Macmillan Caribbean, 1983).

## FLORA & FAUNA

BROWN, ANN B., and JEAN M. OUTERBRIDGE. *Bermuda Houses and Gardens* (Garden Club of Bermuda, 1979).

COLLETT, JILL. *Bermuda: Her Plants and Gardens, 1609–1850* (Macmillan Caribbean, 1987).

MOWBRAY, LOUIS S. *A Guide to the Reef, Shore and Game Fish of Bermuda* (published by author; 3rd ed., 1976).

## ART & ARCHITECTURE

HYDE, BRYDEN B. *Bermuda Antique Furniture and Silver* (Bermuda National Trust, 1971).

RAINE, DAVID R. *Architecture Bermuda Style* (Pompano Publications, 1989).

## FICTION

WILLIAMS, ANN Z. *The Back Yard* (Macmillan, 1988). An account of growing up in Bermuda in the 1930s and '40s.

## FILMS

Film buffs may be surprised to discover that Bermuda has an indirect link to *The Wizard of Oz,* the 1939 movie starring Judy Garland and a host of memorable, magical characters. It is Denslow's Island.

The privately owned island is named after W. W. Denslow, who created the original illustrations for the book on which the movie is based, *The Wonderful Wizard of Oz* (1900) by L. Frank Baum, and thus with his pen gave form to many of the characters depicted on the screen. Denslow lived in Bermuda at the turn of the century. The island, however, despite its famous association, is off limits to visitors.

Several films were shot in and around Bermuda. The most famous is *The Deep* (1977), starring Jacqueline Bisset, Nick Nolte, Robert Shaw, and Lou Gossett—a visually arresting movie about a lost treasure and drugs and, of course, scuba diving off the island's coast. For one of the scenes, a lighthouse near the Grotto Bay Beach Hotel and Tennis Club was accommodatingly blown up.

A movie that was filmed partly in Bermuda is *Chapter Two* (1979), with James Caan and Marsha Mason. Based on the successful Broadway play by Neil Simon, it is the story of a playwright's bumpy romance soon after the death of his wife. The Bermuda scenes were shot at Marley Beach Cottage.

# RECORDINGS

Musical enthusiasts are often pleased to discover that the island's best-known singers and musicians can be heard at many of the hotels and nightclubs. Inquire what group is performing during the cocktail hour at your hotel; chances are it may be one of the most popular.

By virtually everyone's estimate, the musical patriarch of Bermuda is Hubert Smith, the island's official greeter in song. A balladeer of formidable talent and originality, Smith has composed and performed songs for the visits of nearly all the foreign heads of state who have graced Bermuda's shores in recent memory. His performances for members of the British royal family include one of the most famous songs ever written about the island, "Bermuda Is Another World." The song is now the island's unofficial national anthem; it's included in the best-selling album *Bermuda Is Another World* (Edmar 1025).

Almost as popular is a five-member calypso band, the Bermuda Strollers, whose lively rhythms can be heard on gala nights at Bermuda's larger hotels. Look for their album *The Best Of* (Edmar 2005) and also a collection of musical odes to the island's natural beauty, *South Shore Bermuda* (Edmar 1156).

One of the island's youngest and most promising talents is Gene Steede, a balladeer and comic who frequently performs at the Southampton Princess. His most popular album is *Bermuda's Natural Resource* (Edmar 2003).

Another well-known balladeer is Jay Fox. His songs of love, joy, and sorrow may be heard in the album *Island Paradise* (Jay Fox 1601).

Bermuda ballads, songs of love, and calypsos are also performed by Stan Seymour, a popular soloist who has been compared to Harry Belafonte. Look for *Our Man in Bermuda* (Edmar 1070).

The lively calypsos of Trinidad and the pulsating rhythms of Jamaica have also influenced musical tastes in Bermuda. Youth Creation, a dreadlock-sporting local reggae group, adopts the Rastafarian style in *Ja's on Our Side* (Edmar 2002).

For those who find that nothing quite stirs the blood as good old-fashioned oom-pah-pah, there are the live as well as recorded performances of the Bermuda Regiment, whose bagpipes, trumpets, and drum tattoos evoke the finest British military traditions—and must strike a nostalgic chord or two in many a British or Bermudian listener. The regiment's album *Drummers Call Bermuda* (Edmar 1152) is a perennial favorite.

The late Lance Hayward was a Bermuda-born musician who established his musical reputation far from home. His most appreciative audiences were found in the smoke-filled jazz houses of New York's Greenwich Village. With a musical style that has been compared to the soft jazz of George Shearing, his most popular album is *Killing Me Softly* (Island 90683).

Dance aficionados will appreciate the five-member Trinidad-born Clay House Steel Band. They can usually be enjoyed at the New Clay House Inn; three months a year they perform aboard various cruise ships. Their most popular album is *The Real Thing* (Edmar 1111).

A Bermuda-born trio, Steel Groove, performs only instrumentals in the Trinidadian style. Their trademark adaptations use the calypso-derived steel pan combined with a keyboard, an electric guitar, and occasionally a bass guitar. Their most popular album is *Calypso Hits* (produced by Danny Garcia).

A slightly older calypso group (one of the first on the island) is the Esso Steel Band. Their popular albums, among them *The Esso Steel Band* (Sunshine 1003) and *It's a Beautiful World* (produced by Rudy Commissiong), are widely hummed and whistled.

No listing of Bermudian music would be complete, of course, without a mention of gombey (see "Music & Dance" above). A handful of recordings are available from which you can get a fair idea of what this African-based music sounds like, with its rhythmic chanting and rapid drumbeat. Among them, the album *Strictly Gombey Music* (Edmar 1165), performed by four members of the Pickles Spencer Gombey Group, offers a good selection of gombey dances.

Aficionados of the art form, however, will argue that gombey's allure lies not so much in the music as in the feverish, almost trancelike dancing that accompanies it, as well as in the colorful costumes of the dancers. For that reason, they say, audio recordings cannot convey the full mesmerizing power of a gombey dance the way a videotape can. So, while you're in Bermuda, you may consider taping a gombey dance, to show when you get back home and perhaps remind yourself of some of the enchanting sounds and sights of this beautiful island in the sun.

# CHAPTER 2

# BEFORE YOU GO

**G**etting to Bermuda has now become easier than ever, thanks to more frequent flights, often direct ones, from such gateway cities as New York, Boston, and Washington, D.C., among others. For those who'd like to relive the glamorous days of "cruising down to Bermuda," several cruise lines sail there from spring until late autumn.

In this chapter I concentrate on what you need to do before you go. In addition to helping you decide when to take your vacation, I answer questions you might have about what to take, where to gather information, and what documents you need to obtain. I also cover various alternative and specialty travel options, such as educational travel, and include tips for special travelers.

# 1. INFORMATION, ENTRY REQUIREMENTS & MONEY

## INFORMATION

If you want to obtain information about Bermuda before going there, write to the **Bermuda Department of Tourism** at the office nearest you. In the **United States,** the Bermuda Department of Tourism has offices in: *New York,* Suite 201, 310 Madison Ave., New York, NY 10017 (tel. 212/818-9800 or toll free 800/223-6106); *Boston,* Suite 1010, 44 School St., Boston, MA 02108 (tel. 617/742-0405); *Chicago,* Suite 1070, Randolph Wacker Building, 150 North Wacker Dr., Chicago, IL 60606 (tel. 312/782-5486); and *Atlanta,* Suite 803, 245 Peachtree Center, NE, Atlanta, GA 30303 (tel. 404/524-1541). In **Canada,** write to Bermuda Department of Tourism, Suite 1004, 1200 Bay St., Toronto, Ontario, Canada M5R 2A5 (tel. 416/923-9600). In the **United Kingdom,** write to Bermuda Department of Tourism, 1 Battersea Church Road, London SW11 3LY (tel. 071/734-8813).

Other useful sources are, of course, newspapers and magazines. To find the latest articles on Bermuda, check the *Reader's Guide to Periodical Literature* at your local library.

You may also want to contact the U.S. State Department for background information; write to Superintendent of Documents, **U.S. Government Printing Office,** Washington, DC 20402 (tel. 202/783-3238).

A good travel agent can be a source of information. Make sure he or she is a member of the American Society of Travel Agents (ASTA), though. If you get poor service from an agent, you can write to the **ASTA Consumer Affairs,** 1101 King St., Alexandria, VA 22314.

And, the best source of all—friends and other travelers who have just returned from Bermuda.

# ENTRY REQUIREMENTS

A U.S. or Canadian citizen does not need a passport to enter Bermuda, although one would be useful as your required identification. Visitors from Great Britain and Europe do need a passport.

Bermuda Immigration authorities require U.S. visitors to have in their possession any one of the following items: a birth certificate or a certified copy of it, a U.S. naturalization certificate, a U.S. Alien Registration card, a U.S. reentry permit, or a U.S. voter registration card bearing the signature of the holder.

Visitors from Canada must have either a birth certificate (or a certified copy of it), a Canadian certificate of citizenship, or a valid passport plus proof of their Landed Immigrant status.

If you stay longer than three weeks, you must apply to the Chief Immigration Officer for an extended stay. You must have a return or onward ticket.

All travelers must pay a passenger tax under the Passenger Tax Act of 1972; see "Taxes" under "Fast Facts" in Chapter 3, "Arriving in Bermuda."

## PASSPORTS

In the **United States,** citizens 18 or older who meet the requirements are granted a 10-year passport. Applications and information are available at most U.S. post offices or a federal court office. In addition, there are federal passport agencies in the following cities: Boston, Chicago, Honolulu, Houston, Los Angeles, Miami, New Orleans, New York, Philadelphia, San Francisco, Seattle, Stamford, Conn., and Washington, D.C. You can also write to Passport Service, Office of Correspondence, Department of State, 1425 K Street NW, Washington, DC 20522-1075. Ask for form DSP-11 for a new passport or DSP-82 for a renewal by mail.

Youths under 18 are granted a five-year passport. Children under 13 must have their parents apply for their passport, and teenagers 13 to 17 must also have a parent's permission before applying for a passport. If your passport is 12 years old or older, or was granted to you before your 16th year, you must apply in person at a passport agency, post office, or federal or state court office. Otherwise, you can renew it by mail for $42, or for $27 if you're under 18.

To apply for a passport, you'll need a complete government passport application form and you must provide proof of U.S. citizenship—a birth certificate or naturalization papers. An old passport (providing it's not more than 12 years old) is also accepted. You should also have identification with your signature and photograph, such as a driver's license. You'll also need two identical passport-size photographs. You'll wait the longest to receive your passport between mid-March and mid-September; in winter it usually only takes about two weeks by mail. Passports can sometimes be issued quickly in an emergency, providing you present a plane ticket with a confirmed seat.

You can also call 202/647-0518 24 hours for data about agency locations and hours.

In **Canada,** citizens seeking a passport may go to one of the nearly two dozen regional offices in such cities as Ottawa and Montréal. Alternatively, you can mail an application to the Passport Office, Section of External Affairs, Ottawa 1, K1A0G3. Post offices have application forms. Passports, valid for 5 years, cost $25 Canadian, and proof of Canadian citizenship is required, along with two signed identical photographs.

In the **United Kingdom,** citizens may apply at one of the regional officers in Liverpool, Newport, Glasgow, Peterborough, and Belfast, or in London if they reside there. You can also apply in person at a main post office. The fee is £15, and the passport is good for 10 years. Documents required include a birth certificate or a marriage certificate. Two photos must accompany the application.

In **Australia,** locals apply at the nearest post office. Provincial capitals and all big cities such as Sydney or Melbourne have passport offices. The fee is Aus$76, and the passport is valid for 10 years. Those under 18 may apply for a five-year passport for Aus$31. A departure tax stamp for Aus$20, sold at post offices and airports, is also required before leaving home.

**New Zealand** citizens may go to their nearest consulate or passport office or apply by mail. Proof of citizenship is required, and the passport is good for 10 years; cost is NZ$55.50.

In **Ireland,** write in advance for requirements or procedures to the Passport Office, Setanta Centre, Molesworth Street, Dublin 2, Ireland (tel. 01/780-822). The cost is IR£45. Irish citizens living in North America can contact the Irish Embassy, 2234 Massachusetts Avenue NW, Washington, DC 20008 (tel. 202/462-3939). The embassy can issue a new passport or direct you to one of four North American consulates that have jurisdiction over a particular region. If arranged by mail through Irish consulates, an Irish Passport costs U.S. $80.

## DOCUMENT PROTECTION

It is a good policy before leaving home to make copies of your most valuable documents, including the inside page of your passport that has your photograph. You should also make copies of your driver's license, an airline ticket, strategic hotel vouchers, and any other sort of identity card that might be pertinent. You should also make copies of any prescriptions you take. Place one copy in your luggage and carry the original with you. Leave the other copy at your home. The information on these documents will be extremely valuable should you encounter loss or theft abroad.

## CUSTOMS

**U.S. CUSTOMS**  You may take out of Bermuda $400 worth of merchandise duty free if you've been outside the United States for 48 hours or more and have not claimed a similar exemption within the past 30 days. Articles valued above the $400 duty-free limit but not over $1,000 will be assessed at a flat duty rate of 10%. Gifts for your personal use, not for business purposes, may be included in the $400 exemption, and unsolicited gifts totaling $50 a day may be sent home duty free. You are limited to one liter of wine, liqueur, or liquor, and five cartons of cigarettes. U.S. Customs preclearance is available for all scheduled flights. Passengers leaving for the United States must fill out written declaration forms before clearing U.S. Customs in Bermuda. The forms are available at Bermuda hotels, travel agencies, and airlines.

Collect receipts for all purchases made. If a merchant suggests giving you a false receipt, misstating the value of the goods, *beware:* the merchant may be a Customs informer. You must also declare all gifts received during your stay abroad.

Compile a list of expensive carry-on items, and ask a U.S. Customs agent to stamp your list at the airport before your departure. For additional information, write to the **U.S. Customs Service,** 1301 Constitution Avenue, P.O. Box 7407, Washington, DC 20229, for the free pamphlet, *Know Before You Go.*

**CANADIAN CUSTOMS**   For more information, write for the booklet *I Declare,* issued by Revenue Canada Customs Department, Communications Branch, Mackenzie Avenue, Ottawa, ON K1A 0L5. Canada allows its citizens a $300 exemption, and they are allowed to bring back duty free 200 cigarettes, 2.2 pounds of tobacco, 40 ounces of liquor, and 50 cigars. In addition, they are allowed to mail gifts to Canada from abroad at the rate of Can$40 a day, provided they are unsolicited and aren't alcohol or tobacco (write on the package: "Unsolicited gift, under $40 value." All valuables should be declared on the Y-38 Form before departure from Canada, including serial numbers, as in the case of, for example, expensive foreign cameras that you already own. *Note:* The $300 exemption can be used only once a year and only after an absence of seven days.

**BRITISH CUSTOMS**   Citizens can bring in goods valued up to £34; and one must be 17 or older to import liquor or tobacco. Britons are allowed 100 cigarettes or 100 cigarillos, 50 cigars, or 250 grams of tobacco. Two liters of table wine, one liter of alcohol greater than 22% by volume, and two liters of alcohol equal to or less than 22% by volume may also be brought in. British Customs tends to be strict and complicated in its requirements. For details get in touch with Her Majesty's Customs and Excise Office, New King's Bean House, 22 Upper Ground, London SE1 9PJ (tel. 071/382-5468 for more information).

**AUSTRALIAN CUSTOMS**   The duty-free allowance in Australia is Aus$400 or, for those under 18, Aus$200. Personal property mailed back from the United States or Bermuda should be marked "Australian goods returned," to avoid payment of duty. Upon returning to Australia, citizens can bring in 200 cigarettes or 250 grams of tobacco and one liter of alcohol. If you will be returning with valuable goods you already own, such as expensive foreign-made cameras, you should file form B263. A helpful brochure available from Australian consulates or Customs offices is called *Customs Information for All Travellers.*

---

## IMPRESSIONS

*. . . Bermuda is, without doubt, a success. It is, generally speaking, a peaceful place—more so than many Caribbean islands nearby. [Still, there are critics, from whom] you hear complaints about the Americanization of the place, the suggestion that Bermudianism is merely an anomalous cultural hybrid, a mule of a culture, attractive in its own way but of no lasting value or use. And yet it does seem to work; it is rich, it is as content as any place I know, and it is stable.*
—SIMON WINCHESTER, *THE SUN NEVER SETS: TRAVELS TO THE REMAINING OUTPOSTS OF THE BRITISH EMPIRE* (1985)

**NEW ZEALAND CUSTOMS**   The duty-free allowance is NZ$500. Citizens over 16 years of age can bring in 200 cigarettes or 250 grams of tobacco or 50 cigars and 4.5 liters of wine or beer or 1.125 liters of liquor. New Zealand currency does not carry import or export restrictions. A Certificate of Export listing already-owned valuables taken out of the country allows you to bring them back in without paying duty. Most questions are answered in a free pamphlet available at New Zealand consulates and Customs offices called *New Zealand Customs Guide for Travellers.*

**IRISH CUSTOMS**   Irish citizens may bring in 200 cigarettes or 100 cigarillos or 50 cigars or 250 grams (approximately nine ounces) of tobacco; one liter of liquor exceeding 22% volume (such as whisky, brandy, gin, rum, or vodka), or two liters of distilled beverages and spirits with a wine or alcohol base of an alcoholic strength not exceeding 22% volume, plus two liters of other wine; and 50 grams of perfume. Other allowances include duty-free goods to a value of IR£34 per person or IR£17 per person for travelers under 15 years of age.

# MONEY

## CASH/CURRENCY

Legal tender is the Bermuda dollar (BD$), which is divided into 100 cents. Prior to 1972, the Bermuda dollar was pegged to the pound sterling; now it is pegged through gold to the U.S. dollar on an equal basis—BD$1 equals U.S. $1. U.S. currency is generally accepted at par in shops, restaurants, and hotels. Currencies from the United Kingdom and all other foreign countries are not accepted. They can easily be exchanged for Bermuda dollars at banks. Banking and credit-card transactions in all foreign currencies involving currency exchange are subject to exchange rates.

## THE BRITISH POUND & THE U.S. DOLLAR

Here is how British pound sterling breaks down into U.S. dollars. The Bermudian dollar—no longer pegged to pound sterling—has the same value as the U.S. dollar.

| £ | US $ | £ | US $ |
|---|---|---|---|
| .05 | .08 | 8 | 12.80 |
| .10 | .16 | 9 | 14.40 |
| .25 | .40 | 10 | 16.00 |
| .50 | .80 | 15 | 24.00 |
| .75 | 1.20 | 20 | 32.00 |
| 1 | 1.60 | 25 | 40.00 |
| 2 | 3.20 | 30 | 48.00 |
| 3 | 4.80 | 35 | 56.00 |
| 4 | 6.40 | 40 | 64.00 |
| 5 | 8.00 | 45 | 72.00 |
| 6 | 9.60 | 50 | 80.00 |
| 7 | 11.20 | 100 | 160.00 |

## TRAVELER'S CHECKS

Traveler's checks are the safest way to carry cash while traveling, and most banks will give you a better rate on them. (Mergers of traveler's check facilities at several major banks have shortened the list of suppliers, however.) U.S.-dollar checks are accepted virtually anywhere, but in some cases travelers might want checks denominated in other currencies.

When purchasing checks from the following suppliers, ask about refunds and refund hotlines. American Express has probably the greatest number of offices around the world.

**American Express** (tel. toll free 800/221-7282 in the U.S. and Canada) charges a 1% commission. Checks are free to members of the American Automobile Association. The company issues checks denominated in U.S. and Canadian dollars, as well as international currencies, as does **Citicorp** (tel. toll free 800/645-6556 in the U.S. or 813/623-1709, collect, in Canada).

**MasterCard International/Thomas Cook International** (tel. toll free 800/223-9920 in the U.S. or collect 609/987-7300 at the headquarters in Princeton, N.J., from other parts of the world) issues checks denominated in U.S. and Canadian dollars, as well as other international currencies. **Barclays Bank/Bank of America** (tel. toll free 800/221-2426 in the U.S. and Canada) sells VISA traveler's checks denominated in U.S. dollars and other currencies through Barclay's subsidiary, Interpayment Services.

## CREDIT CARDS

Credit cards are accepted in many shops and restaurants, but not all hotels. Check first. VISA and MasterCard are the major cards used, although American Express and, to a lesser extent, Diners Club are also popular.

# WHAT WILL IT COST?

Time is money, and since Bermuda is less than a two-hour flight from most cities on the East Coast, the savings begin even before visitors land on the island. A four-day, three-night vacation in Bermuda really does include four days of vacation for the price of only three nights' accommodation. An 8:30 a.m. flight from New York gets travelers to Bermuda in time for lunch, with the whole afternoon to play.

The variety of accommodations allows travelers to indulge their preferences and tastes while keeping budgets under control. There are luxury resort hotels, small hotels, intimate guesthouses, and cottage colonies. Most large resorts offer money-saving package plans that include meals. If a stay of a week or more is planned, a housekeeping unit or cottage with kitchenette might be a good choice.

No rental cars are available, but Bermuda's local transportation is efficient, and inexpensive, saving visitors up to $250 over the cost of one week's car rental. Options include the simple and comprehensive bus system, ferries, and bicycle or moped rentals.

Golfers will find that greens fees are comparable to or below fees at other destinations. For example, Ocean View Golf & Country Club and St. George's Golf Club charge only $22 and $26, respectively, for 18 holes of golf. There are eight world-class golf courses with varying fees.

Athletic and cultural activities, such as tennis, riding, guided tours, museums, and attractions are good values in Bermuda.

Hotel costs will depend on when you arrive. If you're seeking reductions, perhaps ranging from 20% to 40% per person, go in the off-season. In Bermuda, unlike the Caribbean, this is from November through March.

On the half-board plan (MAP), many hotels ask $125 to $275 per person per day based on double occupancy, with some of the smaller properties charging from $100 to $180 per person per day, double occupancy. A hotel without meals (EP), charges from about $100 to $150 per person daily.

To combat these high tabs, travel agents offer special package deals, which can represent a substantial savings over regular hotel tariffs, for families, golfers, tennis players, or honeymooners and some others.

To cut costs even more, families can rent housekeeping efficiencies, apartments, cottages, or even condominiums (some condos are rented like time-share units when the owners aren't in residence).

In figuring your budget, think about transportation. Getting around the island isn't always easy since visitors aren't allowed to rent cars. You'll therefore have to rely on public transportation or the very expensive taxis. The more agile can rent bicycles or mopeds. (See Getting Around, in Chapter 3, "Arriving in Bermuda," for more information.) Fortunately, once you reach a particular parish, many attractions can be covered on foot, and Bermuda becomes almost one vast walking tour.

Dining out is an expensive undertaking in Bermuda. If you patronize the very expensive establishments, you can end up spending as much as $100 per person, including wine. Even moderate to expensive restaurants charge $30 to $50 per person. Any dinner under $30 per person is considered inexpensive. To cut dining costs, order a picnic lunch or else enjoy pub grub at noon.

If all these hidden or extra costs are intimidating, consider a package tour in which everything will be arranged for you. You'll know the bottom-line vacation cost before you embark on your journey.

| **WHAT THINGS COST IN BERMUDA** | **U.S. $** |
| --- | --- |
| 15-minute taxi ride | 15.00 |
| One-way ride on a bus | 1.25 |
| Local telephone call | .20 |
| Double at Belmont Hotel (deluxe) | 256.00 |
| Double at Rosedon (moderate) | 140.00 |
| Double at Royal Heights Guest House (budget) | 100.00 |
| Lunch for one at La Plage (moderate)* | 15.00 |
| Lunch for one at Bombay Bicycle Club (budget)* | 10.95 |
| Dinner for one at Romanoff Restaurant (deluxe)* | 50.00 |
| Dinner for one at Chancery Wine Bar (moderate)* | 32.00 |
| Dinner for one at Chopsticks Restaurant (budget)* | 22.00 |
| Bottle of beer in a bar | 1.75–5.20 |
| Coca-Cola in a café | 1.50 |
| Cup of coffee in a café | .80–2.50 |
| Glass of wine in a restaurant | 3.00–4.00 |
| Roll of ASA 100 color film, 36 exposures | 7.10 |
| Admission to Elbow Beach | 3.00 |
| Movie ticket | 7.00 |

* Includes tax and tip but not wine.

# 2. WHEN TO GO — CLIMATE, HOLIDAYS & EVENTS

Bermuda enjoys a mild climate, and the term "Bermuda high" has come to mean sunny days and clear skies. Bermuda, being farther north in the Atlantic than the Bahamas, is much cooler in winter. Its slow, or off-season, begins in December and lasts until around the first of March. Many hotels, therefore, quote their low-season rates—discounts of from 20% to 60%—in winter. During the autumn and winter, many hotels also quote some very attractive package deals. Other hotels shut down for a week to a month or two in winter.

The off-season rates, which are also listed in this guide, are a bonanza for cost-conscious travelers who are free to travel to Bermuda from November to March.

## CLIMATE

Bermuda is a semitropical island, and the Gulf Stream, flowing between it and North America, keeps the climate temperate. There is no rainy season, and no normal month of excess rain. Showers may be heavy at times, but the skies clear quickly. In summer temperatures rarely rise above 85° Fahrenheit. There's nearly always a cool breeze in the evening, and accommodations that require it are air-conditioned. Springlike temperatures prevail from mid-December to late March, with the average ranging from the low 60s to 70°F. From mid-November to mid-December and from late March through April, be prepared for either spring or summer weather.

A look at the official chart on temperature and rainfall will show you what to expect during your visit to Bermuda.

### Bermuda's Average Daytime Temperatures & Rainfall

|  | Jan | Feb | Mar | Apr | May | June | July | Aug | Sept | Oct | Nov | Dec |
|---|---|---|---|---|---|---|---|---|---|---|---|---|
| Temp.°F | 65 | 64 | 64 | 65 | 70 | 75 | 79 | 80 | 79 | 75 | 69 | 65 |
| Temp.°C | 19 | 18 | 18 | 19 | 21 | 24 | 30 | 27 | 30 | 24 | 21 | 19 |
| Rainfall (in.) | 4 | 5 | 4.6 | 3 | 3.9 | 5.2 | 4 | 5.3 | 5.3 | 6 | 4.5 | 3.9 |

You can obtain current weather information for Bermuda, as well as other destinations, by calling **Weather Trak** (tel. 900/370-8725). A taped message gives you a three-digit access code to call for the place you're interested in—for Bermuda 809 (area code).

### THE HURRICANE SEASON

The hurricane season—the curse of Caribbean and Bermudian—officially lasts June through November. But don't panic. More tropical cyclones pound the U.S. mainland than hurricanes devastate Bermuda. And Bermuda isn't as likely to be pounded by a

## IMPRESSIONS

*[Above all the attributes of Bermuda is] that uninterrupted health and alacrity of spirit, which is the result of the finest weather and gentlest climate in the world.*
—GEORGE BERKELEY, IN LETTER TO LORD PERCIVAL (1722)

hurricane as is a Caribbean island. Satellite forecasts generally give adequate warning of any really bad weather so that precautions can be taken in time.

If you're really concerned, you can call the nearest branch of the National Weather Service. Look under the U.S. Department of Commerce. Radio and TV weather reports from the **National Hurricane Center** in Coral Gables, Florida, can also keep you posted.

## HOLIDAYS & EVENTS

The following public holidays are observed in Bermuda (the ones without a date change from year to year): New Year's Day (January 1), Good Friday, Easter, Bermuda Day (May 24), the Queen's Birthday (first or second Monday in June), Cup Match Days (cricket; Thursday and Friday preceding first Monday in August), Labour Day (first Monday in September), Christmas Day (December 25), and Boxing Day (December 26). Public holidays that fall on a Saturday or Sunday are usually celebrated on the following Monday.

# BERMUDA CALENDAR OF EVENTS

### JANUARY

✪ **BERMUDA FESTIVAL**  *During the winter months, the Bermuda calendar is jam-packed with such events as golf and tennis invitationals, an international marathon race, a dog show, open house and garden tours, and, of course, the **Bermuda Festival,** the six-week International Festival of the Performing Arts, held in Hamilton and featuring drama, dance, jazz, classical and popular music, and other entertainment by the best international artists.*

*Where: Islandwide. When: January and February. How: Some tickets are reserved until 48 hours before curtain time for visitors. For details, write the Bermuda Festival, Box HM 297, Hamilton HM AX, Bermuda (tel. 809/295-1291).*

☐ **The Bermuda International Marathon,** with international and local runners. For further information and entry forms, contact the International Race Weekend Committee, Bermuda Track and Field Association, P.O. Box DV 397, Devonshire, Bermuda DV BX. (tel. 809/238-2333).

### MARCH

✪ **BERMUDA COLLEGE WEEKS**  *This is an annual spring odyssey for at least 10,000 students who flock here every year. These weeks began as*

*Rugby Weeks in 1933. Rugby teams from Ivy League schools came to compete against British or Bermudian teams. "Where the boys are," to borrow the popular song title, led to "where the girls are." A tradition was born. The Department of Tourism issues a College Week Courtesy Card to those who have a valid college identification card. This becomes a passport to a week of free—courtesy of the Bermudian government—beach parties, lunches, boat cruises, dances, and entertainment.*

***Where:*** *Islandwide.* ***When:*** *March 2–April 13.* ***How:*** *Obtain a list of events from the tourist office.*

---

☐ **Home & Garden Tours:** Each spring the **Garden Club of Bermuda** lays out the welcome mat at a number of private homes and gardens that are open to view. A different set of houses, all conveniently located in the same parish, is open every Wednesday during this springtime viewing. Normally a total of 20 homes participate in the program, many of them dating back to the 17th and 18th centuries.

***Where:*** Islandwide. ***When:*** End of March to mid-May. ***How:*** The tourist office provides a complete list of schedules.

## APRIL

☐ **Beating of Retreat:** Ceremony of the Bermuda regiment and massed pipes and drums, on Front Street in Hamilton at 9pm. Held on the last Wednesday in every month from April through October, except August. (Periodically held in Somerset and St. George's.)

☐ **Peppercorn Ceremony:** His Excellency the governor collects the annual rent of one peppercorn for use of the island's Old State house in St. George's. April 21 (dates may vary).

☐ **An agriculture show:** A three-day exhibit of Bermuda's best fruits, flowers, vegetables, and livestock; and equestrian and other ring events. Dates vary.

☐ **Invitational International Week:** Yachtspeople from the United States, the United Kingdom, Canada, and other countries compete with Bermudians. (Other boat-racing events take place in alternate years.)

## MAY

☐ **Bermuda Game Fishing Tournament:** Special prizes for top catches of 17 species of game fish. All amateur anglers are eligible. Held from May 1–Nov. 30.

☐ **Bermuda Heritage Month:** Culminates in **Bermuda Day,** May 24, a public holiday.

## JUNE

☐ **Queen's Birthday** (first or second Monday in June) is celebrated by a parade on Front Street in Hamilton.

☐ **The Blue Water Cruising Race:** Race from Marion, Massachusetts, to Bermuda is held in June in odd-numbered years, as is the **MultiHull Ocean Yacht Race** from Newport, Rhode Island, to Bermuda. In June of even-numbered years, some 180 of the world's finest yachts compete in the **Bermuda Race,** from Newport to Bermuda.

## JULY

☐ **Marine Science Day:** Lectures, hands-on demonstrations, and displays for adults and children, by Bermuda Biological Station. Call 809/297-1880 for more information. Different date each year.

## AUGUST

☐ **Cup Match and Somers Days:** Spectacular cricket match pits the east against the west end of the island. Held on Thursday and Friday before first Monday in August.

## SEPTEMBER

☐ **Annual American-Bermudian Friendship Festival & Air Show:** Two-day event held entirely at the U.S. Naval Air Station, St. David's, featuring an air show. Gates open 9am–5pm. For information, call Public Affairs Office (tel. 809/293-5515). September 12–13.

## OCTOBER

☐ **Omega Gold Cup International Match Race Tournament:** Top ranking Match Racing skippers compete with Bermudians. Hosted by the Royal Bermuda Yacht Club. October 18–25.

## NOVEMBER

✪ *BERMUDA RENDEZVOUS TIME   During this time walking tours of the historic towns of Hamilton and St. George's (which is as old as Williamsburg), and a tour of the Botanical Gardens are sponsored by the government. Pipe and drum music with Scottish dancers, a fashion show and tea, a thriving craft market, and other special events are offered free to the winter visitor.*

*    **Where:** Islandwide. **When:** November 15 to March 31. **How:** Specific dates for events available in advance from the tourist office, your hotel or guesthouse management, or from local publications.*

☐ **The Opening of Parliament:** Traditional ceremony and military guard of honor connected with the **Opening of Parliament** by His Excellency the governor as the queen's personal representative. November 6.
☐ **World Rugby Classic:** Former international rugby players compete with Bermudians at Bermuda National Sports Club. November 3–11.
☐ **Guy Fawkes Day:** Annual celebration with a minifair starts with the traditional burning of the Guy Fawkes effigy at the Keepyard of the Bermuda Maritime Museum, Royal Naval Dockyard, beginning at 4:30pm. November 7.
☐ **Remembrance Day:** A gala parade is held, with Bermudian police, British and U.S. military units, Bermudians, and veterans' organizations taking part. November 11.
☐ **Bermuda Equestrian Festival:** International Show Jumping Competition at the Botanical Gardens. November 28 and 29.
☐ **Invitation Tennis Weeks:** Over 100 visiting players vie with Bermudians in two weeks of matches.

## DECEMBER

☐ **Bermuda Goodwill Tournament:** Pre/amateur foursomes from international golf clubs play over 72 holes on four of Bermuda's eight courses during golfing activity. December 7–11.

# 3. HEALTH, INSURANCE & OTHER CONCERNS

## HEALTH

If you need treatment while in Bermuda, finding a good doctor is no real problem. See Fast Facts, in Chapter 3, "Arriving in Bermuda," for specific locations and addresses.

It's a good idea to carry all your vital medicines and drugs (the legal kind) with you in your carry-on luggage, in case your checked luggage is lost.

If your medical condition is chronic, always talk to your doctor before leaving home. He or she may have specific advice to give you, depending on your problem. For conditions such as epilepsy, a heart condition, or diabetes, wear a Medic Alert identification tag. This tag provides Medic Alert's 24-hour hotline number, so a foreign doctor can obtain medical records for you. For a lifetime membership, the cost is a well-spent $35. Contact the **Medic Alert Foundation,** P.O. Box 1009, Turlock, CA 95381 (tel. toll free 800/432-5378).

At some point in a vacation, most visitors experience some diarrhea, even those who follow the usual precautions. This is often the result of a change in diet and eating habits, rather than bad or contaminated food and water.

Mild forms of diarrhea usually pass quickly without medication. As a precaution, take along some antidiarrhea medicine, moderate your eating habits, and drink only mineral water until you recover. Drink plenty of fluids to prevent dehydration. Consuming more than your usual intake of salt will help your body retain water. Eat only simply prepared foods at such times, such as plain bread (no butter) and boiled vegetables or some broth. Avoid dairy products, except yogurt.

If symptoms persist, you may have dysentery, especially if you notice blood or mucus in your stool. At this point you should consult a doctor.

Sometimes travelers find that a change in diet will lead to constipation. If this occurs, eat a high-fiber diet and drink plenty of mineral water. Avoid large meals and don't drink wine.

**WATER** Although tap water is generally considered safe to drink, if you have a delicate stomach it is better to avoid it and drink mineral water instead. This applies even to iced drinks. Stick to beer, hot tea, or soft drinks.

**SUNBURN** Actually, one of the most dangerous elements in Bermuda is the very

## IMPRESSIONS

*I find Bermuda is a place where physicians order their patients when no other air will keep them alive.*
—THOMAS MOORE, IN LETTER TO HIS MOTHER (1803)

thing you might have gone there to enjoy: the sun. Take precautions: Wear sunglasses, a hat (wide-brimmed if possible), a coverup for your shoulders, and a sunscreen lotion. Experts also advise that you should limit your time on the beach the first day.

**INSECTS & PESTS**   Mosquitoes are a nuisance, but nothing more than that (the malaria-carrying kind are rare). Among the most annoying insects are the no-see-ums; even if you can't see these little gnats, you can sure "feel-um." They appear mainly in the early evening. Because even screens can't keep them out, you'll have to use your favorite bug repellent.

**VACCINATIONS**   Vaccinations aren't required to enter Bermuda if you're coming from a "disease-free" country such as the United States or Canada.

**MEDICINES**   Take along an adequate supply of any prescription drugs that you need and a written prescription that uses the *generic* name of each drug, not the brand name. Consult your pharmacist about taking such over-the-counter drugs as Colace and Metamucil. Also, if you wear glasses or contact lenses, be sure to take along your prescription (as well as an extra pair).

Other useful items to take along are first-aid cream, insect repellent, aspirin, nose drops, Band-Aids, and hydrogen peroxide. If you're subject to motion sickness, include motion-sickness medicine as well.

# INSURANCE

Insurance needs for the traveler abroad fall into three categories: health and accident, trip cancellation, and lost luggage.

First, review your present policies before traveling internationally—you may already have adequate coverage between them and what is offered by credit-card companies if the trip tickets were purchased with their card. Fraternal organizations sometimes can provide policies that protect members in case of sickness or accident abroad.

Many homeowners' insurance policies cover theft of luggage during foreign travel and loss of documents, for instance, your airline ticket, although coverage is usually limited to about $500. To submit a claim on your insurance, remember that you'll need police reports or a statement from a medical authority that you did in fact suffer the loss or experience the illness for which you are seeking compensation. Such claims, by their very nature, can be filed only when you return from Bermuda.

Some policies (and this is the type you should have) provide cash advances or else transferral of funds so that you won't have to dip into your precious travel funds to settle medical bills.

If you've booked a charter fare, you'll probably have to pay a cancellation fee if you cancel a trip suddenly, even if you cancel because of an unforeseen crisis. It's possible to get insurance that will cover such a fee, either through travel agencies or through a credit card company—for example, VISA and American Express—when such insurance is written into tickets paid for by credit cards.

Companies offering special travel insurance policies include the following:

**Travel Guard International,** 1145 Clark Street, Stevens Point, WI 54481 (tel. toll free 800/826-1300 outside Wisconsin, 715/345-0505 in Wisconsin), offers a comprehensive 7-day policy that covers lost luggage, emergency assistance, accidental death, trip cancellation, and medical coverage abroad. The cost of the package is $52, but there are restrictions that you should understand before you accept the coverage.

**Travel Insurance PAK,** The Travelers Insurance Co., 1 Tower Square, 10 NB, Hartford, CT 06183-5040 (tel. toll free 800/243-3174), offers illness and accident coverage that costs from $10 for 6 to 10 days. For lost or damaged luggage, $500 worth of coverage costs $20 for 6 to 10 days. You can also get trip-cancellation insurance for $5.50 per $100 of coverage to a limit of $5,000 per person.

**Access America,** 6600 West Broad Street, P.O. Box 11188, Richmond, VA 23230 (tel. 804/285-3300 or toll free 800/284-8300), offers travel insurance and 24-hour emergency travel, medical, and legal assistance for the traveler. One call to their hotline center, staffed by multilingual coordinators, connects travelers to a worldwide network of professionals able to offer specialized help in reaching the nearest physician, hospital, or legal advisor, and in obtaining emergency cash or the replacement of lost travel documents. Varying coverage levels are available.

# 4. WHAT TO PACK

## LUGGAGE

Always pack lightly. Airlines are increasingly strict about how much luggage you can bring aboard. Checked luggage should not measure more than a total of 62 inches (width plus length plus height) and weigh no more than 70 pounds. Carry-on luggage should measure no more than 45 inches (width plus length plus height) and fit under your seat or in the overhead bin.

## CLOTHING

In Bermuda, lightweight clothing is best. Avoid nylon or other synthetics, as they become hot and sticky. If possible, don't bring anything that has to be ironed or dry-cleaned. Be prepared to wash your clothes and underwear in the bathroom and hang them to dry overnight. Clothes dry quickly here.

Anyone who burns easily should bring along and wear long-sleeved shirts and long-legged pants. Men might want to wear a jacket and women a light wrap if they're going out at night. Evenings tend to be cooler, and sometimes restaurants and bars keep the air conditioning on too high.

Dress tends to be more formal in Bermuda than it is in the Bahamas and the Caribbean. Thus, when patronizing some of the more elegant restaurants or clubs at night, men are required to wear a jacket and tie. Otherwise, when simply touring around the island, men may wear sports shirts and slacks or walking shorts (certainly Bermuda shorts). Women may wear sun dresses and shifts or blouses with culottes and more modest shorts.

If you're going to be in Bermuda during the winter season, take along appropriate attire—autumn clothes or light woolen articles and especially a raincoat or windbreaker. Yet don't forget your swimsuit, regardless of the season; sunny days are frequent, even in midwinter.

The general rule of packing is to include four of everything, from socks and underwear to shirts, pants, and skirts. You will then have something to wear while other things are drying. And always bring two pairs of comfortable shoes.

## OTHER ITEMS

Bermuda operates on a 110-volt, 60-cycle alternating current. American visitors generally don't need adaptors or converters, but visitors from Britain or France do.

# 5. TIPS FOR THE DISABLED, SENIORS, SINGLES, FAMILIES & STUDENTS

## FOR THE DISABLED

Hotels rarely publicize what facilities, if any, they offer the disabled, so it's always better to contact the hotel directly. A number of agencies can also provide information to help you plan your trip. The **Travel Information Service,** MossRehab, 1200 W. Tabor Road, Philadelphia, PA 19141-3099 (tel. 215/456-9600), charges a nominal fee per package of information. Each package contains names and addresses of accessible hotels, restaurants, and attractions, often based on reports of travelers who have been there.

*Air Transportation of Handicapped Persons,* published by the U.S. Department of Transportation, is free. Writing to Distribution Unit, U.S. Department of Transportation, Publications Division, M-4332, Washington, DC 20590, and ask for Free Advisory Circular No. AC12032.

You may also want to consider joining a tour specifically designed for disabled visitors. Write (and enclose a stamped, self-addressed envelope) to the **Society for the Advancement of Travel for the Handicapped,** 347 Fifth Ave., Suite 610, New York, NY 10016 (tel. 212/447-7284), for a list of such tour operators. Yearly membership dues are $45 for senior citizens or $25 for students. The Bermuda chapter of this society publishes the *Access Guide to Bermuda for the Handicapped Traveler,* which costs $2 and is available at most bookstores on the island.

You might also consider the **Federation of the Handicapped,** 211 West 14th Street, New York, NY 10011 (tel. 212/206-4200), which offers summer tours for members, who pay a yearly fee of $4.

**The Information Center for Individuals with Disabilities,** Fort Point Place, 27-43 Wormwood Street, Boston, MA 02210 (tel. 617/727-5540), is another good source. It has lists of travel agents who specialize in tours for the disabled.

For the blind or visually impaired, the best source is the **American Foundation for the Blind,** 15 W. 16th St., New York, NY 10011 (tel. 212/620-2147, or toll free 800/232-5463). It offers information on travel and various requirements for bringing in seeing-eye dogs. It also issues identification cards, for $10, to those who are legally blind.

## FOR SENIORS

Many discounts are available for seniors, but be advised that you have to be a member of an association to obtain some of them.

Write for *Travel Tips for Older Americans* (publication #8970), distributed for $1 by the Superintendent of Documents, U.S. Government Printing Office, Washington, DC 20402-9375 (tel. 202/512-2164). Another booklet—this one free—called *101 Tips for the Mature Traveler,* is available from Grand Circle Travel, 347 Congress Street, Suite 3A, Boston, MA 02210 (tel. 617/350-7500 or toll free 800/221-2610). This tour operator offers extended vacations, escorted programs, and cruises that feature unique learning experiences for seniors at competitive prices.

**Mature Outlook,** 6001 North Clark Street, Chicago, IL 60660 (tel. toll free 800/336-6330), is a travel club for people more than 50 years of age; it's operated by Sears, Roebuck & Co. Annual membership fee is $9.95, which includes a bimonthly newsletter featuring discounts at hotels.

**SAGA International Holidays** is well known for its all-inclusive tours for seniors, preferably those 60 years old or older. Insurance is included in the net price of any of their tours. Contact SAGA International Holidays, 222 Berkeley Street, Boston, MA 02116 (tel. toll free 800/343-0273).

The **AARP Travel Experience from American Express,** 400 Pinnacle Way, Suite 450, Norcross, GA 30071 (tel. toll free 800/927-0111 for land arrangements, 800/745-4567 for cruises, or 800/659-5678 for TTD), provides travel arrangements for members for the American Association of Retired Persons (AARP). Travel Experience provides a wide variety of escorted, hosted, go-any-day packages. Discounts on car rentals and hotels, and other discounts, are offered through AARP's Purchase Privilege Program, a separate program from Travel Experience.

Information is also available from the **National Council of Senior Citizens,** 1331 F St., N.W. Washington D.C. 20004 (tel. 202/347-8800). A nonprofit organization, the council charges $12 per person or couple, for which you receive a monthly newsletter that is devoted partly to travel tips and often features discounts on hotels and auto rentals.

# FOR SINGLES

One company that has made heroic efforts to match single travelers with like-minded companions is now the largest and best-known such company in the United States. Jens Jurgen, the German-born founder, charges $36 to $66 for a six-month listing in his well-publicized records. New applicants fill out a form stating their preferences and needs. They then receive a minilisting of potentially suitable travel partners. Companions of the same or opposite sex can be requested.

A 34-page bimonthly newsletter also gives numerous money-saving travel tips of special interest to solo travelers. A sample issue is available for $4. For an application and more information, write to **Jens Jurgen,** Travel Companion, P.O. Box P-833, Amityville, NY 11701 (tel. 516/454-0880).

**Singleworld,** 401 Theodore Fremd Avenue, Rye, NY 10580 (tel. 914/967-3334 or toll free 800/223-6490), offers and operates tours geared to solo travel. Two basic types of tours are available: cruises and tours for people in their 20s and 30s, or jaunts for any age. Annual dues are $25.

**Grand Circle Travel,** mentioned above, also offers escorted tours and cruises for singles. Once you book one of their trips, membership is included; in addition, you get vouchers providing discounts for future trips.

# FOR FAMILIES

Bermuda contends for top position on the world list of places for vacations for the entire family. The smallest toddlers can spend blissful hours in shallow seawater or pools constructed with them in mind, while older children can enjoy boat rides, horseback riding, hiking, discoing, or even snorkeling.

Most resort hotels will advise you what there is in the way of fun for all, and many have play directors and supervised activities for various age groups. However, there are some tips for making the trip a success that parents should attend to in advance.

Take along a "security blanket" for your child. This might be a pacifier or a favorite toy or book.

Arrange ahead for necessities such as a crib and a bottle warmer, as well as for cots in your room for larger children. If the place you're staying doesn't stock baby food, bring your own.

Draw up guidelines on bedtime, eating, keeping tidy, being in the sun, even shopping and spending. It will make everybody's vacation more enjoyable.

Take protection from the sun. For tiny tots, this should include a sun umbrella, while the whole family will need sunscreen (a factor of 15 is a good idea) and sunglasses. Also take along anti-insect lotions and sprays. You'll probably need both to repel such unwanted island denizens as mosquitoes and sand fleas, as well as to ease the itching and possible other aftereffects of insect bites.

Don't forget the thermometer, basic first-aid supplies, any medications your doctor may suggest, swimsuits, beach and pool toys, waterwings for tiny mites, flip-flops for everybody, and terrycloth robes.

*Family Travel Times* is published ten times a year by Travel With Your Children (TWYCH), and includes a weekly call-in service for subscribers. Subscriptions cost $55 a year and can be ordered by writing to TWYCH, 45 West 18th Street, 7th Floor, New York, NY 10011 (tel. 212/206-0688).

TWYCH also publishes two nitty-gritty information guides, *Skiing with Children* and *Cruising with Children,* which sell for $29 and $22, respectively, and are discounted to newsletter subscribers. An information packet, which describes TWYCH's publications and includes a recent sample issue, can be purchased by sending $3.50 to the above address.

Most hotels will help you find a babysitter.

## FOR STUDENTS

Bona fide students can avail themselves of a number of discounts on travel. The most wide ranging travel service for students is provided by **Council Travel,** 205 East 42nd Street, New York, NY 10017 (tel. 212/661-1450, ext. 1159), with the main office in New York and 37 other offices throughout the United States. This outfit provides details about budget travel, study abroad, working permits, and insurance. It also compiles a number of helpful publications, including *Student Travels.* This free magazine (with $1 for postage) includes information on study and work opportunities abroad. Council Travel also issues a useful International Student Card (ISIC) for $15.

# 6. HONEYMOONS & WEDDINGS IN BERMUDA

There are good reasons why Bermuda hosts more than 23,000 honeymooners and second honeymooners each year. It offers an ideal environment for couples who prefer active *and* relaxing agendas. While some visitors prefer to fill their days with scuba diving and swimming, others enjoy leisure activities, such as strolling along the beach at sunset or reading poetry to each other while snuggling in a secluded cove. Many of Bermuda's hotels, from luxurious resorts to intimate cottage colonies, have special honeymoon packages. These include airfare, accommodations, meal plans, champagne upon arrival, flowers in the room, and special discounts at local attractions and restaurants. Call toll free 800/BERMUDA for details.

## GETTING MARRIED IN BERMUDA

Couples who wish to get married in Bermuda must file a "Notice of Intended Marriage" with the Register General, accompanied by a fee of $146 (in the form of a bank draft, not a personal check). The draft should be mailed or delivered personally to the Register General at the Government Administration Building, 30 Parliament St., Hamilton HM 12, phone (809/295-5151, fax 809/292-4568). Notice of Intended

Marriage forms can be obtained from the Bermuda Department of Tourism offices in Atlanta, Boston, Chicago, Los Angeles, and New York. Airmail to Bermuda from the United States can take six to 10 days, so plan accordingly.

Once the Notice of Intended Marriage is received, it will be published—including names and addresses—once in any two of the island's newspapers. Assuming there is no formal objection, the Registry will issue the license 14 days after receiving notice. It will be valid for three months.

**CIVIL CEREMONIES** Weddings are preformed at the Registry by appointment only Monday through Friday, 10am to 4pm, and Saturdays between 10am and noon. The fee is $146, which includes the cost of the ceremony and certificate. Copies of the marriage certificate are available for an additional fee.

**RELIGIOUS CEREMONIES** Religious ceremonies for non-Bermudians interested in getting married in a Roman Catholic Church are permitted on a case-by-case basis and arrangements should be made in advance by contacting the Bishop of Hamilton, P.O. Box HM 1191, Hamilton HM EX, Bermuda. Fees for religious ceremonies are arranged individually.

**WEDDING ARRANGEMENTS** Many hotels can help make wedding arrangements, from reserving the church and clergy, to hiring a horse and buggy, ordering the wedding cake, or securing a photographer. In addition, the following on-island wedding consultants can assist with these and other details: **The Wedding Salon,** P.O. Box HM 2085, Hamilton HM HX, Bermuda, tel. 809/292-5677, fax, 809/292-2955; and **Bermuda Wedding Planners,** 12 Tribe Road, #2 Middle Road, Warwick WK 09, Bermuda, tel. 809/236-7309 or 809/234-0695.

---

# 7. ALTERNATIVE/ADVENTURE TRAVEL

---

Offbeat, alternative modes of travel often cost less and yet are far more enriching. Some organizations arranging such travel are listed below.

## EDUCATIONAL/STUDY TRAVEL

The best information is available at the **Council on International Educational Exchange (CIEE),** 205 E. 42nd St., New York, NY 10017 (tel. 212/661-1414), which offers information about working or studying abroad. It's best to request a copy of their 500-page *Work, Study, Travel Abroad: The Whole World Handbook,* costing $14.45. It outlines more than 1,000 study opportunities abroad.

One of the most dynamic organizations offering studies for senior citizens is **Elderhostel,** 75 Federal St., Boston, MA 02110-1941 (tel. 617/426-7788), established in 1975. Most courses last for two or three weeks and are a good value, considering that accommodations (in student dormitories or modest inns), all meals, and tuition are included. Courses involve no homework, are ungraded, and center mostly on the liberal arts. Participants must be age 60 or older. However, if two members go as a couple, only one member need be 60 or over. Write for their free newsletter and a list of upcoming courses and destinations.

## HOMESTAYS OR VISITS

The international, interfaith **Servas** ("to serve" in Esperanto), 11 John St., Suite 407, New York, NY 10038 (tel. 212/267-0252), is a nonprofit, nongovernmental network of travelers and hosts whose goal is to help build world peace, goodwill, and understanding. They do this by providing opportunities for deeper, more personal contacts among people of diverse cultural and political backgrounds. Servas travelers are invited to share living space in a privately owned home, staying without charge for visits lasting a maximum of two days. Visitors pay a $55 annual fee, fill out an application, and are interviewed for suitability by one of more than 200 Servas interviewers throughout the country. They then receive a Servas directory listing the names and addresses of Servas hosts who encourage visitors in their homes. This program embraces 112 countries, including Bermuda.

**Friendship Force,** 575 S. Tower, 1 CNN Center, Atlanta, GA 30303 (tel. 404/522-9490), is a nonprofit organization existing for the sole purpose of fostering and encouraging friendship among people worldwide. Dozens of branch offices throughout North America arrange en masse visits, usually once a year. Because of group bookings, the airfare to the host country is usually less than you'd pay if you bought an individual APEX ticket. Each participant is required to spend two weeks in the host country, one full week of which will be as a guest in the home of a host family.

## HOME EXCHANGES

If you don't mind "staying put," you can avail yourself of a "house swap," as it's often called. It certainly keeps costs low if you don't mind a stranger living in your mainland home or apartment. Sometimes the exchange includes use of the family car.

Possibilities for this type of service are a straight house exchange for vacation purposes, or something more complicated. For example, your teenage child might be housed free in exchange for free room and board when the host child visits your hometown. In this day of increased crime, sometimes the deal is for a "house-sitter." Unfortunately, though, there's no guarantee that you'll find a house or an apartment in the area you're interested in.

For further information, write to **Vacation Exchange Club,** P.O. Box 650, Key West, FL 33041 (tel. 305/294-3720 or toll free 800/638-3841). For a fee of $50 the club will send you four directories a year; your name and address will be listed in one of the directories.

## SPA TREATMENTS

Full-fledged spa facilities are available at the **Sonesta Beach Hotel and Spa,** Southampton (tel. 809/238-8122, or toll free 800/766-3782 in the U.S.), which is recognized by some experts as one of the top 10 health-and-beauty spas of the world. European-staffed, it offers the health-and-fitness regimens so popular at American spas. Many exotic and beneficial treatments are also offered, one being Ionithermie, the inch-reducing treatment from Europe, as well as deluxe facial care from Paris, ancient forms of therapeutic and relaxing massage such as aromatherapy and reflexology, and Swedish massage. Some people check into the hotel on calorie-controlled four- or seven-day programs. The client will be almost totally occupied from 8:30am to 7pm with the likes of aerobics, skin and body care, supervised indoor and outdoor stretching exercises, massages, facials, and beauty regimens.

The facilities can also be used by hotel guests or outsiders who opt for pinpointed treatments rather than the full spa treatment. The up-to-date accoutrements include Universal gym equipment, saunas, steambaths, and massage rooms. The staff directs five-times-a-day exercise classes, which outsiders can join for a fee. Each procedure is priced separately for nonpackage participants. For after-workout pick-me-ups, there's a beauty salon adjacent to the health spa.

# CHAPTER 3

# ARRIVING IN BERMUDA

This chapter explores the different options for getting to Bermuda, treating not only the most obvious choices, but some you may not have thought of. Also suggested are several itineraries to help you get the most out of your vacation time. You'll find tips, too, on determining where to stay and dine and what to buy.

# 1. GETTING THERE

## BY PLANE

From North America's East Coast, you can be in Bermuda in approximately 2 hours by plane.

### THE MAJOR AIRLINES

**American Airlines** (tel. toll free 800/433-7300) usually flies into Bermuda at least once a day from two of its most modern and busiest hubs, Raleigh-Durham, N.C. (lying on almost the same latitude as Bermuda), and New York City. From Raleigh-Durham there is one daily nonstop flight in midwinter and two nonstops every other day throughout the rest of the year, with excellent connections from virtually anywhere within North America on the second daily flights. From New York's JFK Airport, American offers one daily nonstop flight throughout the spring, summer, and autumn. There is no service between December and late March.

**United Airlines** (tel. toll free 800/241-6522) offers daily nonstop flights only between May 1 and September 30 between Washington, D.C.'s Dulles airport and

---

### IMPRESSIONS

*[As you approach Bermuda by air, you'll notice] dozens of small houses, their roofs pyramid-shaped, and whitewashed, their walls picked out in a variety of soft pastels—lemon, bluebell, lilac, primrose. It all looks very prim and ordered: the lawns look neat, the swimming pools glitter in the late morning sun, the sea is the palest of greens and splashes softly against low cliffs of pink and well-washed orange.*
—SIMON WINCHESTER, *THE SUN NEVER SETS: TRAVELS TO THE REMAINING OUTPOSTS OF THE BRITISH EMPIRE* (1985)

Bermuda. Flights depart at 5:30pm, which permits connections from virtually anywhere within United's vast North American network.

**Delta** (tel. toll free 800/221-1212) offers daily nonstop service to Bermuda every day of the year from both Boston and Atlanta. The Boston flight departs early every morning, whereas the Atlanta flight departs around noon, late enough to allow connections from many other cities within Delta's network.

**Continental Airlines** (tel. toll free 800/525-0280) offers daily nonstop service to Bermuda from New Jersey's Newark Airport during spring, summer, and fall, and nonstop service to Bermuda five times a week between mid-December and mid-March.

From Toronto, **Air Canada** (tel. toll free 800/776-3000) offers nonstop flights between six and seven days a week into Bermuda, with frequent connections from Toronto to virtually every other city in Canada. The flight departs around 9:30am, late enough to permit convenient connections through Toronto from both Montréal and Québec City. The airline also offers a once-per-week nonstop flight into Bermuda from Halifax, Nova Scotia, but only between mid-February and early September.

The final contender in the high-stakes routes between North America and Bermuda is **USAir** (tel. toll free 800/428-4322), which at presstime flew nonstop every day of the year to Bermuda from Philadelphia, Boston, Baltimore-Washington, and New York's La Guardia Airport.

The airline of choice for the thousands of annual visitors from the United Kingdom is usually **British Airways** (tel. toll free 800/247-9297), which flies between London's Gatwick Airport and Bermuda between two and three times a week, depending on the season. One offbeat but attractive option offered by this airline are packages combining a visit to Bermuda with an ongoing excursion to London, and then a nonstop flight from London back to the United States. British Airways offers schedules and discounted APEX fares well-suited for midwinter pilgrimages to London's West End theater district and the city's countless shops and museums.

## REGULAR FARES

The best strategy for securing the lowest airfare is to keep calling the airlines, keeping in mind the bonus miles and frequent flyer programs that many of them offer. Most airlines give the best deals on tickets ordered at least 14 days before a traveler's anticipated departure and that include stopovers in Bermuda of at least three days. Airfares fluctuate with the season, but tend to remain competitive among the companies vying for shares of the lucrative Bermuda run.

Peak season—summer in Bermuda—is the most expensive time to go; low season—usually mid-September or early November until mid-March—offers less expensive fares. Few if any of the airlines designate spring and autumn as shoulder (intermediate) seasons, dividing their calendar year into only two instead of three seasons.

At presstime, most airlines flying from North America to Bermuda offer only two classes of service: first class and economy. (Because most aircraft flying to Bermuda are medium-sized, there is no allowance for business class.) Economy class is the lowest-priced regular airfare carrying no special restrictions or requirements.

## OTHER GOOD-VALUE CHOICES

Bear in mind that in the airline industry what constitutes good value is always changing. What was the lowest possible fare one day may not be lowest the next day when a new promotional fare is offered.

**BUCKET SHOPS** A bucket shop (or consolidator) acts as a clearinghouse for blocks of tickets that airlines discount and consign during normally slow periods of air travel. For Bermuda, that usually means November through March. Charter operators (see below) and bucket shops used to perform separate functions, but the line has become blurred lately and many outfits now perform both functions.

Tickets are sometimes discounted up to 35%. Time of payment can vary from 45 days prior to departure to the last minute. Such discount tickets may be purchased through regular travel agents, who, however, usually mark them up at least 8% to 10%, reducing your discount.

Many users of consolidators complain that since they do not qualify for advance seat assignment, they are likely to be assigned a "poor seat" on the plane at the last minute. And in a recent survey many passengers reported no savings at all, since airlines sometimes match the consolidator ticket when they announce a promotional fare. So, carefully investigate all options to make sure you are really saving.

Bucket shops abound. Look for their ads in your local newspaper's travel section. It's much easier to get a bucket shop fare to Europe than to Bermuda, though. Getting a low-cost ticket by this route sometimes pays off, if you're willing to expend a lot of time and effort. In New York, try **TFI Tours International,** 34 W. 32nd Street, 12th Floor, New York, NY 10001 (tel. 212/736-1140 in New York State or toll free 800/825-3834 elsewhere in the United States).

**CHARTER FLIGHTS** Charter flights to Bermuda are severely limited, but not as strictly as they once were. In general, they are not allowed from "gateway" cities such as New York or other points where major international carriers service Bermuda. It is a complicated situation that changes yearly or even monthly, and it's best to go to a good travel agent, who should know the least expensive and most direct route for you.

Essentially, charter flights allow visitors to Bermuda to fly at a less expensive fare than on a regularly scheduled flight, in some cases at 30% or more less than a regular airfare. But this can vary considerably from flight to flight.

Charter flights do have several drawbacks, however. One is the long advance booking often required. For example, many require that you make reservations and purchase your ticket at least 45 days or more before your actual trip. Should you be forced by unforeseen circumstances to cancel your flight, you could lose most of the cash you've advanced. To avoid such a disaster, take out cancellation insurance; ask your travel agent about it.

The charter flight always requires that you go to Bermuda and come back on certain dates. Again, this allows for no flexibility in your scheduling. Some also require that you prebook hotel rooms and pay for certain "ground arrangements."

For a charter flight, work through a travel agent, who will be aware of the business reputation of a packager. If you're a do-it-yourselfer, you can always check the Sunday travel section of your local or a big-city newspaper, looking for the announcements of any charter operators advertising flights to Bermuda.

**GOING AS A COURIER** This cost-cutting technique comes with lots of restrictions, and tickets may be hard to come by, especially to such a popular destination as Bermuda. Basically, you go as both an airline passenger and a courier. Couriers are hired by overnight air-freight firms hoping to skirt the often tedious Customs hassles and delays at the other end. The courier service is absolutely legal; you won't be asked to haul in illegal drugs, for example. As a courier, you don't actually handle the merchandise you're transporting; you just present a manifest to Customs. A courier gets a greatly discounted airfare or sometimes even flies free, but because your baggage allowance is used by the courier firm to transport its cargo, you're allowed only one piece of carry-on luggage.

Upon arrival in Bermuda, an employee of the courier service will reclaim the company's cargo. Incidentally, you must fly alone, so don't plan to travel with anybody. (A friend may be able to arrange a flight as a courier on a consecutive day.) Most courier services operate from Los Angeles and New York, but some operate out of other cities, such as Chicago or Miami.

Courier services are often listed in the Yellow Pages and in advertisements in travel sections or newspapers.

To get you going, check with **Halbart Express,** 147-05 176th Street, Jamaica, NY 11434 (tel. 718/656-8189 from 10am to 3pm daily) or **Halbart Express/ Miami,** 2471 N.W. 72nd Ave., Miami, FL 33122 (tel. 305/593-0260).

You can also try **Now Voyager,** 74 Varick Street, Suite 307, New York, NY 10013 (tel. 212/431-1616, daily from 11:30am to 6pm; at other times an automatic telephone-answering system announces last-minute specials for round-trip fares).

**PROMOTIONAL FARES** Depending on their needs, most airlines also offer promotional fares, which carry stringent requirements concerning advance purchase, minimum stay abroad, and cancellation penalties. The most common (and usually the least expensive) of these fares is the Advance Purchase Excursion (APEX) fare. To take advantage of these deals, however, you'll have to find a good travel agent or do a lot of calling around to learn what's available at the time of your trip.

Land arrangements (that is, prebooking and prepayment of hotel rooms) are often tied in with promotional fares offered by airlines, and can present surprisingly attractive bargains when arranged with the purchase of airline tickets. Most of the larger carriers offer pre-arranged packages where discounted hotel accommodations at reputable hotels can be arranged with a single phone call. Ask about this in advance, or enlist the help of an enlightened travel agent.

**TRAVEL CLUBS** Yet another possibility for low-cost air travel is the travel club, with Bermuda heavily featured in the discounted offerings. A club supplies an unsold inventory of tickets discounted in the usual 20%–60% range. Some deals involve cruise ships and complete tour packages.

After you pay an annual fee to join, you are given a hot-line number to call when you're planning a trip. Many discounts become available several days in advance of an actual departure; many give you at least a week and sometimes as much as a month. Because you're limited to what's available, however, you have to be fairly flexible. Some of the best of these clubs nationwide include the following.

**Discount Travel International,** 114 Forest Ave., Suite 203, Narberth, PA 19072 (tel. 215/668-7184, or toll free 800/334-9294), charges an annual membership of $45. **Last Minute Travel Club,** 132 Brookline Ave., Boston, MA 02215 (tel. 617/267-9800 or toll free 800/LAST-MIN). Trips from Boston and Chicago are arranged at no annual fee. **Moment's Notice,** 425 Madison Ave., New York, NY 10017-1152 (tel. 212/486-0500), is considered one of the best, with a members' hot line (regular phone toll charges) and a yearly fee of $45 per member. **Vacations to Go,** 2411 Fountain View, Houston, TX 77057 (tel. toll free 800/338-4962), charges an annual membership fee of $19.95, or you can save money by paying $50 and joining for three years. **Worldwide Discount Travel Club,** 1674 Meridian Ave., Miami Beach, FL 33139 (tel. 305/534-2082), presents a "travelogue" listing about every three weeks with about 200 discount possibilities. Single travelers pay $40 annually to join, but family membership is only $50.

# BY CRUISE SHIP

Conditions have improved remarkably since that "innocent abroad," Mark Twain, made his rough sea trips to Bermuda. He considered the place "hell to get to," but thought the charms of Bermuda worth the tough sea voyage. He would surely be amazed at the luxurious way today's seagoing passengers travel to sunny Bermuda.

Cruise ships aren't for everyone, but if you'd like to try this method of travel, Bermuda is a good choice for a first-timer. Since you can sail from the east coast of the United States to Bermuda and back in just a few days, you aren't locked into a long time at sea (as you might be on a Caribbean cruise).

Unfortunately, cruise-ship trips to Bermuda are limited, mostly because of the lack of facilities there for big cruise ships. There is a movement to divide the cruise-ship business between Hamilton Harbour (the city of Hamilton) and St. George's on the eastern end of the island. It is hoped that existing facilities will thus not be overtaxed and congestion and other problems can be alleviated.

The cruise-ship season is from April to November. Once only the wealthy could afford such a trip, but package deals and other cost-saving arrangements devised by the travel industry have opened up the decks of the cruise ship to today's middle-income voyager.

Once you've decided to go by cruise ship, it's time to select your cruise line. Some lines want their passengers to have a total vacation—one filled with activities from "sunup to sundown." Others see time at sea as a period of tranquillity and relaxation, with less emphasis on "fun, fun," organized activities (which tend to get a little corny anyway).

To keep costs down, ask for inside cabins, which are usually very small and thus less desirable and cheaper. If you plan to be active during most of the day, you won't be spending much time in your cabin, anyway. Most cabins have a private shower and toilet, so you won't be sharing facilities. Many readers also report that in a midship cabin you are less likely to experience severe rolling and pitching. Cabins on older vessels come in widely different sizes, beginning with deluxe stateroom suites, a throwback to the old days of transatlantic voyages. Modern vessels have more standardized accommodations.

Although "white tie and tails" are no longer de rigueur, it's still a good idea for a man to take along a dark suit, and a woman should bring at least one cocktail dress. Most of the time more casual wear is appropriate for evening: sports coats, slacks, and open shirts for men and sports dresses and pants suits for women.

Unfortunately (considering the investment), one of the most important ingredients for a successful cruise is the hardest thing to know in advance—your fellow passengers. The right crowd can be a lot of fun, an incompatible one can leave you sulking in your cabin.

*Economy tip:* You get considerable savings on 7-day cruises by booking early. See a travel agent or call the cruise line.

**Chandris Celebrity and Fantasy Cruises,** 5200 Blue Lagoon Dr., Miami FL 33126 (tel. toll free 800/437-3111), sails the *Horizon* from New York and San Juan to Hamilton and St. George's. Cruises last five to seven days, with Bermuda only one of several ports of call. (Others are The Bahamas, St. Thomas, and ports on Mexico's Caribbean coast.) The *Meridian* sails from Baltimore, Boston, Charleston, S.C., and Wilmington, N.C., to Bermuda. Schedules vary, and trips are for six or seven nights. Call for more details.

The **Norwegian Cruise Line,** 95 Merrick Way, Coral Gables, FL 33134 (tel. toll free 800/327-7030), sails the *Westward* every Saturday from April 25 to the first of October on a 7-day cruise from New York to St. George's and Hamilton.

The **Royal Caribbean Cruise Line,** 1050 Caribbean Way, Miami, FL 33132 (tel. toll free 800/432-6559 in Florida or 800/327-6700 elsewhere in the U.S.), sails the popular *Nordic Prince,* a handsome 1,038-passenger liner, on a seven-day cruise, leaving New York every Sunday and arriving in Bermuda on Tuesday. The ship leaves Bermuda on Friday, and arrives in New York on Sunday.

**Cunard,** 555 5th Ave., New York, NY 10017 (tel. toll-free 800/221-4700), sails the regal *Queen Elizabeth 2* on four- or five-day cruises from New York to Bermuda at certain times of the year.

# BY PACKAGE TOUR

If you want everything done for you and to save money at the same time, you might consider traveling to Bermuda on a package tour. General tours appealing to the average traveler are offered, but many of the tours are very specific—tennis packages, golf packages, scuba and snorkeling packages, and, only for those who qualify, honeymooners' specials.

Economy and convenience are the chief advantages of a package tour: the costs of transportation (usually an airplane fare), hotel, food (sometimes), and sightseeing (sometimes) are combined in one package, neatly tied up with a single price tag.

If you booked your flight or hotel separately, you would pay more than a package tour—hence their immense and increasing appeal. Also, because tour operators can mass-book hotels and make volume purchases, transfers between your hotel and the airport are often included. Of course, there are disadvantages: You may find yourself in a hotel you dislike immensely, yet you are virtually trapped there because you've already paid for it. The single traveler, regrettably, usually suffers too, since nearly all tour packages are based on double occupancy.

Choosing the right package tour can be a problem, but your travel agent might offer one, and certainly all the major airline carriers will. There are also companies that specialize in package tours.

One company that has specialized in marketing travel to Bermuda since 1978 is the **Bermuda Travel Company, Ltd.,** 420 Lexington Ave., Suite 401, New York, NY 10017 (tel. 212/867-2718, or 800/323-2020). It represents almost 50 of the island's hotels, ranging from modest and out-of-the-way guesthouses to deluxe hotels. Particularly popular are the company's wedding packages. For a set—and sometimes very attractive—price, they include everything: airfare, discounted hotel accommodations, wedding cake, champagne, the services of a minister, the handling of all legal and other paperwork, and arrangements for up to 50 wedding guests. Bermuda Travel also arranges vacation packages for horseback riders, scuba enthusiasts, golf and tennis players, and honeymooners. Hours are 9am to 9pm Monday through Friday.

Other companies that offer well-organized packages to Bermuda include **American Express Vacations,** 300 Pinnacle Way, Norcross, GA 30093 (tel. toll free 800/241-1700; 800/421-5785 in Georgia); **Delta Dream Vacations,** 110 Broward Blvd., Fort Lauderdale, FL 33301 (tel. 305/522-1440 or toll free 800/872-7786); and **Go-Go Tours,** 69 Spring St., Ramsey, NJ 07446 (tel. 201/934-3500 or toll 800/821-3731).

In addition, consider **Travel Impressions,** 465 Smith St., Farmingdale, NY 11735 (tel. 516/845-8000 or toll free 800/284-0044), featuring Bermuda packages that embrace airfare, transfers, accommodations, and often shopping and attraction discounts. This outfit is a wholesaler, so go to a travel agent to avail yourself of its offerings.

Shopping around for the right package can be time-consuming and a bore. To speed up the process, call **Tourscan Inc.,** P.O. Box 2367, Darien, CT 06820 (tel. 203/655-8091 or toll free 800/962-2080). Its computerized list provides both hotel and air package deals not only to Bermuda, but also to the Bahamas and the Caribbean. It usually has the whole range of offerings so you can pick and choose from what's out there. Its *Island Vacation Catalog,* which costs $4, is issued twice yearly and contains complete details. Once you decide on a tour, you can either book it directly through Tourscan, or use any travel agent.

# 2. ORIENTATION

## ARRIVING
### BY PLANE

Chances are, you'll arrive by air, as most visitors do. Arrivals are at the Civil Air Terminal at Kindley Field Rd., St. George's, 9 miles east of Hamilton and about 17 miles east of Somerset at the far western end of Bermuda.

The flight from most East Coast destinations, including New York, Raleigh/ Durham, Baltimore, and Boston takes only about two hours, so you won't have jet-lag upon arrival. Even flights from more remote Atlanta take only 2½ hours, or nearly 3 hours from Toronto.

After clearing Customs, you can pick up tourist information at the airport before heading out to your hotel. Since you aren't allowed to rent a car in Bermuda, you must rely on a bus, taxi, or limousine to reach your hotel.

More than 600 taxis are available in Bermuda, and cabbies meet all arriving flights. Taxis are metered and are allowed to carry a maximum of four passengers. If you and your companion/spouse have a lot of luggage, you will need the taxi all to yourself, of course. Including a tip of 10% to 15%, it costs about $25 to reach a destination in Hamilton. Since you're already near St. George's, the fare there is about $10, or $14 to Tucker's Town. To the fabled south shore hotels, the charge is likely to be $30 or more. To the West End, site of many more resorts, expect to pay $40. Fares go up 25% between 10pm and 6am and all day on Sundays and public holidays. Luggage placed on the roof or trunk carries a surcharge of 25¢ per piece. Expect to pay about $4 for the first mile and $1.40 for each additional mile.

 **FROMMER'S SMART TRAVELER: AIRFARES**

1. Shop all the airlines that fly to your destination.
2. Always ask for the lowest fare, not just a discount fare.
3. Ask about the cost-conscious Advance Purchase Excursion (APEX) fare.
4. Keep calling the airlines. As the departure date nears, additional low-cost seats may become available.
5. Try to fly in winter, when fares are lower.
6. Find out if it's cheaper to fly Monday to Thursday.
7. Read the section "Other Good-Value Choices," which covers bucket shops, charter flights, and promotional fares.
8. Consider air-and-land packages, which offer considerably reduced rates on both accommodations and flights.

A party of four will do better financially to call a limousine and split the cost between two couples. This can be done before you arrive in Bermuda by contacting **Bermuda Hosts Ltd.** at 809/295-2574. This outfit can arrange to have a limousine waiting for your flight. Even if you're a couple and not four passengers you can always ask a waiting limousine at the airport if it has room to take on two extra passengers. That way, you can shave the cost you'd incur by having a taxi all to yourself.

Shuttle service, if prearranged two weeks before your arrival, is provided between the airport and virtually anywhere in Bermuda by the **Airport Transport Department of the Bermuda Aviation Service,** P.O. Box HM 719, Hamilton HM CX (tel. 809/293-2500). The company operates a dozen 26-seat buses to the large resorts, or 8-passenger Volkswagen minibuses to the smaller hotels, charging one-way per-person fares that are determined by the distance from the airport of each final destination. Transit within Zone 1 (between the airport and Grotto Bay Beach Hotel) costs $5; to Zone 2 (St. George's or Flatts Village), $7; to Zone 3 (Hamilton), $13; to Zone 4 (Warwick and part of Southampton Parish), $16; and to Zone 5 (the extreme western tip of Bermuda, within Sandys Parish), $21.

## BY CRUISE SHIP

This is perhaps the easiest way to arrive in Bermuda. The cruise ship staff presents you with a list of tour options long before your arrival in port; everything is virtually done for you, unless you opt to take an independent taxi tour, which is far more expensive of course than an organized tour. Most passengers book shore excursions at the same time they reserve the cruise.

Seven-day cruises out of New York spend four days in the Atlantic, with three days in port. Most cruise ships arrive in the traditional port of Hamilton, which is the capital of Bermuda and its chief commercial and shopping center. If shopping is more important than sightseeing to you, select a cruise that docks here.

If you're more interested in history, arrange to go on a ship that anchors at St. George's, at the eastern tip of the island. With its narrow lanes and old buildings and streets, St. George's has been called the island's equivalent of Colonial Williamsburg in Virginia. It has some shops and boutiques, although not nearly as many as Hamilton does.

It is much more unlikely (because of volume of arrivals) that you'll disembark at Somerset, which is the western end of the island and the farthest cruise port from Bermuda's major attractions. The West End is not without its own charm and sightseeing allure, though. It is, after all, home to the Royal Naval Dockyard, one of the major sightseeing targets of Bermuda. In a shopping mall at the dockyard, craft stores and museums exist side by side.

During your stay in port, you can avail yourself of the waiting taxis outside your vessel, or else you can rent mopeds and bicycles (see "Getting Around," below) and do some independent touring and shopping on your own.

# TOURIST INFORMATION

You can get answers to most of your questions at the **Visitors Service Bureau** at the Ferry Terminal, Hamilton (tel. 809/295-1480); King's Square, St. George's (tel. 809/297-1642); or in Somerset (tel. 809/234-1388). The Visitors Service Bureau is open Monday through Saturday from 9am to 4:45pm.

# ISLAND LAYOUT

## MAIN STREET & ARTERIES

**THE CITY OF HAMILTON AND ENVIRONS**  With Hamilton at the center, Bermuda can be divided into the West End and the East End, the latter the site of the previously mentioned airport. As you leave the Ferry Terminal at Hamilton Harbour, you'll come upon the Visitors Service Bureau and the birdcage policeman.

To your east lies the main shopping artery of Hamilton, Front Street, and to your west is Pitts Bay Road leading to the Princess, Hamilton's leading hotel.

Front Street follows the line of the harbor and boasts many of the stores for which Bermuda is famous, including Trimingham's, established in 1844, and Smith's, established in 1889.

Moving inland and on a parallel line with Front Street are the other many shopping streets of Hamilton, including Reid Street, Church Street, and Victoria Street.

Par-La-Ville Park, lying directly north of the Ferry Terminal, is the city's largest and most central public garden.

North Hamilton is in Pembroke Parish, the name of the parish in which the city of Hamilton is located. The parish of Hamilton is a largely residential area beginning at Victoria Park; it is mainly a working-class district. Unlike a Caribbean island, where it would likely be a slum, it is an area of relatively neat small houses.

East of Hamilton, Fort Hamilton is one of originally 55 forts that once guarded Bermuda. Sitting alone in the Atlantic, it was easy to attack before the installation of these forts. Nearby is the 20-acre Arboretum.

**THE EAST END**  Continuing east from Hamilton, the parish of Devonshire is named after the famous shire in England's West Country, with its rolling hills and "green lungs." The parish's newer name of Devonshire is quite an improvement on its former label: Brackish Pond. One of its major landmarks is Old Devonshire Church, lying to the south of Middle Road.

From Hamilton you can take Middle Road all the way to Flatts Village, which opens onto the landlocked Harrington Sound. It's also possible to go along South Shore Road (also called South Road), which will eventually lead to Tucker's Town, an exclusive residential area of multimillion-dollar properties.

The just-mentioned Harrington Sound is filled with attractions, and if you're in Bermuda for a few days, you'll probably spend much of your time here, seeing the Bermuda Aquarium, the Bermuda Glass Blowing Studio, Crystal Caves, Leamington Caves, Bermuda Perfumery, Spittal Pond, and Verdmont, to name only some of the sights.

Continuing west, follow Blue Hole Hill until you reach the causeway, which takes you east to St. George's, the historic old city of Bermuda and its former capital. St. George's is on an island, also known as St. George's. To explore the town, it's best to take a walking tour (see Chapter 7, "Bermuda Walking Tours").

The eastern end of Bermuda was forever changed when the United States created a sprawling landfill during World War II and used it as a military base. The present-day Bermuda airport grew out of that base. The remaining part of the American base is

# IMPRESSIONS

*Bermuda is essentially a small town in a glamorous setting.*
—DAVID SHELLEY NICHOLL, LETTER TO THE (LONDON) *TIMES* (1978)

used mainly for routine antisubmarine surveillance flights and as a tracking station of the National Aeronautics and Space Administration. (American rights to the base—part of a 99-year lend-lease agreement between the United States and Britain signed in 1941, under which the British received American submarines and other needed war matériel in exchange for use of the base—terminate in the year 2040). Bermuda's only McDonald's is on the base, but it can be visited only on Wednesdays, when the base is open to the public.

The base is on St. David's Island, the most rustic spot in Bermuda. The island lighthouse, dating from 1879, occupies the loftiest point on Bermuda's East End. Some St. David's islanders, the most provincial of whom are said to have never visited Hamilton, refused to be relocated when the naval base was built, stubbornly staying on their homeland. In a section called "Texas," the government built cottages for these islanders, and they and their offspring remain there today.

**THE WEST END**    To the west of Hamilton, a different world unfolds, as visitors explore, in this order, the parishes of Paget, Warwick, Southampton, and Sandys, the last-named lying in the far western corner. The landmass of Sandys along Great Sound juts eastward as if it were trying to reconnect with the city of Hamilton.

South of Hamilton heading west is Harbour Road, which borders the harbor of Hamilton for several miles until it reaches the vicinity of Darrell Island, a tiny green islet that was the site of Bermuda's first airport. You can take ferries from the city of Hamilton to this southern peninsula, which borders the north coast of Paget and Warwick parishes.

Alternatively, you can take Middle Road, which goes through Paget and Warwick parishes. Continue west through Southampton until you reach Somerset Bridge, which you use to cross into Sandys Parish.

Many of the best hotels and beaches, including the Elbow Beach Hotel and Warwick Long Bay along with Horseshoe Bay, lie along the southern coast of the western peninsula, reached by going along South Shore Road (also called South Road). If you continue west far enough, South Shore Road runs into Middle Road for its final push through the parish of Southampton.

Middle Road continues to Somerset Bridge, which leads into the parish of Sandys. This parish consists of Somerset Island, the Royal Naval Dockyard, and Ireland, Watford, and Boaz islands. Although facing the Atlantic on their northern shorelines, these islands and settlements open onto the more protected Great Sound.

Somerset Bridge is best reached by taking the ferry from Hamilton. From the ferry dock at the bridge, you can continue by ferry to Ireland Island and the Dockyard, or you can take the ferry directly from Hamilton to the Dockyard. Sandys Parish is bisected by Somerset Road.

Many visitors come here to visit Mangrove Bay, an idyllic beach strip lying directly east of Somerset Village, the tiny hamlet of the parish dominated by Sandys Boat Club.

Somerset Village is the beginning of Bermuda's Railway Trail, and it's a good place to begin if you wish to take this walk through the island.

## FINDING AN ADDRESS

The island chain of Bermuda isn't the center of Manhattan, and, as such, doesn't follow a system of street addresses too rigidly. Most hotels, even in official government listings, don't bother to include street addresses, although they do include post boxes and zip codes. It's just assumed that everybody knows where everything is, which is fine if you've lived in Bermuda all your life. But, if you're a first-time visitor, you should get a good map and some landmark locations before setting out.

Most of the establishments you will be seeking are on some street plan. Some places use numbers in their street addresses; others, perhaps their neighbors, don't!

The actual street number is not that important in many cases, since a building such as a resort hotel is likely to be set back so far from the main road you couldn't see its numbers anyway. It's far better to look for signs indicating, for example, the Sonesta Beach Hotel than for a street number. Cross streets will also aid you in finding an address.

Plot your itinerary carefully and ask questions. If you get lost, know that some well-traveled people consider that one of the charms of a visit to Bermuda is getting lost along some unmarked country lane. Many interesting discoveries have been made that way.

## MAPS

Bookstores on the island will sell you more detailed maps, but most visitors get by using the free *Bermuda Handy Reference Map* published by the Bermuda Department of Tourism. This tiny pocket map, distributed by the tourist office and available at most hotels, has on one side an overview and orientation map (with key) of Bermuda, highlighting and numbering its major attractions, golf courses, public beaches, and hotels. It does not, however, locate individual restaurants unless they are attached to hotels.

On the flip side of the map is a detailed street plan of the city of Hamilton, indicating all its major landmarks and service facilities, such as the Ferry Terminal and the Post Office.

There is also a detailed map of the Royal Naval Dockyard, the West End, and the East End, plus tips on transportation—ferries, taxis, buses—and other helpful hints, even a depiction of various traffic signs.

# 3. GETTING AROUND

*Driving is on the left,* and the national speed limit is 20 mph in the Bermuda countryside, 15 mph in busier areas. Cars are limited to one per family—and none at all for visitors. In such a far-off Eden, the most popular form of transportation is the motorized bicycle, called a "putt-putt," and the most romantic means of transport is the colorful fringe-topped surrey.

**BY BUS** You can't have a car. Taxis are expensive. You may not want or be able to ride a bicycle or a motor bike. What's left for getting around Bermuda? Buses, of course. All major routes are covered by the bus network, but be prepared for waits. There's even a do-it-yourself sightseeing tour by bus and ferry, and regularly scheduled buses go to most of the destinations that tourists find of interest in Bermuda. However, some routes are not operated on Sunday and holidays, so be sure to find out about routes for the trip you want to make.

Bermuda is divided into 14 zones of about two miles each. At presstime, fare for adults was $1.50 for the first 3 zones and $3 for any longer trip. Children pay 65¢ for all zones. *Note:* You must have the exact change or tokens ready to deposit in the farebox as you board the bus. Drivers do not make change.

You can also purchase tokens at sub-post offices or at the **Central Bus Terminal** on Washington Street in Hamilton, where all routes begin and end. The terminal is just off Church Street a few steps east of City Hall. You can get there from Front Street or Reid Street by going along Queen Street or through Walker Arcade and Washington Mall. Tickets are sold in booklets of 15. You pay $10 for a 3-zone booklet or $18 for a 14-zone packet. Children under 13 pay $5.25 for all zones, and children under 3 ride free. For more information regarding the bus service, telephone 809/292-3854. Nearly all hotels, guesthouses, and restaurants have bus stops close by.

In the east, **St. George's Mini-Bus Service** (tel. 809/297-8199), operates a minibus service around St. George's Parish and St. David's Island. The basic fare is $1.35 for adults or 75¢ for children. Senior citizens ride for 85¢. Buses leave from King's Square in the center of St. George's, but they can also be flagged down along the road. Service is daily from 7am to 11pm March through November. Off-season hours are daily from 7am to 10pm.

The **West End Mini-Bus Service** (tel. 809/234-2344), runs a minibus service leaving from Somerset Bridge and going all the way to the Royal Naval Dockyard on Ireland Island. Fares depend on how far you go, but they're never more than $3 for the entire run. Children and senior citizens go for half price. Passengers can be dropped off where they want, providing it is on the regular bus route. This service operates from May to mid-October daily from 7:20am to 10:20pm. After an autumnal lull, winter service begins in December and runs through March (no service in April); hours are 7:20am to 7pm daily.

**BY TAXI**   An expensive means of getting around, taxis are necessary at times. For more information, including rates, about this form of transportation, refer to "Arriving, By Plane," above.

The hourly charge for taxis is $20 for 1 to 4 passengers. If you want to use one for a sightseeing tour, the minimum is 3 hours. When a taxi has a blue flag on the hood of the vehicle (the locals refer to it as the "bonnet"), the driver, man or woman, is qualified to serve as tour guide. Because he or she is checked out and tested by the government, this is the type of driver you should use if you're planning to use the expensive method of touring Bermuda by taxi. "Blue-bonnet" drivers charge no more than taxi drivers not qualified to serve as guides.

For more information, call **Bermuda Taxi Operators,** 809/292-5600. For radio-dispatched cabs, call **Radio Cabs Bermuda** (tel. 809/295-4141).

**BY CYCLE & SCOOTER**   If you're looking for a lot of exercise, you may want to try a pedal bicycle, the old Bermudian way to travel around the island, although some of the hills may be a real challenge to your stamina.

Many people prefer a motor-assisted cycle—moped, motor scooter, whatever—which you can rent on an hourly, daily, or weekly arrangement. The operator of such a vehicle must be at least 16 years of age, although younger persons may be carried as passengers. Some are large enough for two adults. Both driver and passenger are required by law to wear a helmet, which will be furnished by the place from which you rent your machine. Straps must be securely fastened. *Warning:* Visitors on mopeds have a high accident rate. Exercise extreme caution. Also, *you must,* as mentioned, *drive on the left,* as in England.

In the rentals recommended below, there is a tendency toward price-fixing, so it's not possible to shop around for a better deal, as it was in the past. Nearly all of the agencies charge $20 for a pedal-started moped for the first two days, with a slight discount given on the third or subsequent days. Most of the agencies also charge $36 for a more modern electric-ignition motorscooter, with price breaks given for the third or subsequent days of rentals. There is likely to be a 10% discount during the slower winter months. Almost always a $20 deposit is required, along with some kind of insurance coverage, which costs about $12 per rental.

**Astwood Cycles Ltd.** (tel. 809/292-2245) has shops where you can rent either mopeds or 50-cc scooters: 77 Front Street in Hamilton; at Flatts Village; at the Princess, Sonesta Beach, and Belmont Hotels; Coral Beach Guest Cottages; and at Horizons and Cottages.

Charging comparable prices and renting out either type of vehicle, is **Wheels Ltd.,** Don Donald St., Hamilton (tel. 809/295-0112), or at the Southampton Princess (tel. 809/238-3336).

For motorized vehicles, you can also try **Ray's Cycles, Ltd.,** Middle Road, Southampton, West (tel. 809/234-0629), or at the Lantana Colony Club, Somerset Bridge (tel. 809/234-0141). Another location is at the Royal Naval Dockyard (tel. 809/234-2764). The shops are open daily from 8am to 5pm. Helmets and locks come with each rental.

One of the best rental deals on the island is offered by **Eve's Cycle Livery,** 114 Middle Road, Paget Parish (tel. 809/236-6247). Named after a now-legendary matriarch who founded it 40 years ago, it rents men's and women's pedal bicycles (usually 12-speed mountain bikes well suited to the island's hilly terrain) for $15 for the first day, $10 for the second day, and $5 for each supplemental day. A $10 deposit is required. The shop lies within a 10-minute drive (or a 20-minute leisurely cycle) west of Hamilton. The company also rents a selection of motorized pedal bikes or scooters for between $20 and $36 for the first day, depending on the model, with a descending tier of prices for each additional day.

At **Oleander Cycles Ltd.,** Valley Road, P.O. Box 114, Paget Parish (tel. 809/236-5235), scooters and mopeds tend to be reliable and well maintained. There is another location on Gorham Road in Hamilton (tel. 809/295-0919). Both locations are open daily from 8am to 5pm. Rentals require a $20 deposit and a supplemental charge of $12 for an insurance policy that lasts for the duration of your rental (a day or a week), or until you cause any damage to your rented moped.

**BY FERRY** One of the most interesting methods of transportation is the government-operated ferry service. Ferries crisscross Great Sound between Hamilton and Somerset, charging a $3 fare one way; they also take the harbor route, going from Hamilton to the parishes of Paget and Warwick, where so many hotels are concentrated. The ride from Hamilton to Paget costs only $1.50; children pay half fare. Motorcycles are allowed on the Hamilton to Somerset run (you must pay $3 for your cycle, however). Bicycles are carried free. For ferry service information, telephone 809/295-4506 in Hamilton. Ferry schedules are posted at each landing. They are also available at the Ferry Terminal or the Central Bus Terminal in Hamilton. Actually, most hotels will give you a timetable if you ask.

**BY HORSE-DRAWN CARRIAGE** Being romantics, Bermudians have retained at least some of their horse-drawn carriages. Although once plentiful, there are now only about a dozen left. Drivers congregate on Front Street in Hamilton, adjacent to the No. 1 passenger terminal near the cruise-ship docks. Before 1946 the horse was the principal mode of transport. After that, the first automobiles came to the island. You can book one of these four-wheeled rigs for a chauffeured tour of the island's midriff. Rates range from about $15 to $20 for the first 30 minutes and from $10 to $15 for each additional 30 minutes. If you want to take a ride lasting more than 3 hours, the fee is negotiable. Unless you make special arrangements for a night ride, you aren't likely to find any carriages after 4:30pm.

**HITCHHIKING** There are no special restrictions on hitchhiking that I know of, and it's usually a safe thing to do. However, don't expect to get "picked up" too easily. Taxis, of course, will stop only if you pay them. The only people allowed to have cars other than taxi drivers are local residents (and they are limited to one to a household), so family cars are often filled with friends or relatives. Better count on using public transport in Bermuda instead of your thumb.

**ON FOOT** No island, including all those of The Bahamas and the Caribbean, was designed more for walking than Bermuda. In fact, on foot is about the only way you have of getting around sometimes when public transportation fails you and taxis seem to disappear (or else are beyond your pocketbook).

The city of Hamilton is only explored on foot, but it's an easy, compact place. Our walking tours in Chapter 7, "Bermuda Walking Tours," will concentrate on the most scenic and historic walks, but much of the fun of coming to Bermuda is to walk and explore on your own, especially down those little country lanes that always hold such mysterious surprises.

Walking great distances along the main arteries, especially if it's raining in winter or too hot in summer, appeals only to the most athletic. The trick of "walking" in Bermuda is to take a bus or ferry boat for the long distances, then depend on your trusty feet once you get to a desired area.

# 4. SUGGESTED ITINERARIES

American humorist Mark Twain, a frequent visitor, may have been correct when he claimed that it was the "right country for a jaded man to loaf in." It would take great determination, however, to resist all there is to do in Bermuda.

If you are on a more rushed visit to Bermuda, you might want to skip this section and turn to the "concentrated" Bermuda in Chapter 6, "What to See & Do in Bermuda." Here itineraries are tailor-made for those having anywhere from one to five days for exploring and enjoying.

Golfers or tennis buffs, of course, will likely bypass the following suggestions and concentrate almost every day on their favorite sport. Many visitors come to Bermuda just to play golf, and even the pink sandy beaches can't lure them off the course.

## IF YOU HAVE ONE WEEK

**Day 1**   Do as most visitors do the first day: nothing. Providing you took a morning flight from an East Coast city such as New York, you will arrive in Bermuda and clear Customs in time to have lunch at your hotel. Wind down by the pool or at one of the pink sandy beaches, live the easy life, then have a typical dinner, and retire early in preparation for tackling the charms of Bermuda the following day.

**Day 2**   Head for Hamilton, the capital city, where you'll find the greatest clusters of shops, restaurants, and attractions. Take our walking tour (see Chapter 7, "Bermuda Walking Tours") and get to know the place. If you're still in Hamilton at sundown, go to one of the local pubs for happy hour, maybe have dinner there. If you're booked at your hotel on the half-board plan (MAP), head back there for a refreshing swim in the pool before dinner.

**Day 3**   Today go east to explore the historic former capital of St. George's (take our walking tour [see Chapter 7, "Bermuda Walking Tours"]). You can easily spend the day visiting all the many sights crowded into this small area. There are a number of shops and plenty of places for lunch. If you finish early enough in the day, visit one of the East End beaches, such as St. Catherine Beach.

**Day 4**   Most visitors can occupy a full day exploring Ireland Island, site of the Royal Naval Museum, with its Maritime Museum. While at this, the western, end of the island, you can also shop in the Craft Market and visit the Neptune Cinema, featuring a multimedia show, *The Attack on Washington*. After all this sightseeing, unwind by turning left after leaving the Dockyard and going down Craddock Road to Lagoon Park. Here you will find a good place for a picnic while you enjoy the lagoon and its bird life.

**Day 5**   Head west again this morning to Mangrove Bay and Somerset Village. An ideal spot for a morning at the beach is Somerset Long Bay, a sandy stretch that is part of the Long Bay Nature Reserve. Bird-watchers especially are fond of the place. Because of the calm waters, families with small children are attracted to the sands, and the beach has toilets and changing facilities. Have lunch at Somerset Country Squire Restaurant, overlooking Mangrove Bay, then spend the rest of the afternoon exploring Somerset Village.

**Day 6**   Make this a beach day, exploring Horseshoe Bay Beach in Southampton, the most photographed beach in Bermuda. You can spend the good part of a day here discovering the hills in the background and the cave-like formations at the western end. If you wish, you can walk east to Chaplin Bay, seeking out hidden coves. There's a lunch concession at Horseshoe Bay if you don't want to leave the beach. Then after a rest at your hotel, sample some Bermudian nightlife (see Chapter 10, "Bermuda Nights").

**Day 7**   To continue your first week—for many their final day—head for Flatts Village in the east, in Smith's Parish. Here you can partake of several attractions, including Spittal Pond, the largest wildlife sanctuary in Bermuda, and the Bermuda Aquarium, Museum, and Zoo. Consider an undersea walk offered by the Hartley family (see Chapter 6, "What to See & Do in Bermuda"). Have lunch at Palmetto Hotel & Cottages, then in the afternoon explore Devil's Hole and go for a swim at Shelly Bay Beach.

# IF YOU HAVE TWO WEEKS

**Days 1–7**   See above.

**Day 8**   In the morning, visit Paget Parish. Go inside the Botanical Gardens for a visit, (see Chapter 6, "What to See & Do in Bermuda"). While in the area, call at Birdsey Studio at Stowe Hill, the home of Bermuda's best known painter. Have lunch at Paraquet Restaurant and spend the rest of the day at Elbow Beach.

**Day 9**   Explore Crystal Caves and other attractions in Hamilton Parish (see Chapter 6, "What to See & Do in Bermuda"). Have a Swizzleburger for lunch at the Swizzle Inn; in the afternoon, visit Leamington Caves. For your evening entertainment, go to Henry VIII pub restaurant.

**Day 10**   Go to Elbow Beach in the morning, then spend the afternoon having lunch and shopping in Hamilton. Make sure you buy your duty-free liquor to take back with you. Visit Marriott's Castle Harbour Resort at Tucker's Town for afternoon tea. Spend the evening attending an island show of limbo dancers, a steel band, and calypso artists. Ask at your hotel for current offerings.

**Day 11**   Explore the sights of Warwick Parish in the morning. Have lunch at Paw Paws, then spend the rest of the afternoon at Warwick Long Bay Beach.

**Day 12**   Take the Looking Glass Cruise in the morning (see Chapter 6, "What to See & Do in Bermuda"). After lunch, return to your favorite beach or indulge in your favorite sport, such as golf or tennis.

**Day 13**   In the morning, visit Pembroke Parish and take in its attractions. At the end of your tour, have lunch at a pub in the city of Hamilton and browse more among the shops. Have tea at one of the cafés and head early back to your hotel for a relaxing swim and lounge around the pool.

**Day 14**   To cap your final week, head for Southampton Parish to see its attractions. Visit Gibbs Hill Lighthouse and get some beach time in one more time at Horseshoe Bay Beach.

## IF YOU HAVE THREE WEEKS

**Days 1–14**   See above.

**Day 15**   In the morning, visit Verdmont, Bermuda's finest house museum, then head for St. David's Island. You can also visit the St. David's Lighthouse, occupying the highest point in the East End. Have lunch at Black Horse Tavern and return to St. Catherine's Beach for two hours of relaxation. In the late afternoon continue up Barry Road to visit Fort St. Catherine.

**Day 16**   Take a tour of Smith's Parish. Have lunch at one of the restaurants in the parish, perhaps in the Palmetto Hotel and Cottages.

**Day 17**   In the afternoon arrange a charter boat rental at the harbor at Salt Kettle. That evening, have dinner at Rum Runners.

**Day 18**   Explore Devonshire Parish and visit Old Devonshire Church. After lunch, explore a new beach such as Church Bay in Southampton, a secluded small beach of pink sand. Scuba diving and snorkeling are available here.

**Day 19**   Go to the Princess Hotel in Hamilton; at their dock you can charter a sailboat or Sunfish, or even go parasailing. After a morning of water sports, have lunch at a restaurant along Front Street. Try out a new beach in the afternoon. A suggestion is Astwood Cove in Warwick, suitable for lazy days in the sun or swimming. Some Bermudians would like to keep this beach a secret.

**Day 20**   Go to the tourist office and pick up a copy of *The Bermuda Railway Trail.* This trail stretches all across the island and you could spend three days following all of it. However, take only the section that interests you the most; if its a hot day, the walk can get very tiring. If you'd like to see some of the trail—and not exert yourself too much—take Section No. 1 of the trail. It takes about 1½ hours and its length is only 1¾ miles, but it covers some major scenery, including the Springfield & Gilbert Nature Reserve. You could easily make a morning of the tour, especially if you take time out to explore Fort Scaur, one of Bermuda's largest forts. After lunch in the West End visit another beach, maybe the secluded stretch at Church Bay in Southampton.

**Day 21**   After all this activity, you deserve a day of rest and recreation before your return to the mainland. Pack at your leisure, lounge on your favorite beach or around the hotel pool, and plan your next visit to Bermuda.

# 5. WHERE TO STAY

Accommodations in Bermuda basically fall into six major categories, descriptions of which are given below.

**RESORT HOTELS**   These often sprawling properties are Bermuda's best, offering many facilities, services, and luxuries—but also charging the highest prices, especially in summer. It's usually cheaper to check into them on MAP rates (breakfast and dinner) than it is to order all your meals à la carte. They charge the lowest rates from mid-November to March, usually about 20% less. Most of the large resorts have their own beaches or beach clubs, along with swimming pools. Some even offer their own golf courses.

**COTTAGE COLONIES** A uniquely Bermudian offering, these colonies are usually a series of bungalows constructed around a main clubhouse, which is the center of social life, drinking, and dining. The cottages are usually placed scenically on landscaped grounds. Most of them have been built to give guests maximum privacy, and nearly all have their own kitchenettes (used mainly for preparing light meals). Most of the colonies have either their own beaches or swimming pools.

**HOUSEKEEPING COTTAGES & APARTMENTS** These accommodation units are usually called efficiencies in the United States. Most of them lie on landscaped estates, have swimming pools, and usually are built around a main clubhouse. All of them offer kitchen facilities, and some are designed as wings or modern apartment-style units surrounding a pool or else opening onto a beach. Most of them offer minimal daily maid service.

**GUESTHOUSES** These accommodations are the cheapest means of living in Bermuda. Most of the large ones are old Bermuda homes, with garden settings. Generally, they have been modernized, with comfortable guest rooms. Some of them have their own pools. A number of these guesthouses are small, modest places, offering breakfast only; the bath is often shared with other guests. You will usually have to commute to the beach if you stay in one of these places.

**HOME EXCHANGES & HOMESTAYS** See "Alternative/Adventure Travel" in Chapter 2, "Before You Go."

**RENTAL VILLAS & VACATION HOMES** You might rent a big villa, a good-sized apartment in someone's condo building, or even a small beach cottage (more accurately called a cabaña).

Private apartments are also available with or without maid service. These are more of a no-frills option than the villas and condos. The apartments may not be in buildings with swimming pools, and they may not have a front desk to help you.

Cottages, or cabañas, offer the most freewheeling life-style available in this category of vacation accommodations. Many ideally open onto a beach, although others may be clustered around a communal swimming pool. Most of them are fairly simple, containing no more than a simple bedroom plus a small kitchen and bath. In the peak summer season, reservations should be made at least five or six months in advance.

Several agents throughout the United States and Canada offer these types of rentals. To get you going, try **Rent-a-Home International,** 7200 34th Ave. NW, Seattle, WA 98117 (tel. 206/789-9377), which specializes in condos and villas. It arranges both daily and weekly tariffs, although longer bookings are preferred.

# 6. WHERE TO DINE

Whenever possible, it is best to stick to local food; for a main dish, that usually means fish caught in the deep sea. But let me state at the very beginning that food is not one of the reasons people go to Bermuda. So-called "gourmet fare" often isn't, although the prices charged would make you think that you're getting something really special. To find the many dishes that *are* truly worthy, you'll have to pick and choose your way carefully through the menu.

In general, it is unwise to order too many meat dishes. Red meats have probably been flown in, and may have been resting on the island for some time.

Dining in Bermuda also is generally more expensive than it is in the United States and Canada. Because virtually everything except the fish has to be imported, restaurant prices are more in tune with those of Europe than with those of America. Service is automatically added to most restaurant tabs, usually 10% to 15%. Even so, if service has been good, it is customary to leave something extra.

If you're booked into a hotel on MAP rates (half board), which hotels sometimes require in the peak summer season, you can sample some of the local restaurants at lunch. That way, your stomach won't become completely "hotel bound."

In some establishments, men are required to wear jackets. Ties are not usually required—an open-neck shirt usually suffices. If in doubt, check the policy of a restaurant before going there.

At the better places, women usually appear casually chic in the evening. During the day, no matter what the establishment, wearing a coverup is the proper thing to do—do not arrive for lunch attired in a bikini.

Because of the lack of inexpensive transportation on the island, many economy-minded people eat at their hotel at night to avoid adding an expensive taxi fare to their already overburdened dinner cost. If you like to dine around, find a hotel in and around Hamilton that has a number of restaurants. That way, you can walk to and from the restaurant.

# 7. WHAT TO BUY

Retailers on less prosperous islands have claimed that the endless popularity of Bermuda is a result of its superb climate and its many years of sophisticated marketing. Indeed, no one has ever accused the Bermudians of not knowing how to market themselves or their rich inventories of retail goods. Bermuda, perhaps better than any other island in the world, draws richly upon its British antecedents to produce a battery of shops and stores, both large and small, whose charm and desirability is almost breathtaking. Even if your goal is only to window-shop (a highly engrossing art form in its own right) you'll find ample quantities of some of the most realistically priced, discreetly elegant merchandise anywhere. Much of it seems to literally beckon through the display windows for the time and attention of vacationing foreign visitors.

What produces this alluring jumble of saleable goods? Much of it might have to do with the built-in sense of conservative style that permeates much of Bermuda. Most stores take full advantage of their placement within charming cottages or historically important buildings. Shopkeepers are for the most part both polite and discreet, and merchandise is often unusual and well made. Despite the fact that much of it seems to exude a kind of upscale quality and innate tastefulness, most of it is significantly cheaper than you might have expected.

Some frequent visitors to Bermuda take careful stock of their needs for porcelain, crystal, silverware, jewelry, timepieces, and perfume, perhaps anticipating several months in advance a needed wedding gift. The island is filled with merchandisers of fine tableware, the prices of which are between 25% and 50% less than you might have found at home. Famous makers whose goods fill the shops of Bermuda include Royal Copenhagen, Wedgwood, and Royal Crown Derby. Crystal is also an excellent bargain in Bermuda, with many of the finest manufacturers in Europe and North America providing wide selections of glittering merchandise. For a fee, all of these can be shipped, usually in impressively well-wrapped packages that keep breakage to a minimum.

Not all the acquisitional temptations of Bermuda, however, derive from goods imported from abroad. The island produces endless quantities of unusual merchandise of its own. These include elegantly evocative watercolors of Bermuda landscapes, etchings of its famous rooflines, oil paintings executed on pieces of aromatic local cedar, and jewelry configured into shapes inspired by the island's nautical traditions. They also include such culinary delights as sherry peppers preserved in herb-laced vinegar, or buttery cakes laced with Bermuda rum.

Antique lovers appreciate the mixture of the British aesthetic with mid-Atlantic charm. And, naturally, anyone interesting in carrying home a piece of the island's nautical heritage will find oversized ship's propellers, captain's bells, brass nameplates, scale models of the sailing ships of long ago, or perhaps an old-fashioned ship's steering wheel from a salvaged shipwreck. Then there is the island's wealth of antique engravings, 19th-century furniture, modern artwork, and handmade pottery and crafts, all of which make for richly elegant heirlooms. In fact, the island's material (and saleable) allures are almost endless.

How does Bermuda maintain prices that many visitors consider low and/or at least extremely fair? Many of the merchandisers buy their inventories directly from manufacturers in Europe or North America, thereby avoiding high distribution costs. Duties imposed on goods imported into Bermuda are low, and there is no sales tax. In fact, some prices are low enough, and the merchandise tempting enough, to equalize whatever import duties might be imposed upon them by your government's Customs. (For more information on this, refer to the section on Customs in Chapter 2, "Before You Go."

 **BERMUDA**

The desk personnel at your hotel are usually reliable dispensers of information. If you're staying at a guesthouse, your host or hostess will probably be able to supply any information you need on the immediate vicinity of your parish.

**American Express**   The representative in Hamilton is **L. P. Gutteridge, Ltd.,** 34 Bermudiana Road, P.O. Box HM 1024 Hamilton HM DX (tel. 809/295-4545). The office provides complete travel service, sightseeing tours, airport transfers, hotel reservations, traveler's checks, and emergency check cashing.

**Area Code**   The area code for Bermuda is 809. It can be dialed directly from the mainland.

**Babysitting**   Arrangements for babysitting can often be made at your hotel, but never at the last minute. Always ask as far ahead as possible, and be prepared to be turned down. Each financial arrangement has to be personally negotiated.

**Banks**   There are three banks, all with their main offices in Hamilton:

The **Bank of Bermuda Ltd.,** Front Street, Hamilton (tel. 809/295-4000), has branches on Church Street, Hamilton; Par-la-Ville Road, Hamilton; King's Square, St. George's; in Somerset; and at the airport.

The **Bank of N. T. Butterfield Ltd.**, Front and Reid Streets, Hamilton (tel. 809/295-1111), has branches on Church Street West, Hamilton; in St. George's; in Somerset; and at the Southampton Princess.

The **Bermuda Commercial Bank Ltd.** is at 44 Church St., Hamilton (tel. 809/295-5678).

All banks and their branches have the same hours (with the exception of the airport branch of the Bank of Bermuda). They are open Monday through Thursday from 9:30am to 3pm, on Friday from 9:30am to 3pm and 4:30 to 5:30pm (9:30am to 4:30pm at the Bank of Bermuda). The Bank of Bermuda airport branch is open Monday through Friday from 11am to 12:30pm and 1 to 4pm. All banks are closed Saturday, Sunday, and on public holidays. Many of the big hotels will cash traveler's checks.

**Barbers**   See "Hairdressers/Barbers" below.

**Bookstores   Bermuda Book Store (Baxters) Ltd.,** Queen Street (tel. 809/295-3698), stocks everything that is in print about Bermuda. Some books are available only through this store. There are books on gardening, flowers, local characters, and poets, among other subjects. There are also many English publications not easily obtainable in the United States, as well as a fine selection of children's books. You can also buy maps and prints here. The store has an extensive stationery department.

**Business Hours**   Most businesses are open Monday through Friday from 9am to 5:30pm. Stores are generally open Monday through Saturday from 9am to 5:30pm. Several shops open at 9:15am, closing at 5pm. A few shops are also open in the evening, but usually only when big cruise ships are in port.

**Cameras**   See "Photographic Needs" below.

**Car Rentals**   There are no car-rental agencies in Bermuda.

**Cigarettes**   Tobacconists and other stores carry a wide array of tobacco products, generally from either the United States or England. Prices vary but tend to be high. At most tobacconists you can buy classic cigars from Havana, but you must enjoy them on the island, since they can't be taken back to the United States because of Customs restrictions. Smoking in public places such as restaurants is generally allowed, but check first before lighting up. If your guests at the next table happen to be American, you may encounter objections to your smoking because of increased concerns about inhaling "secondary smoke." Movie theaters set aside a section for nonsmokers.

**Cleaners**   See "Laundry/Dry Cleaning" below.

**Climate**   See "When to Go—Climate, Holidays & Events," in Chapter 2, "Before You Go."

**Crime**   See "Safety" below.

**Currency**   See "Information, Entry Requirements & Money" in Chapter 2, "Before You Go."

**Currency Exchange**   Because the U.S. dollar and the Bermudian dollar are on par, both currencies can be used and it's not necessary to convert U.S. dollars into Bermudian dollars. It will be necessary to, however, convert Canadian dollars into local currency because of different valuations between the Canadian dollar and the Bermuda dollar.

**Customs**   Visitors going through **Bermudian Customs** may bring into Bermuda duty-free apparel and articles for their personal use, including sports equipment, cameras, 200 cigarettes, one quart of liquor, one quart of wine, and approximately 20 pounds of meat. Other foodstuffs may be dutiable. All imports may be inspected on arrival. Visitors entering Bermuda may claim a duty-free gift allowance.

**Dentist** Try Dr. David Roblin, Outerbridge Building, Pitts Bay Road, Pembroke Parish (tel. 809/292-7676).

**Doctor** Try Dr. Gordon Campbell, Sea Venture Building, Parliament Street, Hamilton (tel. 809/295-8106).

**Documents Required** See "Information, Entry Requirements & Money" in Chapter 2, "Before You Go."

**Driving Rules** There are no specific automobile-driving requirements for visitors for a very simple reason—there are no car-rental agencies in Bermuda. However, motor-assisted cycles are available (see "Getting Around" earlier in this chapter), but they may not be operated by children under 16. All cycle drivers and passengers are required by law to wear safety helmets that are securely fastened.

*Driving is on the left side of the road.* The speed limit is 20 mph, 15 mph in busy areas.

**Drug Laws** Importation of, possession of, or dealing with unlawful drugs, including marijuana, is an offense under Bermuda laws, with heavy penalties levied for infraction. Customs officers, at their discretion, may conduct body searches for drugs or other contraband goods.

**Drugstores** In Hamilton, try **Bermuda Pharmacy,** Church Street West (tel. 809/295-5815). It's in the Russell Eve Building and is open Monday through Saturday from 8:30am to 5:30pm. Under the same ownership is the **Phoenix Drugstore,** 3 Reid St. (tel. 809/295-3838), open Monday through Saturday from 8am to 6pm.

In Paget Parish, you can go to **Paget Pharmacy,** 130 South Road (tel. 809/236-7275), open Monday through Saturday from 8:30am to 8:30pm. At 49 Mangrove Bay, the **Somerset Pharmacy** in Somerset Village (tel. 809/234-2484) is open Monday through Saturday from 8am to 6pm.

**Electricity** Electricity is 110 volts, 60 cycles, AC. American appliances are compatible without converters or adapters.

**Embassies and Consulates** Except for Portugal and Greece, no European country, not even Great Britain, maintains an embassy or consulate in Bermuda. Nor does Canada. However, the United States has a representative. You'll find the **U.S. Consulate** at 16 Middle Rd. in Devonshire (tel. 809/295-1342). Hours are Monday through Friday from 8:30am to 4:30pm.

**Emergencies** To call the police in an emergency, dial 911; if it's not an emergency, dial 295-0011. To report a fire, dial 911; to summon an ambulance, call 911. For Air-Sea Rescue, dial 297-1010.

**Etiquette** Well-tailored Bermuda shorts are acceptable on almost any occasion, and many men wear them with jackets and ties at rather formal gatherings. But aside from that, the people are rather conservative in their attitude toward dress—bikinis, for example, are banned more than 25 feet from the water.

**Eyeglasses Argus Optical Company** (Henry Simmons, O.D.), Parliament Street, Hamilton (tel. 809/292-5452), works with both prescription glasses and contact lenses.

**Film** See "Photographic Needs" below.

**Firearms** Bringing in any firearm, part of a firearm, or ammunition is forbidden except under a license granted by the commissioner of police. Such a permit will not usually be granted except to visiting rifle club members attending a sports meeting in Bermuda. Spearguns and a variety of dangerous weapons are treated as firearms, but antique weapons made 100 or more years ago may be imported if you can show that they are antique. Breaches of the firearms import law are punishable by imprisonment or heavy fines.

**Gasoline** Since you aren't able to rent a car, you won't have to worry much about gasoline or "petrol" as some call it here. Mopeds take a mixture of oil and gas, and there's always a separate pump at gasoline stations for these vehicles. Honda scooters take regular unleaded gasoline, and it costs about $8 to fill up a tank. If you tour the distance of most bikers, you'll need only one refill per week. Both Honda scooters and mopeds are rented with full tanks. Gasoline stations are conveniently placed throughout the islands.

**Hairdresser/Barbers** Bermuda is well supplied with beauty shops and hairdressers. Nearly all the major hotels (for example, the Southampton Princess) have them on the premises.

You can always head for the **Bosun's Chair,** Front Street, Hamilton (tel. 809/295-5743). Open Monday through Saturday from 9am to 5:30pm, the store is sometimes so busy that an advance appointment is necessary.

Women can also head for the **BerSalon** on Front Street West, Hamilton (tel. 809/292-8570), for an array of hair and skin treatments. Open from 8am to 8pm, it too requests appointments.

BerSalon is the leading hairdressing, health, and beauty therapy organization in Bermuda, with shops not only in Hamilton, but also at Marriott's Castle Harbour Hotel, Elbow Beach Hotel, Southampton Princess Hotel, Sonesta Beach Hotel, Belmont Hotel, and Cambridge Beaches.

**Hitchhiking** See "Getting Around" earlier in this chapter.

**Holidays** See "When to Go—Climate, Holidays & Events" in Chapter 2, "Before You Go."

**Hospital** **King Edward VII Memorial Hospital,** 7 Point Finger Rd., Paget Parish (tel. 809/236-2345), has a staff of many nationalities and high qualifications. It has Canadian accreditation. Take bus no. 1 to reach it.

**Hotline** Call Helpline at 292-5159 for personal crisis; Lifeline at 236-0224 from 9am to 5pm or 236-3770 from 5pm to 9am, for any life-threatening emergency.

**Information** For information before you go, refer to "Information, Entry Requirements & Money" in Chapter 2, "Before You Go." Once on the island, you can also obtain information: see Tourist Information under "Orientation" in this chapter.

**Laundry/Dry Cleaning** If you're staying at a hotel, service will be provided in most cases—but with a very expensive price tag. One sure bet in Hamilton is **Coral Cleaners,** 9 Victoria St. (tel. 809/292-4059), open Monday through Thursday from 7:30am to 6pm and Friday from 7:30am to 5:30pm.

If you're trying to save money, try one of the local laundries, such as the **Quickie Lickie Laundromat,** 74 Serpentine Rd., Pembroke Parish (tel. 809/295-6097). It is open Monday through Saturday from 7am to 10pm, on Sunday from 8am to 7pm. Another convenient laundromat is called **Soaps,** the Market Place, Shelly Bay Plaza (tel. 809/293-2303), open Monday and Thursday through Saturday from 8am to 10pm; Sunday from 8am to 5pm. Closed Tuesday and Wednesday.

If you're out in Somerset, try **Sandy's Laundromat,** Market Place Plaza (tel. 809/238-9426). **Pembroke Laundry,** 18 Parsons Rd., Pembroke Parish (tel. 809/292-9055), is open daily from 6am to 10pm. It maintains a branch, the **West End Laundry,** at 57 Main Rd., Somerset Parish (tel. 809/234-3402), which is open Monday through Friday from 7am to 10pm; Saturday from 6am to 10pm; and Sunday from 6am to 7pm.

**Legal Aid** Should you become ill or injured in Bermuda, American citizens may need the services of the U.S. Consulate (see "Embassies and Consulates" above). The staff there can suggest where you might get medical help and will notify close relatives. Should your problem be a legal one, such as a drug arrest, the consulate will inform you of your rights (limited) and offer a list of attorneys. However, the consulate's office cannot interfere with law-enforcement officers in Bermuda.

A hot line in an emergency—useful for questions about U.S. citizens arrested abroad—is the Citizens' Emergency Center of the Office of Special Consular Services in Washington, DC (tel. 202/647-5225). They'll also tell you how to get money to U.S. citizens arrested abroad.

**Libraries**   The **Bermuda Library,** Queen Street, Hamilton (tel. 809/295-2905), is open Monday through Friday from 9:30am to 6pm (on Saturday to 5pm). It stands in Par-la-Ville, occupying the former house of the celebrated postmaster, W. B. Perot. There are two branch libraries—one in Somerset (tel. 809/234-1980) and another in St. George's (tel. 809/297-1912). The branches are open on Monday, Wednesday, and Saturday from 10am to 5pm.

**Liquor Laws**   Bermuda sternly regulates the sale of alcoholic beverages. The legal drinking age is 18, and most bars close at 1am. Sometimes nightclubs and bars in hotels can serve liquor until 3am, depending on the hotel. Many places are closed on Sunday.

**Lost Property**   Call the police with a full description of your lost property.

**Luggage Storage/Lockers**   There are no facilities unless private arrangements are made with a hotel.

**Mail**   Regular mail can be deposited in red pillar boxes on the streets. You'll recognize them by the monogram of Queen Elizabeth II. The postage rates for airmail letters up to 10 grams and for postcards is 55¢ to the United States and Canada, 70¢ to the United Kingdom. Air mail letters and postcards to the North American mainland can take 6 to 10 days, and perhaps the same time or even longer to reach Britain. Often visitors have returned home before their postcards arrive.

**Maps**   Visitors wanting a more detailed map than the previously mentioned *Bermuda Handy Reference Map* can pick up a map entitled *Bermuda Tourist Map,* on sale at the Public Works Department, next to the General Post Office on Parliament Street in Hamilton. The yard-wide map is extremely detailed, pinpointing specific buildings, with a scale of two inches to the mile.

**Newspapers/Magazines**   One daily newspaper is published in Bermuda, the *Royal Gazette.* Three weekly papers, the *Bermuda Sun, The Bermuda Times,* and the *Mid-Ocean News,* are issued on Friday. Major U.S. newspapers, including the *New York Times* and *USA Today,* and magazines (such as *Time* and *Newsweek*) are delivered to Bermuda on the day of publication on the mainland. *This Week in Bermuda* is a weekly guide published for tourists.

**Passports**   See "Information, Entry Requirements & Money" in Chapter 2, "Before You Go."

**Pets**   If you want to take your pet with you to Bermuda, you'll need a special permit issued by the director of the Department of Agriculture, Fisheries & Parks, P.O. Box HM 834, Hamilton HM CX, Bermuda (tel. 809/236-4201). Dogs and cats entering Bermuda from any country other than the United Kingdom, Australia, or New Zealand must have received a vaccination against rabies at least one month and not more than one year before the date of their intended arrival. Some guesthouses and hotels will permit you to bring in small animals, but others will not, so be sure to check into this in advance.

**Photographic Needs**   Many hotels, gift shops, camera dealers, and drugstores offer 24-hour service on Kodacolor, Ektachrome, and black-and-white film. Kodacolor 110, 120, 126, 127, and 135 pocket Instamatic film sizes can be developed and printed in Bermuda on Kodak quality-controlled equipment. In most cases, you can get same-day service on color prints (except Saturdays, Sundays, and holidays) if you bring in your film before midmorning. Most varieties of film are available.

For film or camera equipment, try **Camera Store,** 21 Queen St. (tel. 809/295-0303). It's Hamilton's leading camera store.

**Police**   In an emergency, call 292-2222; otherwise, call 295-0011.

**Post Offices**   The General Post Office is at 56 Church St., Hamilton (tel. 809/295-5151), and is open Monday through Friday from 8am to 5pm, on Saturday from 8am to noon. Post office branches and the Perot Post Office, Queen Street, Hamilton, are open Monday through Friday from 8am to 5pm. Some take a lunch break from 11:30am to 1pm. Airmail service for the United States and Canada closes at 9:30am in Hamilton, leaving daily. Also see "Mail" above.

**Radio and TV**   News is broadcast on the hour and half hour over AM stations 1340 (ZBM), 1230 (ZFB), and 1450 (VSB). The FM stations are 89 (ZBM) and 95 (ZFB). Tourist-oriented programming, island music, and information on activities and special events are aired over AM station 1160 (VSB) daily from 7am to noon.

The television channel, 10 (ZBM), is affiliated with America's Columbia Broadcasting System (CBS).

**Religious Services**   Nobody can call Bermuda the "Isles of Devils" today. It's an archipelago of houses of worship. In this relatively small area, numbering 57,000 in population, the following religions are represented, several by more than one congregation:

African Methodist Episcopal, Anglican, Apostolic Faith, Baha'i, Baptist, Brethren, Christian Science, Church of Christ, Church of God, Church of God in Christ, Church of God of Prophecy, Church of Jesus Christ of Latter Day Saints, Church of the Nazarene, Ethiopian Orthodox, Evangelical, Greek Orthodox, Jehovah's Witnesses, Jewish, Lutheran, Methodist, Muslim, New Testament Church of God, Pentecostal Assemblies of Canada, Presbyterian, Roman Catholic, Salvation Army, Seventh Day Adventist, Twentieth Century Gospel Crusade, United Holy Churches of America, Unity, and Worldwide Church of God. If you're contemplating attending a service, go to the tourist office Friday or Saturday and ask about the particular denomination with which you'd like to worship. When you give them the location of your hotel, someone will direct you to the nearest place of worship and provide the times of services. You may have to show up on a moped, however.

**Restrooms**   Hamilton and St. George's provide public facilities, but only during business hours. In Hamilton, toilets are found at City Hall, in Par-la-Ville Gardens, and at Albouy's Point. In St. George's, they are at Town Hall, Somers Gardens, and Market Wharf. Outside of these towns, you'll find restrooms at the public beaches, the Botanical Gardens, in several of the forts, at the airport, and at service stations; but, often you'll have to use the facilities in hotels, restaurants, and whatever else you can find.

**Safety**   There is no particular need for a crime alert regarding Bermuda. For the Bermudians are generally a peaceful people, not given to the expression of violence. To be sure, the island has experienced racial tensions in the past, but now relations between its white and black residents seem to be harmonious, as blacks assume a greater role in Bermuda's affairs.

Crimes, violent or otherwise, against tourists are rare, but don't be lulled into any false security, either. Crime does exist, as in any society—for instance, someone might try to pick your wallet in Hamilton. Protect your valuables, especially when you're at the beach. Lock your moped each time you leave it. Very valuable items should be placed in your hotel safe (if your hotel is big enough to have one) and never left carelessly in your room.

It is usually safe to go anywhere in Bermuda, but, here again, caution should be exercised, particularly late at night and especially if you're a woman traveling alone.

**Shoe Repair**   One of the most popular establishments is **Reid Johansen,** Washington Lane, Hamilton (tel. 809/295-2151). Hours are Monday through Friday from 8am to 5:30pm.

**Taxes**   Visitors to Bermuda are levied a tax before departing from the island. For those who leave by air, the tax, collected at the airport, is $15 for adults and $5 for children between the ages of 2 and 11 (children under 2 are exempt). For those who leave by ship, the tax, collected in advance from the cruise ship company, is $60 (children under 2 are exempt).

All room rates, regardless of the category of accommodation or the plan under which you stay, are subject to a 6% Bermuda government tax, to be paid when you check out of your hotel.

**Taxis**   See "Getting Around" earlier in this chapter.

**Telegrams/Telexes/Faxes**   Worldwide cable and overseas phone service is available, and charges may be reversed. Direct dialing is possible from Bermuda to the United States and Canada. To send telegrams, telexes, or faxes, go to the **Cable and Wireless Office** on 20 Church St. (west) in Hamilton, open Monday through Saturday from 9am to 5pm; or else telephone 809/295-7000.

**Telephone**   In conjunction with the **Bermuda Telephone Co. Ltd.,** Cable & Wireless (see above) provides International Direct Dialing (IDD) to more than 150 countries. Country codes and calling charges may be found in the current edition of the Bermuda telephone directory. Telephone booths are provided at the office and customers have the choice of prepaying for calls, or purchasing Cash Cards in $10, $25, and $50 denominations. Making long distances calls here can be a lot cheaper than at your hotel, which might impose stiff surcharges. To make a local call, deposit 20¢ (either Bermudian or U.S.). Hotels often charge from 20¢ to $1 for local calls.

Special telephones are also in place at passenger piers in Hamilton, St. George's, and the Dockyard, connecting directly to AT&T, U.S. Sprint, and MCI operators in the United States, thus permitting collect or calling card calls.

**Time**   Standard time in Bermuda is Greenwich mean time minus four hours, which makes it one hour ahead of eastern standard time. Daylight saving time is in effect from the first Sunday in April to the last Sunday in October, as it is in the United States. Thus when it's 6am in New York, it's 7am in Bermuda.

**Tipping**   In most cases, a service charge is added to your hotel and/or restaurant bill. In hotels, this is in lieu of tipping the various individuals such as the bellman, maids, and restaurant staff (for meals included in a package or in the daily rate). Otherwise, a 15% tip for service is customary.

**Tourist Offices**   See "Tourist Information" above.

**Transit Information**   For information about ferry service, call 809/295-4506. For bus information, call 809/292-3854.

**Useful Telephone Numbers**   For time and temperature, call 909. To learn "What's On in Bermuda," dial 974.

**Visas**   See "Information, Entry Requirements & Money" in Chapter 2, "Before You Go."

**Water**   See "Health, Insurance & Other Concerns" in Chapter 2, "Before You Go," and "Food & Drink" in Chapter 1, "Getting to Know Bermuda."

**Weather**   This might be an all-important consideration for your Bermuda plans. In addition to the newspaper and the radio, you can call 977 at any time of the day or night for forecast covering the next 24-hour period.

***Yellow Pages***   All Bermuda telephone numbers appear in one phone book, revised annually. The helpful *Yellow Pages* in the back outline all the goods and services you are likely to need.

# CHAPTER 4

# WHERE TO STAY IN BERMUDA

1. **BIG RESORT HOTELS**
- **FROMMER'S SMART TRAVELER: HOTELS**
- **FROMMER'S COOL FOR KIDS: HOTELS**
2. **SMALL HOTELS**
3. **COTTAGE COLONIES**
4. **HOUSEKEEPING UNITS**
5. **GUESTHOUSES**

**B**ermuda offers a wide selection of lodgings, ranging from small guesthouses to large luxury hotels. You'll find variations in size and facilities in each category. The Bermuda Hotel Association requires two nights' deposit within 14 days of confirmation of a reservation; full payment 30 days prior to arrival; and cancellation advice 15 days prior to scheduled arrival or your deposit will be lost. Some smaller hotels and other accommodations levy an energy surcharge, so you should ask about this when you make your travel arrangements.

All room rates, regardless of what plan you're staying on, are subject to a 6% Bermuda tax, which is added to your bill. A service charge ranging from 10% to 15% is added to your room rates in lieu of tips. Service charges do not cover bar tabs. Third-person rates are lower for those occupying a room with two other people, and children's tariffs vary according to their ages.

Generally, there are two major seasons in Bermuda, winter and summer. Bermuda has the reverse of the Bahamian or Caribbean high season, with its major season in spring and summer. Most establishments start to charge their high-season tariffs in March (Easter is the peak period) and lower their rates again around mid-November. A few hotels have all-year rates, and others charge in-between, or "shoulder," prices in spring and autumn. If business is slow, many smaller places will shut down in winter.

What follows is only a rough guideline to price ranges. In several large old resorts, because of the wide range of accommodations, prices are not uniform. Thus, while

---

## IMPRESSIONS

*No, ne'er did the wave in its elements steep*
*An island of lovelier charms;*
*It blooms in the giant embrace of the deep,*
*Like Hebe in Hercules' arms.*
*The blush of your bowers is light to the eye,*
*And their melody balm to the ear;*
*But the fiery planet of day is too nigh,*
*And the Snow Spirit never comes here.*
—THOMAS MOORE, "THE SNOW SPIRIT," IN *POEMS RELATING TO AMERICA* (1806)

one guest at the Elbow Beach Hotel, for example, might be staying at a "moderate" cost, another guest might be booked in at a "very expensive" rate. It all depends on your room assignment.

In general, "very expensive" hotels in Bermuda offer double rooms for $275 and up—and we do mean *up*, perhaps in the $420 to $565 region. These rates are on the modified American plan (MAP) or half board.

Hotels considered "expensive" offer MAP doubles for anywhere from $200 to $275. Hotels classified as "moderate" charge from $110 to $200 for a double, but are likely to include only breakfast. Hotels or guesthouses classified as "inexpensive" ask around $100 for a double room, most often including breakfast. Any guesthouse charging less than $100 for a double is considered "budget," at least by the standards of Bermuda.

In many of the cottage colonies, breakfast is not offered. You can either go out for breakfast or else pick up supplies the night before and prepare your own morning meal

# EMERGENCY ACCOMMODATIONS

If you haven't had time to reserve rooms before going to Bermuda, you may avail yourself of the services offered by the Visitors Service Bureau at the airport (tel. 809/292-0030). Located near where newcomers clear Customs, it is open from 9am to 4pm. Unless you have a hotel reservation and a return airplane ticket, you will not be allowed to proceed beyond this point. In the event that you do not have prebooked reservations, the bureau will help you make a reservation from the airport. But if you don't want to take a chance on such last-minute reservation attempts, you can make prior arrangements by writing to or calling the **Visitors Service Bureau,** P.O. Box HM 655, Hamilton HM CX (tel. 809/295-1480). The staff there must know the exact dates of your arrival and departure, the number of people in your party, the type of accommodation you prefer, and the maximum rate you can pay per person.

# 1. BIG RESORT HOTELS

The big resort hotels can promise enough amenities to make it unnecessary for their

---

## VARIOUS RATE PLANS

**AP (American Plan)**   Includes three meals a day (sometimes called full board or full pension).

**BP (Bermuda Plan)**   Popularized first in Bermuda, this option includes a full American breakfast (sometimes called an English breakfast).

**CP (Continental Plan)**   A continental breakfast (that is, bread, jam, and coffee) is included in the room rate.

**EP (European Plan)**   This rate is always cheapest, as it offers only the room—no meals.

**MAP (Modified American Plan)**   Sometimes called half board or half pension, this room rate includes breakfast and dinner (or lunch, if you prefer).

patrons to leave the premises, although most visitors tend to want to see what's on the outside. Most of the large hotels have their own beaches or beach clubs and swimming pools. Some have their own golf courses. Most hotels in this category offer luxury resort facilities, such as porter and room service, planned activities, sports facilities, shops (including a cycle shop), beauty salons, bars, nightclubs, entertainment, and taxi stands.

Few hotels or guesthouses include taxes and service charges in the prices quoted, so be aware that they will be added to your bill. The hotel tax is 6%, and service charges range from 10% to 15%.

# VERY EXPENSIVE

**BELMONT HOTEL GOLF & COUNTRY CLUB, Middle Rd., P.O. Box WK 251, Warwick WK BX, Bermuda. Tel. 809/236-1301,** or toll free 800/225-5843 in the U.S. and Canada. Fax 809/236-6867. 144 rms (all with bath), 7 suites. A/C MINIBAR TV TEL **Transportation:** Ferry from Hamilton.

**$ Rates** (EP): Mar 22–Nov 15, $234–$286 single; $256–$312 double; from $412 suite; off-season, $140–$160 single; $160–$210 double; from $310 suite. MAP $36 per person per day extra. AE, DC, MC, V.

Overlooking Hamilton Harbour with views over Great Sound, this British-inspired, country-club resort is situated on 110 acres of manicured grounds. The Forte hotel chain, the managing company, poured millions of dollars into the creation of one of the most desirable properties in Bermuda.

The hotel's exterior is a modern interpretation of a Bermuda colonial building. Wide latticed porches flank the entrance portico, which leads into a formal reception area paneled in Virginia cedar and dotted with Sheraton and Chippendale reproductions. Plushly upholstered English sofas and comfortable wing chairs are illuminated by light streaming through big windows with views of the lawn and the scattered cays of the Bermuda coast. The luxurious rooms and suites feature designer decor and Queen Anne–style furniture. The hotel has a garden with a limestone moon gate, plus summer-only outdoor bars.

**Dining/Entertainment:** Guests enjoy their meals in the main dining room, called the Gallery, with a view of the golf course. The hotel offers continental cuisine and Bermudian specialties. My favorite place for a drink is the Harbour Sights Bar, off the main lobby; it's one of the most elegant modern bars in Bermuda, with a decor featuring beautifully finished hardwoods and panoramic views—all adding up to a sophisticated ambience.

**Services:** Complimentary taxi to Horseshoe Bay Beach in summer, a seven-minute ride; the hotel pier serves as a stopping point for the government ferryboat that travels ever 30 minutes to and from Hamilton. Also laundry, babysitting, room service (breakfast and dinner only), two boutiques. A friendly staff answers questions and assists with many planned activities.

**Facilities:** An 18-hole championship golf course, designed by Robert Trent Jones; three floodlit tennis courts; an outdoor swimming pool.

**ELBOW BEACH HOTEL, 60 South Shore Road, P.O. Box HM 455, Hamilton HM BX, Bermuda. Tel. 809/236-3535,** or toll free 800/882-4200 in the U.S. Fax 809/236-6043. 220 rms, 80 suites. A/C MINIBAR TV TEL **Bus:** No. 1, 2, or 7 from Hamilton.

**$ Rates** (MAP): Mar 16–Nov 16, $270–$465 single; $295–$465 double; from $515 suite; off-season, $165–$260 single; $215–$310 double; from $345 suite. AE, DC, MC, V.

## FROMMER'S SMART TRAVELER: HOTELS

VALUE-CONSCIOUS TRAVELERS SHOULD TAKE ADVANTAGE OF THE FOLLOWING:

1. Off-season reductions. Most hotels grant such reductions (ranging from 20% to 60%) from November through March.
2. Greatly reduced rates for children who stay in a parent's room. Sometimes children stay free.
3. Reductions in rates if you pay cash.
4. Accommodation in a Bermudian guesthouse in a room most often with a private bath.
5. Air-and-land packages, which in the long run are usually cheaper for you.
6. The modified American plan (MAP), which invariably is less expensive than ordering meals à la carte.
7. Any special full packages offered for honeymooners, divers, tennis players, golfers, and so on.

### QUESTIONS TO ASK IF YOU'RE ON A BUDGET

1. Is there a surcharge for local or long-distance calls? Usually there is. In some hotels it can be an astonishing 40%.
2. Is service included in the rates quoted, or will 10% to 15% be added to your final bill? It makes a big difference.
3. Is breakfast included? If it's not, it can easily add as much as $80 more per week to your final bill.
4. Is the 6% government tax included in the quoted rate? It can make a big difference in your final bill after a few days.

★ This self-contained Wyndham resort, set in 34 acres of gardens some 10 minutes by taxi from the center of Hamilton, has its own quarter-mile pink-sand beach on the South Shore. Originally built in 1908, it has been enduringly popular over the decades. Usually it attracts the tradition-minded guest, but during spring College Weeks it draws the largest concentration of young students in Bermuda.

After a $20-million restoration, Elbow Beach is better than ever. Guests can select from a wide array of air-conditioned hotel rooms or suites, including everything from bedrooms with balconies overlooking the water to duplex cottages. Some lanai rooms overlook the pool and the Atlantic, and others are surfside. In the restoration, the rooms were completely gutted and rebuilt. Most rooms were given Italian marble baths with up-to-date plumbing, and bedroom walls draped in silk.

**Dining/Entertainment:** All guests, including those on MAP, may choose dinner at any of the hotel's three restaurants, all with ocean views, or from one outdoor theme party nightly. The main dining room, Ondine's, is the most formal of the restaurants; its pastel pink-and-green decor is reminiscent of an elegant garden gazebo. Here, a sumptuous breakfast buffet is served daily, as is classic French cuisine at dinner. Spazzizzi's on the pool level, the most casual of the three eateries, has been endowed with a rustic tavern look. A wood-burning pizza oven and selection of pastas complement salads, sandwiches, and snacks at lunch and a range of grilled and sautéed seafood, steaks, chicken, and veal at dinner. At Café Lido, the resort's beachfront restaurant, seafood with a Mediterranean accent is the focus. Lunch is served on the outdoor terrace overlooking the beach, while dinner is served indoors in a greenhouse ambience. Casual poolside dining at Elbow Beach's Pool Terrace Barbecue features steak, chicken, and corn-on-the-cob Monday through Thursday evenings and on Saturday evenings. St. David's Island Buffet on Friday evenings offers dining under the stars, accompanied by mellow music. Bermuda specialties headline the menu: conch chowder, fresh local fish, curried chicken, mussel pie, and more. After dinner the festivities continue with "bamboo dancing," or limbo. Every Sunday a lively Elbow Beach Party and barbecue is held on the resort's pink sand beach, featuring music and entertainment. Some of the island's top musical performers appear nightly in Spazzizi's Bar, and piano music fills the lounge, adjacent to the cozy Library Bar and Orangerie sun room, during the evening.

**Services:** Room service, babysitting, laundry, beauty salon, moped rental.

**Facilities:** Private beach, five all-weather tennis courts, large swimming pool with controlled temperatures, game room, health club with exercise room and whirlpool.

**MARRIOTT'S CASTLE HARBOUR RESORT, Paynters Town Rd., Tucker's Town, P.O. Box HM 841, Hamilton HM CX, Bermuda. Tel. 809/293-2040,** or toll free 800/228-9290 in the U.S. and Canada. Fax 809/293-8288. 405 rms (all with bath), 19 suites. A/C TV TEL **Bus:** No. 2 from St. George's.

**$ Rates** (EP): Mar 28–Nov 6, $210–$335 single or double; from $450 suite; off-season, $105–$150 single or double; from $250 suite. Breakfast buffet $15 per person extra. AE, DC, MC, V.

Originally built of coral blocks in the 1920s on a hilltop overlooking Castle Harbour and Harrington Sound, this prestigious property had fallen into disrepair before Marriott poured $60 million into one of the loveliest renovations in Bermuda late in 1986. The renovation added more than 100 bedrooms, landscaped the gardens, and enhanced the public rooms into one of the most strikingly elegant array of spaces of any hotel on the island. The 250 acres of prime real estate surrounding the property are maintained by at least 50 gardeners. From the outside, the place looks almost severe, a bit like a modernized version of a Tuscan fortress with abruptly angular outbuildings. One of these is connected to the main building by an elevated concrete catwalk. The most dramatic wing slopes like a modern version of a Mayan pyramid down to the sea.

The '20s-era core was entirely transformed. What might be the most glamorous room in Bermuda is an 18th-century salon, much like what you'd find in an English country house. Filled with copies of Chippendale and Queen Anne furniture, and sheathed with mahogany paneling, it's a showplace for morning coffee, afternoon fish chowder, four o'clock tea, six o'clock hot hors d'oeuvres (to the playing of a live pianist), and after-dinner dance music. Adjacent to it is an elegant dining room, where copies of the original Castle Harbour china from the 1920s are part of the meal service. Throughout the property are such refined touches as the Cascade Terrace, stone moon gates, and formal garden terraces built around a Bermuda cedar.

Depending on your tastes, your room might be within one of at least three different buildings on the property. The accommodations are either predominantly pink or predominantly yellow, and they are invariably furnished with a sense of tradition, usually with good copies of English furniture.

**Dining/Entertainment:** The hotel has a disco and three restaurants: the Windsor Room, the Golf Club Grill, and the Mikado (reviewed separately).

**Services:** Massages, laundry, babysitting, room service.

**Facilities:** Health club, sauna, golf course, beach club (accessible by minivan), scuba-diving facilities, outdoor swimming pool.

**THE PRINCESS, 76 Pitts Bay Rd., P.O. Box HM 837, Hamilton HM CX, Bermuda. Tel. 809/295-3000,** or toll free 800/223-1818 in the U.S., or toll free 800/268-7176 in Canada. Fax 809/295-1914. 411 rms (all with bath), 36 suites. A/C TV TEL **Bus:** No. 7 or 8.

**$ Rates** (EP): Apr 11–Nov 27, $185–$275 single or double; suites from $350; off-season, $130–$160 single or double; from $215 suites. MAP $50 per person per day. AE, DC, MC, V.

On the edge of Hamilton Harbour, you'll find a regal pink "wedding cake" landmark. Often called the Hamilton Princess, it's been graced with countless visits from British aristocrats, Hollywood and European movie stars, and discreetly wealthy yachting enthusiasts since it opened, with international fanfare, in 1887. The hotel is named for Princess Louise, Queen Victoria's daughter, who stayed here shortly after its opening.

Today, this is the flagship of the Princess Hotel chain and undoubtedly the one hotel with the most glamorous history. It was initially designed as a wintertime palace for the very wealthy and boasted an all-wood construction to "guarantee against dampness." Before 1932, it had been reconstructed no fewer than four times. By World War II, the Princess's role as a deciphering center and inspection headquarters for each piece of mail transported from Europe to North America ensured its place in history (see "History & Politics" section in Chapter 1).

The elegantly colonial core is flanked by well-designed modern wings, each of which is pierced with row upon row of balconied loggias. One of the hotel's more unusual salons is the Wedgwood-inspired Adam Lounge; originally built in 1927, it's the central and most formal salon of this prestigious hotel where prewar weekly balls were the social event of the colony. The property was designed around a concrete pier extending into the harbor, off which lies a Japanese-style floating garden, complete with lily ponds, waterfalls, fountains, and towering trees. The botanical theme is repeated in the lobby, where a rivulet of water cascades past rock-climbing orchids near the huge windows.

In 1992 management renovated the already tastefully decorated bedrooms and public salons, continuing a program of making a good property even better. Most of the guest rooms have private balconies; each room was designed "to create the feeling that you'd choose the same kind of bedroom if you owned a home here." Some 40% of the guests are repeat visitors.

**Dining/Entertainment:** The hotel maintains a wide array of drinking and dining facilities; for more information, refer to "City of Hamilton" in Chapter 5, "Where to Dine in Bermuda," and "Evening Entertainment" in Chapter 10, "Bermuda Nights."

**Services:** Frequent ferryboat service between the Hamilton Princess and the Southampton Princess, laundry, room service, babysitting.

**Facilities:** Heated freshwater swimming pool; unheated saltwater swimming pool; guests can take the ferryboat to the Southampton Princess for tennis, sailing, white-sand beaches, and golf. Moped rental available.

**SONESTA BEACH HOTEL & SPA, South Shore Rd., Southampton Parish, P.O. Box HM 1070, Hamilton HM EX, Bermuda. Tel. 809/238-8122,** or toll free 800/766-3782 in the U.S. Fax 809/238-8463. 365 rms, 37 suites. A/C MINIBAR TV TEL **Bus:** No. 7.

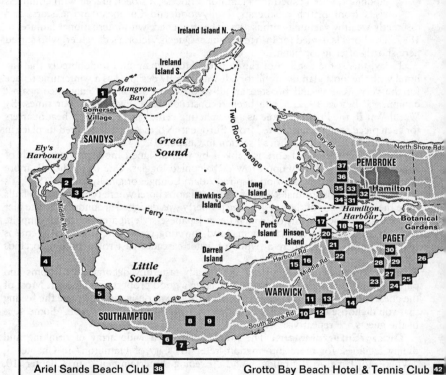

# Atlantic Ocean

Ireland Island N.

Ireland Island S.

Mangrove Bay

Somerset Village

SANDYS

Ely's Harbour

Great Sound

Two Rock Passage

Bay Rd

PEMBROKE

North Shore Rd.

Hamilton

Long Island

Hawkins Island

Ferry

Middle Rd

Ports Island

Hinson Island

Darrell Island

Little Sound

Hamilton Harbour

Botanical Gardens

PAGET

Harbour Rd.

Middle Rd.

WARWICK

South Shore Rd.

SOUTHAMPTON

| Ariel Sands Beach Club **38** | Grotto Bay Beach Hotel & Tennis Club **42** |
|---|---|
| Astwood Cove **11** | Harmony Club **30** |
| Belmont Hotel Golf & Country Club **16** | Hillcrest Guest House **44** |
| Cambridge Beaches **1** | Horizons and Cottages **23** |
| Edgehill Manor **36** | Lantana Colony Club **3** |
| Elbow Beach Hotel **24** | Longtail Cliffs **10** |
| Fourways Inn **22** | Loughlands **29** |
| Glencoe Harbour Club **17** | Marley Beach Cottages **12** |
| Granaway Guest House & Cottage **15** | Marriott's Castle Harbour Resort **41** |
| Greenbank Guest House **18** | Newstead **19** |
| Greene's Guest House **5** | Oxford House **32** |

# BERMUDA ACCOMMODATIONS

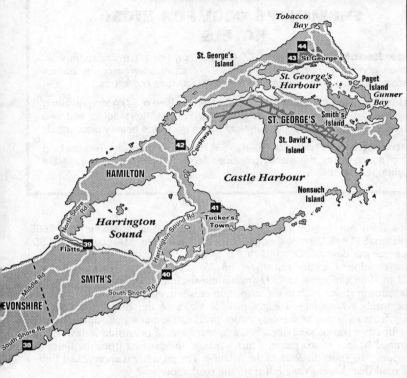

## FROMMER'S COOL FOR KIDS: HOTELS

**Elbow Beach Hotel** *(see p. 77)* Children stay free in parents' room. Ask, however, about the "Family Value Package," which includes accommodations, transfers, daily breakfast buffet, and a host of activities and extras.

**Grotto Bay Beach Hotel & Tennis Club** *(see p. 84)* A long-enduring family favorite, this hotel features a "Family Special" (two adults and two children under 16), requiring a four-night minimum. Rates heavily discounted.

**Southampton Princess** *(see p. 83)* This pocket of posh offers the best children's program on the island. It includes parties for the kiddies and reliable babysitting services.

**$ Rates** (EP): Apr 1–Nov 15, $220–$535 single or double; suites from $635; off-season, $118–$238 single or double; from $268 suite. MAP supplement $50 per person per day. AE, DC, MC, V.

This long-established luxury resort, set on 25 acres of prime seafront property, benefited in 1986 and again in 1992 from a massive multimillion-dollar restoration and enlargement. It was built in the shape of a crescent, curving along the spine of a rocky peninsula whose jagged edges provide views of the Bermudian coastline. Benefiting from its status as the only major hotel in Bermuda built directly on the beach, it boasts a trio of sandy beaches, ample lengths of oceanside walkways, and well-trimmed hedges of sea grape, which separate the gardens from the limestone cliffs dropping the short distance to the Atlantic. The property is approached from a winding road that descends the hill from the road above it.

A uniformed doorman greets visitors in front of a glass tunnel stretching over a flowering ravine and eventually opening into the tasteful art deco–inspired lobby. With its big windows, wood trim, and pastel shades of pink and violet, the lobby is like a 1920s interpretation of the view from a sailboat. The hotel contains a spa facility, and many clients check in on a weight-reduction and muscle-toning regime that is strictly supervised by the staff.

The resort also incorporates a favorite beach on the island, Boat Bay, into its facilities. Shaped like a circle and flanked by limestone cliffs and sandy beaches, the bay was used long ago by gunpowder smugglers and later by rum-runners because of its well-camouflaged entrance. From the sea, the rocky coastline almost conceals the narrow inlet that supplies the bay's waters. With its encircling palm-covered cabañas and bars and its soft sandy bottom, the bay looks like a small corner of Polynesia transported onto the buccaneer sands of Bermuda.

Each room contains a radio alarm and private terrace, plus a floral kind of charm and all the conveniences you'd expect. Rates are based solely on the view. MAP clients are served well-prepared evening meals in the La Sirena dining room. Be sure to ask about the reduced honeymoon packages, if applicable, when you call.

**Dining/Entertainment:** The hotel has an upscale Italian restaurant, Lillian's (see Chapter 5, "Where to Dine in Bermuda").

**Services:** Room service, laundry, babysitting.

**Facilities:** Beach, outdoor swimming pool, indoor swimming pool, complete dive shop for snorkelers and scuba divers, children's playground, six tennis courts (illuminated for night play) and full-time tennis pro, who offers complimentary group lessons twice weekly.

**SOUTHAMPTON PRINCESS, 101 South Shore Rd., P.O. Box HM 1379, Hamilton HM FX, Bermuda. Tel. 809/238-8000,** or toll free 800/223-1818 in the U.S. Fax 809/238-8245. 600 rms, 34 suites. A/C MINIBAR TV TEL **Transportation:** Private hotel ferry boats.

**$ Rates** (BP): Apr 5–Nov 28, $272–$422 single; $325–$475 double; from $487 suite; off-season, $125–$160 single or double; from $280 suite. AE, DC, MC, V.

At the Southampton Princess, perhaps the most desirable hotel in Bermuda, you receive superlative service and sumptuous accommodations. The 100-acre resort is the biggest and best maintained on the island and was built on top of a verdant knoll between two views of the sea, at a point where Bermuda narrows to a spit of rock and sand. Since its erection, a team of landscape architects have turned the grounds into the most idyllic large-scale gardens on the island. The hotel also has convention facilities, and many international companies hold annual get-togethers here.

Guests who never want to leave the shelter of the beautifully paneled public rooms enjoy a self-contained village of bars, restaurants, shops, and athletic facilities. These public rooms, scattered over three plushly carpeted or tiled floors, are connected by baronial staircases, the intermediate landings and well-crafted angles of which provide absorbing vantage points for looking out over the well-dressed clientele. What might be the most dramatic chandelier in Bermuda—a glass, brass, and wrought-iron Spanish-inspired piece especially designed for the space—illuminates three floors of festivities. The furnishings throughout the hotel are well-upholstered pieces, reflecting a kind of 18th-century English dignity.

The guest rooms are arranged in three soaring wings that radiate more or less symmetrically from a central core. This design allows each of the luxurious bedrooms to incorporate a private veranda with a sweeping view of the water.

But some of the best parts of the resort are scattered throughout the gardens of the surrounding acreage. The scenic beach and private harbor lie within a five-minute walk. Although the terrace pool is ideal for a tropical drink in the sunlight, my preferred pool is a re-creation of a Polynesian waterfall, where streams of heated water spill off an artificial limestone cliff, while cascades of flowering vines bloom above the foaming waterjets of the swirling basin. Swimming is possible here even during colder weather because of the greenhouse constructed above. If you crave the salty waters of the sea, the hotel beach is sheltered in a jagged cove, flanked by cliffs and studded with rocky outcroppings lashed by the tides.

**Dining/Entertainment:** Meals are taken in one of the hotel's restaurants (see "Southampton Parish" in Chapter 5, "Where to Dine in Bermuda"). Dining rooms include Windows on the Sound, a three-tiered palace that seems like a happy medley of London's Mayfair of the 1930s and New York's Rainbow Room. Through arched windows rising 20 feet are views of the islands of Great Sound. It's almost a nostalgic re-creation of the grand dining of an earlier era. Other choices include Wickets Brasserie, Newport Room, Rib Room, Whaler Inn, and Waterlot Inn.

Bar and restaurant facilities are also available on the beach, plus the main building is rich in entertainment facilities, covered separately in this guide.

**Services:** A shuttlebus runs among the various hotel facilities; hotel ferryboats make runs along Little Sound into Hamilton. Also available are room service, laundry, babysitting, beauty salon, moped rental, massages.

**Facilities:** Private beach, indoor and outdoor swimming pools, 11 tennis courts, 18-hole golf course (see Chapter 8, "Sports & Recreation"), business center, dive club.

### GROTTO BAY BEACH HOTEL & TENNIS CLUB, 11 Blue Hole Hill, Hamilton Parish CR 04, Bermuda. Tel. 809/293-8333, or toll free 800/582-3190 in the U.S. Fax 809/293-2306. 201 rms (all with bath), 3 suites. A/C MINIBAR TV TEL **Bus:** No. 1, 3, 10, or 11.

**$ Rates** (CP): Apr–Oct, $198–$240 single or double; off-season $110–$130 single or double. Suite from $350 year-round. MAP $48 per person extra. AE, MC, V.

The only major complaint any guest could have about this top-notch resort is that it's slightly isolated from the rest of the island; however, the natural surroundings and other advantages of the hotel make up for any inconvenience.

The resort is named after the subterranean caves that perforate the 21 acres surrounding it. The organizers have turned these caves to their best advantage and conduct tours, communal swimfests, and spelunking expeditions through them, thus creating one of the most unusual hotel attractions in Bermuda. One of the caves has been turned into a disco, Prospero's. Furthermore, the property is rife with tropical fruit trees, allowing patrons to eat loquats, oranges, papayas, and a local kind of kiwi called "locust and wild honey."

The swimming pool is blasted out of natural rock and ringed with serpentine edges, much like a grotto in its own right. Under a peaked Bermuda roof, swimmers enjoy the swim-up bar, where a handful of underwater chairs permit guests to "sip and dip." A sandy beach nearby offers a view of an unused series of railroad pylons, leading onto forested Coney Island across the bay. A lighthouse there was demolished for one of the explosion scenes in the film *The Deep*.

From the sea side, the airy public areas look like a modernized version of a mogul's palace, with big windows, thick white walls, and a trio of peaked roofs with curved eaves. The hotel's stylishly lighthearted decor includes quilted wall hangings and pendulous macramés.

The double accommodations are contained in 11 three-story "lodges" (actually modern buff-colored buildings with prominent balconies and sea views). Several package rates are available for those who remain more than six nights and for families who stay more than four. Scuba-diving, tennis, and golf packages are also available for stays of more than five nights.

**Dining/Entertainment:** Nightly live entertainment is provided in the Rum House Lounge, and there are a handful of other bars on the property. Guests can also enjoy the afternoon tea and the daily happy hour.

**Services:** Nature walks, twice-weekly "cave crawls," daily cave swim, complete program for children, frequent tennis clinics, daily "Jazzercise" in the Rum House Lounge before breakfast, scavenger hunts, communal croquet near the bar, fish feeding, bridge competitions, organized activities for teenagers. Also laundry, room service, babysitting.

**Facilities:** Beach, swimming pool with swim-up bar, four tennis courts, and a golf course nearby.

### PALM REEF HOTEL, 1 Harbour Rd., P.O. Box HM 1189, Hamilton HM EX, Bermuda. Tel. 809/236-1000, or toll free 800/221-1294 in the U.S. Fax 809/236-6392. 91 rms (all with bath), 3 suites. A/C TEL **Transportation:** Bus No. 7 or private hotel ferry.

**$ Rates** (EP): Mar 15–Nov 15, $125–$160 single; $150–$162 double; from $190 suite; off-season, $75–$90 single; $96–$116 double or suite. Continental breakfast $8 extra. AE, MC, V.

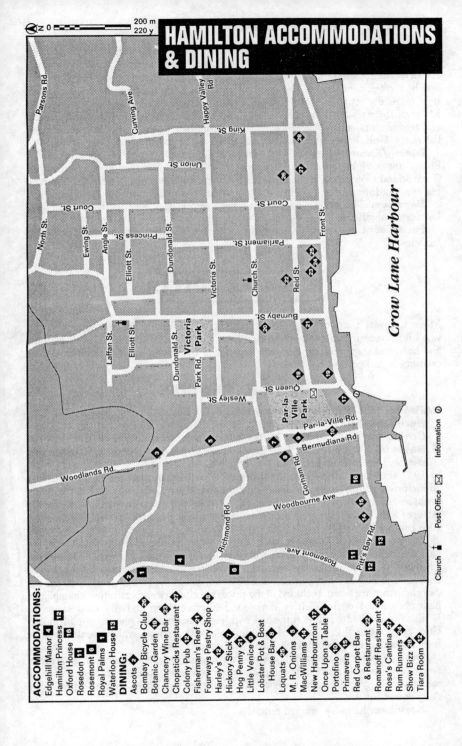

# HAMILTON ACCOMMODATIONS & DINING

Z 0 — 200 m / 220 y

*Crow Lane Harbour*

Parsons Rd.
Curving Ave.
Happy Valley Rd.
King St.
Union St.
Court St.
North St.
Ewing St.
Angle St.
Princess St.
Elliott St.
Dundonald St.
Victoria St.
Church St.
Parliament St.
Front St.
Reid St.
Burnaby St.
Laffan St.
Elliott St.
Dundonald St.
Park Rd.
Wesley St.
Queen St.
Par-la-Ville Park
Victoria Park
Par-la-Ville Rd.
Bermudiana Rd.
Woodlands Rd.
Gorham Rd.
Woodbourne Ave.
Richmond Rd.
Rosemont Ave.
Pitt's Bay Rd.

Church ✝   Post Office ⊠   Information ⊘

**ACCOMMODATIONS:**
Edgehill Manor 4
Hamilton Princess 10
Oxford House 11
Rosedon 5
Rosemont 6
Royal Palms 1
Waterloo House 13

**DINING:**
Ascots 4
Bombay Bicycle Club 28
Botanic Garden 19
Chancery Wine Bar 23
Chopsticks Restaurant 27
Colony Pub 12
Fisherman's Reef 24
Fourways Pastry Shop 10
Harley's 12
Hickory Stick 7
Hog Penny 21
Little Venice 20
Lobster Pot & Boat
House Bar 9
Loquats 26
M. R. Onions 5
MacWilliams 14
New Harbourfront 11
Once Upon a Table 3
Portofino 15
Primavera 13
Red Carpet Bar
& Restaurant 22
Romanoff Restaurant 29
Rosa's Cantina 21
Rum Runners 28
Show Bizz 26
Tiara Room 12

Located on Harbour Road and Cobbs Hill Road where Paget and Warwick parishes meet, the Palm Reef Hotel has had a loyal following for more than three-quarters of a century. The resort overlooks Hamilton Harbour, with Hamilton only a 10-minute ride by the frequent ferries. The main buildings, in Bermuda pink, have a decorative style originally set by Dorothy Draper and are surrounded by landscaped grounds. Many of the well-furnished bedrooms have separate dressing rooms, coffeemakers, and refrigerators, and all have sliding glass doors that open onto private terraces or balconies. Golf, honeymoon, and family plans are featured.

**Dining/Entertainment:** The hotel has a cocktail lounge, a dining room, Le Bistro, and a nightclub called Le Cabaret. Good food is served in the Waterfront Great Sound House, and an English afternoon tea is offered daily. The Marine Terrace features outdoor dining, dancing, and entertainment under a night sky.

**Services:** The hotel's own ferry takes visitors back and forth to Hamilton. Laundry, babysitting.

**Facilities:** Large open-air, temperature-controlled swimming pool, scuba diving facilities.

# 2. SMALL HOTELS

More informal than the big luxury and first-class hotels are the places in the small-hotel category. Many of these establishments have their own good dining rooms and bars, and some feature their own beaches or beach clubs. All of them have their own pools and patios.

## VERY EXPENSIVE

**HARMONY CLUB, South Shore Rd., P.O. Box PG 299, Paget PG BX, Bermuda. Tel. 809/296-3500,** or toll free 800/225-5843 in the U.S. and Canada. Fax 809/236-2624. 71 rms (all with bath). **Bus:** No. 2 or 7.
**$ Rates** (AP): Apr 22–Oct 15, $415 per couple per day: off-season $330 per couple per day. No children accepted. AE, DC, MC, V.

In 1987 the Forte hotel chain transformed a well-landscaped resort into the first all-inclusive, couples-only hideaway in Bermuda. It was originally called Harmony Club; and even earlier, in the 1830s, it had been known as Harmony Hall, the family estate of a Bermudian shipping merchant. It remained a private dwelling until the early 20th century.

Using a touristic format that has been frequently employed in the Caribbean, the package includes all meals, drinks, and diversionary activities, giving participants the advantage of knowing exactly what their vacation will cost in advance. Visitors walk beneath a pink-and-white portico, leading them inside the reception area, where the daily activities are listed. Included in the prices are all taxes and gratuities; champagne, bathrobes, and French toiletries; dining and entertainment; and all facilities.

Each of the bedrooms is furnished with reproductions of Queen Anne furniture. Units are contained in a series of rambling pink-sided wings, which usually encircle formal gardens containing gazebos and well-tended roses.

**Dining/Entertainment:** There is a full English tea every afternoon, an array of constantly available snacks, free and open-bar privileges, carefully prepared evening meals served by candlelight on fine china and crystal, nightly cocktail parties, and daily entertainment.

**Services:** Laundry, moped rental.

**Facilities:** Freshwater swimming pool; whirlpool; tennis courts; Jacuzzis; two saunas; video library; complimentary beach club privileges; unlimited use of a double-seat motorscooter (one per couple) during a week's stay; reduced greens fees at nearby Belmont golf course.

**POMPANO BEACH CLUB, 32 Pompano Beach Rd., Southampton SB 03, Bermuda. Tel. 809/234-0222,** or toll free 800/343-4155 in the U.S. or Canada. Fax 809/234-1694. 33 rms (all with bath), 21 suites. A/C MINIBAR TV TEL **Transportation:** Hamilton ferry to Somerset.

**$ Rates** (MAP): Apr 16–Nov 14, $269–$312 single; $289–$332 double; from $319 suite; off-season, $180–$220 single; $200–$240 double; from $230 suite. No credit cards.

On the southwest shore, the Pompano Beach Club was Bermuda's first fishing club when it opened in 1956. Today, it's also one of the most delightful smaller hotels on the island. Part of its allure stems from its setting on the side of a limestone hill, adjacent to the Port Royal Golf Club. Years ago, it was cut in a stair-shaped series of terraces to accommodate the various buildings of this well-maintained property. Each of them is painted in a shade of rose called "Pompano pink."

From the terraced beach below the clubhouse, it's possible for water lovers to walk waist-deep along a clean sandy bottom for the length of 2½ football fields before finally reaching deep water. The renovated accommodations present this view to its best advantage and offer balconies or terraces from each of the hillside villas scattered over the landscaped property. Suites cost a bit less than the most expensive deluxe rooms. That's because these deluxe accommodations are larger, although they don't contain a division between the sleeping and the living areas. For guests who prefer to admire the sunlit ocean from the edge of a pool, the resort offers a crescent-shaped freshwater oasis with an adjacent bar, and a mosaic depiction of a pompano, the fish that made these waters famous. Other extras include a fireplace in one of the stone-trimmed lounges for colder evenings, and a moon gate.

**Dining/Entertainment:** Meals in the dining room, the Cedar Room, are international. Nonresidents can reserve a place for the fixed-price evening meal, which offers a wide selection of courses and costs from $35 per person. Each dish is prepared by a team of five chefs. The hotel also has a British style pub.

**Services:** Laundry, babysitting.

**Facilities:** Freshwater swimming pool; oceanside Jacuzzi, clay tennis court; easy access to the government-owned Port Royal Golf Course, designed by Robert Trent Jones, with a par of 71 (six of its holes lie immediately adjacent to the hotel); sunfish and windsurfer rentals.

**THE REEFS, 56 South Shore Rd., Southampton SN 02, Bermuda. Tel. 809/238-0222,** or toll free 800/223-1363 in the U.S. or Canada. Fax 809/238-0222. 65 units (all with bath). A/C TEL **Bus:** No. 7.

**$ Rates** (MAP): Apr 1–Nov 15, $276–$340 single; $286–$350 double; off-season, $186–$246 double. No credit cards.

This lanai colony on Christian Bay is arranged along a low coral ridge. The uncrowded cluster of salmon-pink cottages faces a private beach of pink-flecked sand surrounded by palm trees and jutting rocks. On a ledge with an ocean view is a kidney-shaped swimming pool. The Reefs offers lanais decorated with rattan furniture and island colors, all with private sun decks and ocean views.

**Dining/Entertainment:** There is a choice of dining either in the plant-filled Terrace Dining Room or al fresco at Coconuts, the popular beach deck between palm trees. A continental and North American cuisine is served. The main clubhouse has a beam-ceilinged nautical lounge offering entertainment seven nights a week, ranging from calypso to pub-style sing-along favorites.

**Services:** Laundry, babysitting, room service.
**Facilities:** Beach, swimming pool, two all-weather tennis courts.

## STONINGTON BEACH HOTEL, South Shore Rd., P.O. Box HM 523, Hamilton HM CX, Bermuda. Tel. 809/236-5416, or toll free 800/223-1588 in the U.S., or toll free 800/268-0424 in Canada. For reservations and information, contact Prima Reservations Systems, 747 Third Ave., New York, NY 10017 (tel. 212/223-2848). Fax 809/236-0371. 64 rms (all with bath). A/C TEL

**Bus:** No. 7.
**$ Rates** (MAP): May 1–Nov 15, $260–$275 single; $360–$390 double; off-season, $155–$185 single; $270–$330 double. AE, DC, MC, V.

Overlooking South Shore in Paget Parish, this hotel is set in what used to be a grape arbor. The $6 million structure is owned and operated by the Bermuda Department of Hotel Technology, whose classrooms and headquarters lie at the top of a nearby knoll. Some of the employees are students, supervised by professional international staff and trainers. Few deluxe hotel resorts can offer such a high standard of service, and the students are likely to be more helpful than some other battle-trained, jaded personnel in the hotel field.

A lamplit drive leads visitors through foliage up to the buff-colored facade. A stucco passageway follows a trail to an inner octagonal courtyard where a palm tree grows as a centerpiece. The reception area is high-ceilinged, its dark pine beams alternating with white plaster.

The accommodations are contained in four outlying buildings. Rooms are comfortably spacious, each with a wide balcony or patio, plus a view of the ocean. They are furnished with Drexel-Heritage pieces and have ceiling fans, small refrigerators, and love seats that become extra folding beds. The hotel's sandy beach is reached via steps cut through foliage and limestone.

**Dining/Entertainment:** A library bar with a fireplace is most inviting, as is a very attractive restaurant, the Norwood Room (see "Paget Parish" in Chapter 5, "Where to Dine in Bermuda").

**Services:** Laundry, babysitting.
**Facilities:** Beach, freshwater swimming pool with terrace bar, two tennis courts, business center.

## WATERLOO HOUSE, Pitts Bay Rd., P.O. Box HM 333, Hamilton HM BX, Bermuda. Tel. 809/295-4480, or toll free 800/468-4100 in the U.S. Fax 809/295-2585. 25 rms (all with bath), 7 suites. **Bus:** No. 1, 2, 10, or 11.

**$ Rates** (BP): Apr–Nov, $160–$230 single; $220–$350 double; $250–$350 suite; off-season, $120–$160 single; $160–$210 double; $190–$210 suite. AE, MC, V.

On the edge of Hamilton Harbour in Pembroke Parish is a remake and an extension of a 19th-century house, lying on the outskirts of town center. Terraced gardens descend to the water in the style of the Italian Riviera. Behind salmon walls, the gardens are filled with palms and magnolias, poinsettias, and urns of ivy; a splashing fountain; and white iron garden furniture with fringed parasols. Guests can observe the British custom and take afternoon tea on the lawn at the water's edge. There are nooks for drinks and sunbaths. Shade trees stand on the fringe of an open-air, freshwater swimming pool. There are, as well, a private dock, a waterside barbecue area, and a terrace for rum-swizzle parties.

Inside, the drawing room is furnished with English antiques and decoratively tiled floors. The main dining room, overlooking the terrace and harbor, is dignified with Queen Anne chairs. On the lower terrace level is a bar lounge, with eclectic decorations, Moorish arches, English armchairs, and hand-woven pillows. The bedrooms vary in size and decorative treatment, each with its own flair, suggesting a country-house guest room.

# EXPENSIVE

**GLENCOE HARBOUR CLUB, P.O. Box PG 297, Salt Kettle Lane, Paget PG BX, Bermuda. Tel. 809/236-5274,** or toll free 800/468-1500 in the U.S. toll free 800/463-1469 in Canada. Fax 809/236-9108. 34 rms (all with bath), 7 suites. A/C TEL **Transportation:** Ferry from Hamilton every 30 minutes.

**$ Rates** (MAP): Apr 15–Nov 30, $205–$300 single; $225–$250 double; from $320 suite; off-season, $135–$165 single; $165 double; from $195 suite. AE, MC, V.

During racing season this clublike hotel is likely to be filled to capacity with yachting enthusiasts. It's built at the edge of a cove lined with private houses and filled with boats in any season. Reggie Cooper, who runs the place, was captain of Bermuda's yachting team in the 1964 and 1968 Olympics. Today, Reggie and his wife, Margot, welcome nautically minded guests, many of whom reserve the best rooms months in advance.

The oldest core of this property dates from the 18th century. (Some of the ceiling beams of the original house are visible below the billiard tables.) Soon after the house was built, it was sold to Josiah Darrell for 10 shillings, two peppercorns, and three hogsheads of rum. When it was still a private residence, it was visited many times by Woodrow Wilson, who stayed here before he became president.

The Coopers have expanded it with pink-walled extensions containing the guest rooms, all of which have verandas. Tariffs do not include service and taxes. Each of the public rooms faces a waterfront terrace, where a black ebony tree blooms every year on May 1, according to Reggie. Reggie has also added a nautically inspired conference room whose windows open onto views of the harbor and the Princess Hotel.

**Dining/Entertainment:** The sophisticated decor includes a paneled bar with a working fireplace. There's entertainment nightly from calypso bands or a live pianist. The dining room serves an international cuisine. Meals in summer or barbecues are often presented on the terrace.

**Services:** Laundry, babysitting, room service (8–10am).

**Facilities:** Dock, outdoor swimming pool.

**NEWSTEAD, 25 Harbour Rd., P.O. Box PG 196, Paget PG BX, Bermuda. Tel. 809/236-6060,** or toll free 800/468-4111 in the U.S. Fax 809/236-7454. 48 rms (all with bath), 2 suites. A/C TEL **Transportation:** Ferry from Hamilton.

**$ Rates** (MAP): Apr–Nov, $165–$258 single; $230–$298 double; from $338 suite; off-season, $140 single; $190 double; from $200 suite. AE, MC, V.

On Harbour Road in Paget Parish, overlooking Hamilton Harbour, Newstead is owned by a prominent local family. It is a Bermuda landmark, with a long and colorful history. The original guesthouse accommodated only 12 guests when it opened in 1923, but nowadays there is room for 107 guests. Part of the property, Lyndham, was the former home of Sir Richard and Lady Fairey. It was long ago expanded to include adjoining properties, forming a waterfront resort on a flowering hillside overlooking Hamilton Harbour. (From the estate, it's a 10-minute ferry ride to Hamilton.)

The ancestral home, painted in three shades of green, has become the hub of social activities. It is popular with the sailing set, and it's impossible to get in here during race week in Bermuda. The setting is traditional, with drawing rooms, a library, and lounges, furnished in part with English antiques, a true country-house flavor, and many informal touches.

On the extensive grounds are well-designed and furnished bungalows, with a view of either the harbor or the garden with its flowering hibiscus, coconut palms, and cut-flower beds. Accommodations are in either the main house or the garden bungalows.

**Dining/Entertainment:** Dining is available through the Bermuda Collection, a fraternity of seven different properties, allowing you to dine at a different hotel every night for seven days, all part of the MAP plan of the hotel. At an outdoor terrace, guests can enjoy waterside barbecue buffets, rum-swizzle parties, calypso music, and dancing, according to the season. For dining in the Pickwick Room, refer to Chapter 5, "Where to Dine in Bermuda." Newstead also operates Brellas, a casual dining spot overlooking Hamilton Harbour. Both Bermudian and international specialties are served here for lunch and dinner from June to early October, and evening entertainment is often provided.

**Services:** Laundry, babysitting, room service.

**Facilities:** Swimming pool (swimming is also possible from two private docks); sauna room; two clay tennis courts; privileges of the Coral Beach Tennis Club, which are extended to guests of Newstead; a nine-hole mashie golf course at Horizons, also available to guests.

**PALMETTO HOTEL & COTTAGES, Harrington Sound Rd., P.O. Box FL 54, Flatts FL BX, Bermuda. Tel. 809/293-2323,** or toll free 800/982-0026 in the U.S. for reservations. Fax 809/293-8761. 42 units (all with bath). A/C TEL **Bus:** No. 10 or 11.

**$ Rates** (MAP): Apr–Oct, $149–$189 single; $220–$260 double; off-season, $111–$138 single; $172–$224 double. AE, MC, V.

Palmetto Hotel & Cottages, in Flatts Village, Smith's Parish, was the ancestral home of the Bermudian Tucker family, whose best-known member is Teddy Tucker. He became famous in the 1950s for dredging up treasures from wrecked ships of the 17th century.

The walls of the hotel are pink, as are a cluster of cottages and outbuildings. The main building's reception area is paneled in Bermuda cedar.

Palmetto's location is on the waters of Harrington Sound, about 4½ miles east of Hamilton. A raised beach rests on the side of the sound, with access for both swimming and snorkeling to the sandy bottom of the bay.

The rooms are attractively furnished. In addition to 26 double rooms with bath in the hotel, there are 16 double units with bath in separate cottages, all with views of the water and private pools. The hotel also offers several special package plans.

**Dining/Entertainment:** Dinner can be taken on an à la carte basis or booked for your entire stay at the MAP rate. The Inlet Restaurant (see "Smith's Parish" in Chapter 5, "Where to Dine in Bermuda") overlooks the moon gate, which frames a view of Harrington Sound. The Ha' Penny Pub is a darkly intimate hideaway with big windows behind the dark-grained bar. Afternoon tea is served here. In summer, barbecues are held on the terrace.

**Services:** Complimentary taxis take guests to a beach, five minutes away on the South Shore. There is also laundry service, as well as babysitting.

**Facilities:** Swimming pool that overlooks the water; swimming and snorkeling in bay; boat rentals; windsurfing instruction.

**WHITE SANDS HOTEL & COTTAGES, 55 White Sands Rd., Paget Parish PG BX Bermuda. Tel. 809/236-2023,** or toll free in the U.S. 800/548-0547. Fax 809/236-2023. 40 rms (all with bath). A/C TV TEL **Bus:** No. 7 or 8.

**$ Rates** (MAP): Apr 1–Nov 15, $159.50–$194.30 single; $237.80–$295.80 double; off-season, $95.70–$130.50 single; $168.20–$203 double. AE, MC, V.

One of the less known but eminently charming small hotels of Bermuda sits within a compound of salmon-colored buildings amid terraced gardens a short walk uphill from the semiprivate beach at Grape Bay. Originally built in 1953 by members of the Browne family (who visibly continue its management today), it has steadily expanded its size, the number of its facilities, and its loyal clientele. In fact, of all the hotels of Bermuda's South Shore this is the closest to the shops and restaurants of Hamilton, a 10-minute taxi or bus ride away.

Bedrooms contain wall-to-wall carpeting, large closets, small refrigerators, a radio, a coffeemaker, comfortable beds, and carefully coordinated color schemes of pink, green, or blue. Each is spacious, airy, and bright, and for the most part filled with conservatively modern furniture in light-grained woods. Especially noteworthy is a tower room (Room 222) whose five oversized windows provide an eagle's-nest view over the surrounding shoreline. Eight of the establishment's 40 bedrooms lie within a trio of two- and three-bedroom cottages. These are usually rented as complete units to extended groups of friends and family vacationing together.

**Dining/Entertainment:** A formal but relaxed dining room, The Captain's Table, outfitted in a colonial English motif; the Terrace Club poolside restaurant for breakfast and lunch; and an English-inspired pub, the Sandbar, open every night for food and drink.

**Services:** Room service 8–8:45am and 7–8:30pm; babysitters if advance notice is given.

**Facilities:** A freeform swimming pool; a garden path leading to a wide, semiprivate beach, whose sands are finer than those of many other Bermuda beaches; easy access to nearby tennis, golf, and watersports facilities of other South Shore hotels; an on-site kiosk for the rental of mopeds.

# MODERATE

**ROSEDON, Pitts Bay Rd., P.O. Box HM 290, Hamilton HM AX, Bermuda. Tel. 809/295-1640.** For information and reservations, contact Jenkins-Gibson, Ltd., P.O. Box 10685, Towson, MD 21285; tel. 410/321-1219, or toll free 800/225-5567. Fax 809/295-5904. 42 rms (all with bath). TV TEL **Bus:** No. 7 or 8.

**$ Rates** (BP): Apr–Nov, $130–$196 single; $140–$206 double; off-season, $105–$160 single; $110–$170 double. No credit cards.

Situated on the outskirts of Hamilton, in Pembroke Parish, this 1906 manor house is just across the lawn from the Princess Hotel and is surrounded by extensive gardens and lawns. Look for the loquat tree, a Bermuda trademark. Other shrubs include hibiscus, banana plants, and birds of paradise. Rosedon resembles a colonial-era plantation Great House, with a pristine white exterior and shutters painted a royal blue. It was once occupied by an English family, and was the first house in Bermuda with gas lights. The formal entry hall is dominated by an open staircase and a midway landing window. There are two antique-filled lounges. Guests can sit on a flagstone terrace under parasol tables around a large, temperature-controlled pool. The honor system prevails at Nigel's Bar.

Individually decorated bedrooms with private baths are rented out. The back modern veranda rooms—called lanai suites—open onto a pool, and there are, as well, fully air-conditioned colonial-style rooms in the main house; each unit has a private refrigerator. The Bermuda Plan rates include a full breakfast, room service, English afternoon tea, and unlimited tennis and beach use at Elbow Beach, with free round-trip taxi service (10 minutes).

# 3. COTTAGE COLONIES

These cottage colonies are considered uniquely Bermudian. Each has a main clubhouse with a dining room, lounge, and bar, plus its own beach or pool. The cottage units are spread throughout landscaped grounds and offer privacy and often luxury. Most have kitchenettes suitable for beverages and light snacks, but not for full-time cooking.

## VERY EXPENSIVE

**ARIEL SANDS BEACH CLUB, 34 South Shore Rd., Devonshire, P.O. Box HM 334, Hamilton HM BX, Bermuda. Tel. 809/236-1010,** or toll free 800/468-6610 in the U.S.; call collect from Canada. Fax 809/236-0087. 48 rms (all with bath). TEL **Bus:** No. 1.

**$ Rates** (MAP): Apr 15–Nov 15, $252–$330 single or double; off-season $178–$250 single; $198–$270 double. AE, MC, V.

This is one of the best-established cottage colonies in Bermuda. You'll reach it by going down a winding lane that leads through a park and eventually deposits you near a lime-green clubhouse with forest-green shutters.

The grounds are well landscaped, with flowering trees and coconut palms; each of the grounds offers a view of the ocean. One of the most original sculptures on the island is the stainless-steel statue of Ariel, who dances like a water sprite on the surf. The statue was made in Princeton, N.J., by Seward Johnson. The resort contains a series of public rooms, where a double-hearth fireplace throws cold-weather light and heat into both a reception lounge and a conservatively attractive bar area designed in cardinal red to look like an English library. Those who want to explore Hamilton can take a public bus, which stops nearby. The 2½-mile ride takes about 15 minutes.

The accommodations have a private entrance and a simple but attractive decor of white walls, Bermudian flower paintings, and bentwood furniture. Most have private porches as well. Each of them lies adjacent to other units, which can be connected to create units of up to eight rooms—ideal for large families or reunions of old friends.

**Dining/Entertainment:** An international cuisine is served, and in season a local calypso band often entertains.

**Service:** Laundry, room service, babysitting.

**Facilities:** Water lovers can swim in an oval freshwater pool, in a rectangular saltwater pool whose waters are replenished every day by rising tides, or at a sandy beach. The resort contains three tennis courts, two of which are lit for night games.

**CAMBRIDGE BEACHES, Cambridge Rd., Sandys MA 02, Bermuda. Tel. 809/234-0331,** or toll free 800/468-7300 in the U.S., 800/463-5990 in Canada. Fax 809/234-3352. 59 units (all with bath), 16 suites. A/C MINIBAR TEL **Bus:** No. 7.

**$ Rates** (MAP): Apr 6–Nov 15, $235–$340 single; $275–$380 double; from $410 suite; off-season, $155–$230 single; $195–$270 double; from $290 suite. No credit cards.

On a peninsula overlooking Mangrove Bay in Somerset, Cambridge Beaches has qualities no other cottage colony has, and for that reason heads the list of desirables in its category. Its position is one of a kind, for it occupies the entire western tip of the island—25 acres of semitropical gardens, lush green lawns, and a choice of five palm-fringed private beaches.

As the pioneer of Bermudian cottage colonies, Cambridge Beaches has at its center an old sea captain's house. The main lounges are tastefully furnished with some antiques; one lounge has a beamed pitched ceiling, chintz-covered sofas, and chairs placed around a fireplace. The prevailing flavor is that of a country estate.

Scattered throughout the gardens are well-furnished, pink-and-white units, some of which are nearly 300 years old and retain Bermudian architectural features. The restrained furnishings are color- and fabric-coordinated. All cottages, several of which were once private homes, have sun-and-breakfast terraces, mostly with unmarred views of the bay and gardens. Each unit also has a small refrigerator.

Transportation to Hamilton is provided by the hotel's ferry; from Hamilton you may take the Somerset bus.

**Dining/Entertainment:** Informal lounges for drinks include the Port O' Call Pub and the residents' piano bar. Calypso and other entertainment are often offered six nights a week. Dining is in the air-conditioned main room or else out on the terrace, where barbecues are sometimes held. The establishment has long been known for serving some of the finest food in Bermuda.

**Services:** Massage facilities, room service, laundry.

**Facilities:** The hotel has three all-weather tennis courts and a golf course, Port Royal, designed by Robert Trent Jones and only seven minutes away; the resort has its own putting green. Guests swim in a temperature-controlled pool or from the many beaches. Cambridge Beaches has a full marina with Boston whalers and various kinds of sailboats. Water sports include windsurfing with instruction, canoeing, kayaking, snorkeling, and fishing with equipment available. Parasailing, sailing, and snorkeling trips, plus glass-bottom-boat excursions and fishing voyages, are offered from the property. Adjacent to the colony are two bone fishing flats. In 1992, Cambridge Beaches opened a full service spa; it features exercise equipment, a whirlpool, steam, a sauna, hair dressing, and some 50 types of skin, beauty, and relaxation treatments.

**HORIZONS AND COTTAGES, South Shore Rd., P.O. Box PG 198, Paget PG BX, Bermuda. Tel. 809/236-0048,** or toll free 800/468-0022 in the U.S. Fax 809/236-1981. 50 units (all with bath). A/C TEL **Bus:** No. 7.

**$ Rates** (MAP): Mar 15–Nov 30, $252–$400 single; $272–$420 double; off-season, $182–$280 single; $202–$300 double. No credit cards.

Horizons and Cottages has as its core a converted manor farm (circa 1690), where much of the romantic atmosphere of the past has been retained. A Relais & Châteaux member, it is set on a 25-acre estate with terraced gardens and lawns, atop a hill overlooking Coral Beach. The manor house has fine reception rooms, containing old Bermudian architectural details. Throughout are some antiques from England and the continent; several drawing rooms have open fireplaces.

The complex consists of double accommodations in either the cottages or the main building. All are handsomely furnished—with Italian terra-cotta tile floors, scatter rugs, traditional tray ceilings, and ceiling fans—and all have separate dressing areas as well as private terraces overlooking the ocean. Some units are split-level. Minibars and TVs are provided on request.

**Dining/Entertainment:** The main dining room serves superb French *cuisine naturelle* that uses all fresh products, as guests sit on country chairs before an open fireplace. Lunch can be served on a terrace furnished with white garden furniture. In the evening, the terrace is transformed into an entertainment area, with informal dancing and often calypso music. Lunches and dinners, by reservation, can be exchanged at Newstead and Waterloo House.

**Services:** Laundry, room service, babysitting.

**Facilities:** It has its own nine-hole mashie golf course, 18-hole putting green, and tennis courts, as well as a heated freshwater swimming pool.

**LANTANA COLONY CLUB, P.O. Box SB 90, Somerset Bridge SB BX, Bermuda. Tel. 809/234-0141,** or toll free 800/468-3733 in the U.S., 800/468-0036 from Canada. Fax 809/234-2562. 56 suites, 6 cottages. A/C MINIBAR TV TEL **Transportation:** Hamilton ferry to Somerset Bridge.

**$ Rates** (MAP): Apr 16–Oct 31, $237–$295 single; $274–$390 double; $630 cottage for 4; off-season, $150–$210 single; $200–$300 double; $440 cottage for 4. No credit cards.

Lantana is like a private club where dining is a strong asset. Overlooking Great Sound, this fashionable cottage colony lies in a far-out location, attracting those seeking peace more than action (a 25-minute ferry ride to Hamilton). It is spread over 23 acres of cultivated gardens, with both poolside and bay swimming, along with tennis courts.

Placed around the main building are clusters of Bermudian cottages and lanai suites. Accommodations are restrained and traditional in decor, with the emphasis on comfort; you'll even find an iron and hairdryer. One cottage has its own private swimming pool.

A popular rendezvous point is the clubhouse, which has a large fireplace.

**Dining/Entertainment:** The hotel's restaurant is open to the public (see "Sandys Parish" in Chapter 5, "Where to Dine in Bermuda"). A superb dinner is served in the midst of much greenery and flowers. The chef skillfully prepares a continental cuisine, and the staff is well trained.

**Services:** Laundry, room service.

**Facilities:** Solarium, outdoor patio, freshwater pool, sundeck, two all-weather tennis courts, croquet lawn, putting green, and water sports from a private dock.

**PINK BEACH CLUB & COTTAGES, South Shore Rd., P.O. Box HM 1017, Hamilton HM DX, Bermuda. Tel. 809/293-1666,** or toll free 800/422-1323 in the U.S. Fax 809/293-8935. 81 units (all with bath) A/C TEL **Bus:** No. 1.

**$ Rates** (MAP): Apr 17–Oct 31, $290–$355 single; $300–$365 double; $620–$645 cottage for four; off-season, $190–$233 single; $200–$243 double, $429–$456 cottage for four. MC, V. **Closed:** Second week of Jan, Feb.

In Smith's Parish you'll find this luxurious colony of pink cottages surrounding two private South Shore beaches. The largest cottage colony on the island, it enjoys an 18-acre garden setting, filled with bay grape trees and flowering hibiscus bushes. The drawing room is harmoniously decorated with mahogany wooden pieces.

A maid will come around to one of the little kitchenettes located just outside your door and prepare breakfast for you (just as you requested it the night before). The staff is one of the best on the island, including many who have been with Pink Beach since its inception in 1947.

The resort attracts a loyal list of international habitués. Its cottages range from a studio (bed-sitting room, bath, and patio) to a full individual unit (living room, two bedrooms, two baths, and two private terraces), the latter suitable for four people.

**Dining/Entertainment:** The heart of the colony is the limestone clubhouse, painted pink, with its natural-wood dining room, where "backyard" vegetables and fresh seafood are served. Every table has a view of the ocean and the South Shore breakers. An excellent international cuisine is served.

**Services:** Laundry, babysitting.

**Facilities:** On extensive landscaped grounds are found a large saltwater pool, a sun terrace, and two tennis courts.

**ST. GEORGE'S CLUB, Rose Hill, P.O. Box GE 92, St George's GE, BX, Bermuda. Tel. 809/297-1200.** Fax 809/297-8003. 61 cottages. A/C TV TEL **Bus:** No. 6, 8, 10, or 11.

**$ Rates** (EP): Year round, $250 cottage for up to four; $450 cottage for up to six. AE, DC, MC, V.

This resort, on 18 acres atop Rose Hill, off York Street, in St. George's, features clusters of traditionally designed Bermudian one- and two-bedroom cottages. The luxurious accommodations offer private balconies or patios, comfortable living and dining areas, fully equipped kitchens, and baths with sunken tubs and marble vanities. The units have views of the ocean, the pool, or the golf course.

**Dining/Entertainment:** An elegant restaurant, the Margaret Rose, is on the premises and is open to the public. Refer to the dining suggestions for St. George's in Chapter 5, "Where to Dine in Bermuda." The Sir George Pub is also a popular rendezvous point.

**Services:** Laundry, babysitting.

**Facilities:** A convenience store, the Ample Hamper, may be found in the spacious clubhouse. There are three freshwater swimming pools, one of which is heated, plus three all-weather tennis courts, one of which may be lit for night games. The beach club at Achilles Bay is connected by a short shuttle bus ride. Golfers receive preferential tee time at reduced rates on the adjacent 18-hole golf course, designed by Robert Trent Jones.

# 4. HOUSEKEEPING UNITS

Housekeeping apartments, Bermuda's efficiency units, vary from modest to superior. Most have kitchens or kitchenettes and minimal daily maid service. Housekeeping cottages all have fully equipped kitchens, are either on or convenient to a beach, and are air-conditioned. The cottages offer privacy and casual living.

## EXPENSIVE

**FOURWAYS INN, 1 Middle Rd., P.O. Box PG 294, Paget PG BX, Bermuda. Tel. 809/236-6517,** or toll free 800/962-7654 in the U.S. Fax 809/236-5528. 5 rms, 5 cottages (all with bath). A/C MINIBAR TV TEL **Bus:** No. 8.

**$ Rates** (CP): Apr 1–Nov 15, $190–$280 single or double, $590 two-bedroom cottage for four; off-season, $140–$180 single or double, $360 two-bedroom cottage for four. AE, MC, V.

Pink-sided, airy, and stylish, this cluster of Bermudian cottages was added to the garden of one of the best restaurants on the island, the Fourways Inn Restaurant (see Chapter 5, "Where to Dine in Bermuda"). Its core is a former private home that dates from 1727. Each of five cottages contains two accommodations, with a view of Hamilton Harbour or Great Sound, a patio, a private safe, a fully equipped kitchenette, conservatively comfortable furniture, a satellite-connected TV, and lots of extra touches. The cottages ring a communal swimming pool and a well-maintained garden. The beaches of the South Shore lie nearby.

**SOMERSET BRIDGE HOTEL, 162 Somerset Rd., P.O. Box SB 149, Sandys SB BX, Bermuda. Tel. 809/234-1042.** Fax 809/234-1860. 20 rms (all with bath). A/C TEL **Transportation:** Bus no. 7 or 8 or Hamilton ferryboat.

**$ Rates** (MAP): Apr 1–Nov 15, $157 single; $214 double; off-season, $125 single; $154 double. AE, DC, MC, V.

The Somerset Bridge Hotel was skillfully designed to fit into its hillside terrain and is almost completely hidden from the road on which it sits. Consequently, you climb down, rather than up, a flight of steps after registering at the upper-level reception area. This establishment is owned by the Roberts family, whose head serves in the Bermudian Parliament. The property is managed by the owner's charming daughter, Karen. A swimming pool is set between the hotel and Ely's Bay, where guests can also swim. A government ferryboat stops at a nearby wharf five or six times a day on its way to Hamilton.

Each unit is like an urban studio apartment, complete with kitchenette and private bath. There's also a double bed contained in one of the foldaway couches. When the bed is folded up and out of sight, the area becomes a comfortably furnished living room, with large glass doors opening onto a private balcony. The Blue Foam Restaurant (see "Sandys Parish," in Chapter 5, "Where to Dine in Bermuda") is the establishment's dining hideaway, opening onto the water.

## MODERATE

**ASTWOOD COVE, 49 South Shore Rd., Warwick WK 07, Bermuda. Tel. 809/236-0984,** or toll free 800/541-7426 in the U.S. Fax 809/236-1164. 20 rms (all with bath). A/C TEL **Bus:** No. 7 from Hamilton.

**$ Rates** (EP): Apr 16–Nov 15, $98–$108 single; $98–$128 double; off-season, $55–$75 single; $70–$86 double. No credit cards.

Nigel (Nicky) and Gabrielle (Gaby) Lewin own this homestead, built in 1720, on a dairy farm. The cove house has tradition. Three Astwood sisters, Maude, Ada, and Mary, willed the house with the stipulation that it always carry their name. The apartment resort enjoys a peaceful setting overlooking lightly wooded meadows and the South Shore, with such extra features as a sauna, a pool, and gas-fired barbecue stations. The pool opens onto a subtropical garden, where you can help yourself to papayas, grapefruit, bananas, and oranges, depending on the season.

Each of the 20 self-contained, fully air-conditioned rental units has a private bath with shower (no tubs), a telephone (no charge for local calls), a radio, ceiling fans, and a terrace or porch. Some of the units have sitting rooms, and all have fully equipped kitchenettes, with English bone china, wine glasses, and even salt and pepper shakers. Guests prepare their own breakfast. An all-apartment building added in 1985 has a communal terrace and pavilion, with TV and an exercise cycle. From here, the closest large beach, Long Bay, is a quarter of a mile away; however, Astwood's Beach and Mermaid Beach are only a three-minute stroll from the compound.

**LONGTAIL CLIFFS, 34 South Shore Rd., P.O. Box HM 836, Hamilton HM CX, Bermuda. Tel. 809/236-2864.** Fax 809/236-5178. 13 units (all with bath). A/C TV **Bus:** No. 7 from Hamilton.

**$ Rates** (EP): Apr 1–Nov 15, $110 one-bedroom apartment for one or two, $250 two-bedroom apartment for three or four; off-season, $75 one-bedroom apartment for one or two, $150 two-bedroom apartment for three or four. AE, MC, V.

You'll find this resort in a scenic spot in Warwick Parish. Bird-watchers will enjoy the dozens of longtails (a longtail is a form of seagull) that nest in the cliffs below. A swimming pool is set into a lawn, and a row of hedges signals the beginning of a steep drop-off toward the sea. Beachcombers can walk a short distance to one of the neighboring coves.

The facade that you'll see from the road may not appear very dramatic, but once you're inside one of the rooms, especially those on the upper floor, you'll be rewarded with lots of space, cathedral-like ceilings, and comfortable accommodations. Each unit has a kitchen, where you can prepare your own breakfast or other meals; a radio and a wall safe; and a panoramic view of the sea. Twelve of the units contain two bedrooms and two baths. On the premises is a coin-operated laundry.

**MARLEY BEACH COTTAGES, South Shore Rd., P.O. Box PB 278, Warwick PG BX, Bermuda. Tel. 809/296-8910.** Fax 809/236-1984. 14 cottages. A/C TV **Bus:** No. 2 or 7.

**$ Rates:** (EP): Apr 1–Nov 15, $155–$228 single or double, $253–$286 cottage for four; off-season, $110–$171 single or double, $200 cottage for four. AE, MC, V.

These pink-walled cottages are set in a steep but beautifully landscaped plot of land, on the South Shore near Astwood Park, that was used for scenes in the movies *The Deep* and *Chapter Two*. A trio of narrow beaches lies at the bottom of the slope that leads to the sea, and a curved heated freshwater swimming pool and a whirlpool are on the premises. The attractively airy cottages have their own sea-view patios and sense of spaciousness, as well as fully equipped kitchens. Each cottage offers both a suite and a studio apartment, which can be rented as one unit or two, depending on your needs. Guests prepare their own meals or else dine out. These housekeeping cottages have been called complete "do-it-yourself" retreats.

**PARAQUET GUEST APARTMENTS, South Shore Rd., P.O. Box PG 173, Paget PG BX, Bermuda. Tel. 809/236-5842.** Fax 809/236-1665. 12 apartments (all with bath). A/C TV **Bus:** No. 7.

**$ Rates** (EP): Apr–Oct, $80–$95 apartment for one; $100–$125 apartment for two; off-season, $65–$75 apartment for one or two; $75–$98 apartment for two. No credit cards.

This buff-colored collection of Bermudian houses attractively landscaped into a gentle knoll is a five-minute walk from Elbow Beach. Built in the mid-1970s, the resort is owned by the Portuguese-born Correia family. Eight of the units have kitchenettes, and each has a private bath, maid service, and functional but comfortable modern furniture. The focal point here is a restaurant and coffee shop (see Paraquet Restaurant in "Paget Parish" in Chapter 5, "Where to Dine in Bermuda").

**PRETTY PENNY, 7 Cobb's Hill Rd., P.O. Box PG 137, Paget PB BX, Bermuda. Tel. 809/236-1194,** or toll free 800/541-7426 in the U.S. Fax 809/236-1662. 9 apartments. A/C TEL **Transportation:** Hamilton ferry. **Bus:** No. 8.

**$ Rates** (EP): Apr–Nov, $115 single or double; off-season, $86 single or double. AE, MC, V.

**$** The owner and manager of this charming home, located in an excellent neighborhood, is a Bermudian citizen, Stephen Martin. You'll be welcomed into a bright and airy living room, his personal residence, for a weekly cocktail party. A fire usually burns in a stone hearth during cooler weather, but in summer Martin entertains on an outdoor terrace. A food market is within easy reach, so that guests can replenish their provisions, especially for breakfast. The ferryboat to Hamilton is just a two-minute walk from the front desk. A selection of beaches lies within a 10-minute walk of the premises, and there's a deck-ringed pool on the grounds.

Some of the names of the accommodations evoke a smile: Tuppence, Thruppence, Sixpence, Playpenny, and Sevenpence. Each is contained in its own hillside bungalow, with kitchenette and attractive furnishings; one unit contains a fireplace. Each of the units is suitable for at least two guests.

**ROSEMONT, 41 Rosemont Ave., P.O. Box HM 37, Hamilton HM AX, Bermuda. Tel. 809/292-1055,** or toll free 800/367-0040 in the U.S. Fax 809/295-3913. 35 units (all with bath), 2 suites TV TEL **Bus:** No. 7 or 8.

**$ Rates** (EP): Mar 16–Nov 15, $118–$200 single or double; from $200–$580 suite; off-season, $90–$94 single or double; from $180–$500 suite. No credit cards.

Rosemont is a cluster of gray-walled cottages set on a flowered hillside a short distance from the Hamilton Princess Hotel. The harbor, with its passing ships, is visible from the raised terrace beside the small L-shaped swimming pool. The policy of the Rosemont is to "keep it quiet," so that the commercial travelers, families, and mature couples who stay here won't be disturbed; for that reason, the hotel usually doesn't accept college students or large groups. A grocery store is within a few minutes' walk, and the heart of the city lies only 10 minutes away. Elbow Beach, a 15-minute ride, provides saltwater swimming. Upon request, the hotel will arrange for a motor scooter.

Each of the well-furnished rooms has lots of sunlight, a kitchenette, a radio/alarm clock, and a full bath. It's possible to connect as many as three rooms together, which some families prefer to do. In addition to the regular rooms, the hotel offers two deluxe penthouse suites, with private entrances and luxurious furnishings. Tariffs do not include service and taxes. Laundry and babysitting can be arranged.

## SANDPIPER APARTMENTS, South Shore Rd., P.O. Box HM 685, Hamilton HM CX, Bermuda. Tel. 809/236-7093. Fax 809/236-3898. 9 units (all with bath), 5 suites. A/C TV TEL **Bus:** No. 7.

**$ Rates** (EP): Mar 16–Nov 15, $115 single or double; from $150 suite; off-season, $68 single or double; from $98 suite. AE, DC, MC, V.

Built in 1979 and frequently upgraded, this apartment complex is an excellent choice for a budget-conscious vacation and is within a short walk of several beaches. You can relax in the outdoor whirlpool and swimming pool or lounge in the inviting gardens. Nine of the units are studios suitable for single or double occupancy. The studios have bedrooms with two double beds, baths, and fully equipped kitchenettes. Five of the units have bedrooms with king-size or twin beds, kitchens, baths, and living and dining areas with two double pull-out sofa beds. All the apartments have radios, balconies, and daily maid service. The Sandpiper is only minutes away from restaurants and the supermarket.

## SKY-TOP COTTAGES, 65 South Shore Rd., P.O. Box PG 227, Paget PG BX, Bermuda. Tel. 809/236-7984. 11 units (all with bath). A/C MINIBAR TEL **Bus:** No. 7.

**$ Rates** (EP): Mar 1–Nov 15, $72–$103.50 single; $80–$115 double; off-season, $58.50–$76.50 single; $65–$85 double. MC, V.

Set on a hilltop above Paget's southern shoreline, opposite the Elbow Beach Hotel, this collection of cottages provides some of the most comfortably isolated accommodations in their price bracket. The units are contained in four cozy, English-style cottages, two of which, dating from early this century, were assembled into a single unit by the English-born wives of two local doctors, Marion Stubbs and Susan Harvey. Each cottage contains a tastefully conservative decor of well-chosen furniture and thick carpeting, and each has a private bathroom as well as a small private terrace. Nine of the units contain fully equipped kitchenettes.

The units take their names from some of the flowers in the gardens, so you may find yourself staying in Morning Glory, Pink Corallita, or Allamanda. On all sides of the property, emerald-colored lawns encompass shrubs and trees whose sightlines stretch down to a sweeping view of the sea. Few social activities are planned, except for an occasional rainy-day party to cheer everybody up. Nevertheless, a kind of

English-inspired camaraderie sometimes permeates the consciously private accommodations. The sands of Elbow Beach are only a five-minute walk away, and Hamilton can be reached in about 10 minutes by cab, bus, or moped.

**SURF SIDE BEACH CLUB, South Shore Rd., P.O. Box WK 101, Warwick WK BX, Bermuda. Tel. 809/236-7100,** or toll free 800/553-9990 in the U.S. Fax 809/236-9765. 36 units. A/C TEL **Bus:** No. 2 or 7.
**$ Rates** (EP): Apr–Oct, $165 single or double; $240 apartment for up to four, off-season, $95 single or double; $160 apartment for up to four. No credit cards.
The Surf Side Beach Club was terraced into a steeply sloping hillside that descends, after passing through gardens, to a crescent-shaped sweep of private beachfront. The property was purchased by Norway-born Erling D. Naess and his wife, Elisabeth, who designed it nearly a quarter of a century ago and who still maintain the varied array of flowering trees and panoramic walkways. The stonemasons added several quiet vantage points at various places in the gardens, from which visitors can see grouper and other fish swimming among the distant rocks of the shallow sea.

Accommodations include one-bedroom apartments near the terrace pool. Other lodgings are in hillside buildings. Each of the units is simple and sunny, furnished in bright colors with comfortable accessories; and each is self-contained, with a fully equipped kitchenette (English bone china, wine glasses, even salt and pepper shakers), a shower (no tubs), a radio, ceiling fans, and a private balcony or patio. Some of the accommodations have sitting rooms as well. There is no charge for local calls. An all-apartment building added in 1985 has a communal terrace and pavilion with TV and an exercise cycle. From here, the closest large beach, Long Bay, is a quarter of a mile away; however, Astwood's beach and Mermaid beach are only a three-minute stroll from the compound.

# 5. GUESTHOUSES

Guesthouses are usually comfortable old converted manor houses in garden settings. Some have pools and terraces. The smaller ones have fewer facilities and are much more casual. Most guesthouses serve only breakfast. Those taking fewer than 12 guests are usually small private homes; some have several housekeeping units, while others provide shared kitchen facilities for the preparation of snacks.

## MODERATE

**GRANAWAY GUEST HOUSE & COTTAGE, Harbour Rd., P.O. Box WK 533, Warwick, WK BX, Bermuda. Tel. 809/236-1805.** Fax 809/236-0609. 4 rms, 1 cottage (all with bath). **Transportation:** Ferry from Hamilton.
**$ Rates** (CP): Apr–Oct, $80–$98 single; $90–$100 double; $130 cottage; off-season, $60 single; $65 double; $80 cottage. MC, V.
Dating from 1734, this well-built Bermudian house with a self-contained cottage—originally the home of a British sea captain—opens onto views of Great Sound. Today, it's painted a pastel pink with a soft white roof. Its wide-girted chimney is somewhat of an architectural landmark. The owners, Michael and Carol Ashton, are your hosts, directing guests to the cottage—often a honeymoon special—or to one of their cozy rooms upstairs. The decor has a Laura Ashley

aura, with hardwood floors. TVs are provided upon request. Breakfast is served on Herend china, either in bed or in the garden patio. A private swimming section lies across Harbour Road.

**OXFORD HOUSE, Woodbourne Ave., P.O. Box HN 374, Hamilton HM BX, Bermuda. Tel. 809/295-0503,** or toll free 800/548-7758 in the U.S. Fax 809/295-0250. 12 rms (all with bath). A/C TV TEL **Bus:** No. 1, 2, 10, or 11.

**$ Rates** (BP): Mar 16–Nov 30, $95 single; $112 double; off-season, $83 single; $99 double. No credit cards.

Oxford House is one of the best and most centrally located guesthouses in Hamilton. Said to be the only property in Bermuda constructed specifically as a guesthouse, it lies on a side street leading into Front Street, near the Bermudiana Hotel. It was built in 1938 by a doctor and his French wife, who requested that some of the architectural features follow French designs.

The white- and cream-colored entrance portico is flanked by Doric columns, corner mullions, and urn-shaped balustrades. Inside, a curved stairwell sweeps upward to the spacious, well-furnished bedrooms, each of which is named after one of Bermuda's parishes. There's even an upstairs sitting room, bathed in sunlight. Each accommodation gives the feeling of a private home and contains a private bath, high ceilings, dressing areas, and a coffeemaker. Included in all rates is the Bermudian breakfast which features, in season, fresh-fruit salad made with oranges and grapefruit grown in the yard. The gracious overseer of the establishment is Welsh-born Ann Smith.

**ROYAL PALMS HOTEL, 24 Rosemont Ave., P.O. Box HM 499, Hamilton HM CX, Bermuda. Tel. 809/292-1854,** or toll free 800/441-7087 in the U.S. Fax 809/292-1946. 12 rms (all with bath). A/C TV TEL **Bus:** No. 1, 2, 10, or 11.

**$ Rates** (EP): Apr–Oct, $89–$99 single; $109–$119 double; off-season, $85 single; $98 double. AE, MC, V.

Situated in Pembroke Parish, close to Hamilton, the Royal Palms Hotel is one of the most sought-after guesthouses in the city, thanks to the care and extensive renovation work of its owners, Richard and Sallyann Smith. The date of the house is uncertain, but it's definitely a century old. Residents nearby often walk by its gardens just to admire the masses of marigolds and zinnias that bloom in the front yard. The house, a fine example of Bermudian architecture, is one of the prettiest around, with coral-colored walls, white shutters, and a white roof, plus a wraparound front porch dotted with rocking chairs and sofas. The guest rooms were converted from the living rooms, parlors, and bedrooms of what used to be a grand private house. Today, each of them is spacious, sunny, and comfortably furnished. Rich fabrics are used throughout, and most units have tall ceilings and high windows. Available in each unit is a tea- or coffeemaker. In a building in the rear are four additional guest rooms. This annex was once, presumably, a stable; its restaurant, Ascots, serves both a European and a Bermudian cuisine.

**EDGEHILL MANOR, Rosemont Ave., P.O. Box HM 1048, Hamilton HM EX, Bermuda. Tel. 809/295-7124.** Fax 809/295-3850. 9 rms (all with bath). TV **Bus:** No. 7 or 8.

**$ Rates** (CP): Mar 16–Nov 15, $92–$98 single; $98–$110 double; off-season, $60–$70 single; $70–$80 double. Children under 12 are charged $10 when staying in parents' room. No credit cards.

Directly outside the city limits, in a quiet residential area that is nevertheless convenient to restaurants and shopping in Hamilton, Edgehill Manor just might become your "little home in Bermuda." Painted green, it was built around the time of the American Civil War and still exudes an old-fashioned, homelike quality, attracting a rather middle-aged clientele. Your landlady is British-born Bridget Marshall, who still observes the custom of English tea in the afternoon, which she serves in a flowery nook. Some of her well-lit, airy units are cooled by ceiling fans and some have air conditioning. At least two units are equipped with kitchenettes, and all come with small balconies or patios. Each unit, however, has its own style. If you're interested, ask Ms. Marshall about her special honeymoon rates.

**GREENBANK GUEST HOUSE, 17 Salt Kettle Rd., P.O. Box PG 201, Paget PG BX, Bermuda. Tel. 809/236-3615.** Fax 809/236-2427. 8 units (all with bath), 2 suites. A/C TEL **Transportation:** Hamilton ferry.

**$ Rates** (EP): Apr 1–Nov 15, $85–$110 single or double; $165–$185 suite; off-season, $65–$90 single or double; $155–$165 suite. AE, MC, V.

On the water's edge in Salt Kettle, this resort stands across the bay from Hamilton, which is reached by a 10-minute ferry ride. It's an old Bermuda home, hidden under pine and palm trees, with shady lawns and flower gardens. The manager welcomes guests to an antiques-filled drawing room with its original floor, a fireplace, and a grand piano. The atmosphere is relaxed and personalized. Greenbank offers accommodations with private entrances, baths, and kitchens—either waterside cottages or garden-view apartments. There is maid service daily, but guests provide their own breakfast. Greenbank has a private dock for swimming, plus a boat rental and charter operation on the property where sailing, snorkeling, motorboats, and sailboats are offered.

**GREENE'S GUEST HOUSE, 71 Middle Rd., P.O. Box SN 395, Southampton SN BX, Bermuda. Tel. 809/238-0834.** Fax 809/238-8980. 6 rms (all with bath). A/C TV TEL **Bus:** No. 7 or 8.

**$ Rates** (CP): Year-round, $75 single; $100 double. No credit cards.

**S** The outside of this place, which overlooks Great Sound, appears well maintained, clean, and unpretentious. A look on the inside reveals a pleasant and conservatively furnished environment that's even better than you might have initially supposed. The entryway is flanked by a pair of lions resting on stone columns. The dining room, which can be closed off from the adjacent kitchen by a curtain, is set with a full formal dinner service throughout the day. Wall-to-wall carpeting covers the floors of the entrance lobby as well as the spacious and well-furnished living room. Guests are free to use this room, as well as the sun-washed terraces in back. A swimming pool is in the back garden. The owners are Walter (Dickie) Greene and his wife, Jane.

Each of the bedrooms contains an ironing board and iron, a coffeemaker, a TV and radio, a telephone, a refrigerator, and air conditioning. Facing the sea there's a cozy bar, where guests use the honor system to record their drinks. Dinners can be prepared upon request. A public bus that stops at the front door runs into Hamilton. The beach and the Port Royal Golf Course are both about five minutes away.

**LOUGHLANDS, 79 South Shore Rd., Paget PG 03, Bermuda. Tel. 809/236-1253.** 25 rms (19 with bath). A/C **Bus:** Nos. 2 and 7 stop nearby.

**$ Rates** (CP): Mar 15–Nov 14, $75 single without bath; $110 double with bath; off-season, $55 single without bath; $70 double with bath. No credit cards.

Loughlands is a stately, once-private residence built in 1920 as the home of the president of the Staten Island Savings Bank in New York, who bestowed his name, Lough, on the estate. It is now the largest guesthouse in Bermuda. Set on nine acres of landscaped grounds in the center of the island, it is plantation chalk-white, and its entry hall contains a large portrait of Queen Victoria. Loughlands was purchased in

1973 by Mary Pickles, who sold her large country house in Cornwall, England, and shipped many of her antiques to Bermuda. The bedrooms at Loughlands are handsomely decorated, some with high-post beds and antique chests. Rates include a continental breakfast, with such Bermudian touches as fresh citrus fruit or bananas and homemade preserves. On the grounds are a swimming pool and a tennis court; bus service to all parts of the island is available. Elbow Beach is just a short walk away.

**ROYAL HEIGHTS GUEST HOUSE, Lighthouse Hill, P.O. Box SN 144, Southampton SN BX, Bermuda. Tel. 809/238-0043,** or toll free 800/247-2447 in the U.S. Fax 809/238-8445. 7 rms (all with bath) A/C TV **Bus:** No. 7 or 8.

**$ Rates** (BP): Apr–Nov, $100 single or double, $150 triple; off-season, $90 single or double, $120 triple. Children under 12 $40 when staying in parents' room. No credit cards.

The strange thing about this amply proportioned guesthouse is that it isn't better known. Set at the top of a steeply inclined driveway near the summit of Lighthouse Hill, it's convenient to the Southampton Princess Hotel and its assorted nightlife and restaurant facilities. This is a modern, turquoise-trimmed building, whose pair of wings embrace the front entryway. Terraced near the foundation, a sparkling swimming pool encompasses a view of the passing ships of Great Sound. Guests are welcome to congregate in the stylish modern living room of the owners, Russel Richardson and his wife, Jean, who will suggest activities for you. Each of the very clean bedrooms has a balcony and comfortable furniture.

## BUDGET

**HILLCREST GUEST HOUSE, 1 Nea's Alley, P.O. Box GE 96, St. George's GE BX, Bermuda. Tel. 809/297-1630.** Fax 809/297-1630. 10 rms (all with bath). A/C **Bus:** No. 6, 8, 10, or 11.

**$ Rates** (EP): Year-round, $45 single, $65 double, $84 triple. No credit cards.

Hillcrest is a green-and-white, early-18th-century home, spread on the rise of a hill off Old Maid's Lane. With its wide verandas and its lawns (with a moon gate) and trees, it has a homelike look. The interior is pleasant and comfortable, filled with clutter and antiques. The small entry hall has Edwardian furnishings, and all the rather sparse but clean accommodations have private bathrooms and clock radios. A small honeymoon cottage is on the grounds. Hillcrest is about five minutes away from several restaurants, where you can go to eat breakfast; also to be found nearby are shops, golfing, the bus route, and all points of interest in the historic town of St. George's. Write to E. Trew Robinson at the address above for a reservation; the place has been in her family since World War I. By the way, in 1804 the Irish poet Thomas Moore roomed here for several weeks. He was quite taken with Nea Tucker next door and wrote her some romantic verse.

# CHAPTER 5

# WHERE TO DINE IN BERMUDA

**W**ahoo steak, shark hash, mussel pie, fish chowder laced with rum and sherry peppers, Hoppin' John (black-eyed peas and rice), and the succulent spiny Bermuda lobster (called guinea-chick) are some of the unusual dining experiences awaiting you in Bermuda. Trouble is, you'll have to search hard to find these off-beat dishes, since many hotels and a large number of restaurants serve typical international resort cookery. For a more detailed description of Bermudian cookery, refer to the "Food & Drink" section in Chapter 1, "Getting to Know Bermuda."

Bermudian food has improved in recent years, but dining out is still not the major reason to visit these islands. British dishes such as steak-and-kidney pie are common, as are American ones. Most of the meat has to be imported, so whenever possible it's best to stick to selections from the briny. The fish is generally excellent, especially Bermuda rockfish.

Sunday brunch is a Bermuda tradition. Hot and cold dishes are served buffet style at several restaurants, including my favorite for brunch, the Waterlot Inn in Southampton Parish (see below).

Most restaurants, at least the better ones, insist on a dress code, preferring men to wear a jacket and tie after 6pm. Note that all lunch and dinner prices quoted are per person.

---

## IMPRESSIONS

*Had America ever suffered from land hunger . . . she would have seized Bermuda long ago. Wise, she took it not with soldiers, but with tourists, and today she controls it with dollars and an air base. There is nothing to be sorry about. The Bermudans stand on their tradition and their cash tills.*
—CECIL ROBERTS, *AND SO TO AMERICA* (1946)

Restaurants rated "very expensive" charge more than $50 per person, excluding drinks and service, the latter most often added at 15%. Restaurants judged "expensive" ask from $38 to $50 per person for dinner; "moderate," $25 to $38, and "inexpensive," any dinner for one for less than $25.

# 1. CITY OF HAMILTON

The location of Hamilton restaurants and pubs is shown on the map "Hamilton Accommodations and Dining," which appears in Chapter 4, "Where to Stay in Bermuda" (page 85).

## VERY EXPENSIVE

**ROMANOFF RESTAURANT, 34 Church St., just west of Burnaby. Tel. 809/295-0333.**
   **Cuisine:** RUSSIAN/CONTINENTAL/FRENCH **Reservations:** Required. **Bus:** No. 1, 2, 10, or 11.
   **$ Prices:** Appetizers $9–$15; main courses $22–$29. AE, DC, MC, V.
   **Open:** Lunch Mon–Fri noon–2:30pm; dinner Mon–Sat 7–10pm.
In the last few years, this restaurant has established itself as the most prestigious gourmet restaurant in Bermuda. In an atmosphere evoking the style of Old Vienna, the haute cuisine of the Continent is dispensed. Fine Wedgwood china, Damask linen, brass lamps, and crystal accompany your elegant repast in the extensively renovated burgundy-colored room with smoked-glass mirrors. And the service, as you may expect, is impeccable.
   Appetizers include snails in garlic butter and smoked rainbow trout. The chef prepares crêpes filled with assorted seafood and also makes tempting kettles of soup, including the traditional Russian borscht, lobster bisque, and French onion soup. Dover sole is prepared in classic ways, but if you want something fresh from local waters, try either the broiled wahoo filet or the Bermuda lobster. Shashlik is served Georgian style (that is, flambéed with vodka), or you might prefer chicken Kiev or duckling à l'orange. However, the chef's pièce de résistance is his tournedos flambé Alexandra, which is beef tenderloin flamed with cognac and served with a superb sauce made at your table. Each night you can also select the chef's creation of the evening from a silver trolley. For dessert, there are marvelous soufflés and crêpes, or perhaps a zabaglione.
   Lunch is a business repast with six choices. Men are asked to wear jackets and ties to dinner.

## EXPENSIVE

**NEW HARBOURFRONT RESTAURANT, Front St. between Queen St. and Par-la-Ville Rd. Tel. 809/295-4207.**
   **Cuisine:** ITALIAN/SEAFOOD **Reservations:** Recommended. **Bus:** No. 1, 2, 10, or 11.
   **$ Prices:** Lunch appetizers $4–$6; lunch main courses $6–$11; dinner appetizers $5–$11; dinner main courses $15–$23. AE, DC, MC, V.
   **Open:** Lunch Mon–Sat 11:30am–6pm; dinner Mon–Sat 6:30–10pm.
On the second floor of an old Hamilton building across from the ferry station in the center of town, this spacious restaurant was stylishly renovated with marine-blue and

**FROMMER'S SMART TRAVELER:**
**RESTAURANTS**

VALUE-CONSCIOUS DINERS SHOULD CONSIDER THE
FOLLOWING:

1. Daily specials, which are often cheaper than the regular fare on the à la carte menu.
2. The cost of alcohol. Your tab will mount rapidly with liquor and wine, especially. Seek out places that have a happy hour and do your drinking early. Most happy hours end at 7pm.
3. A meal at a local Bermudian restaurant such as Clyde's Café & Bar in St. George's or the Paraquet Restaurant in Paget Parish. These places are invariably cheaper than the French/continental restaurants.
4. Having a light lunch of sandwiches and hamburgers at one of the local cafés during the day, saving your big meal for the evening. Better yet, pack a picnic lunch or purchase your lunch from one of the lunch wagons along the beach.
5. Fixed-price menus, which are usually more economical than ordering from the à la carte menu, where extras add up fast.
6. Whether service is included. Most restaurants add 10% to 15% to the bill. Most visitors, not knowing that, add yet another—unnecessary—10% to 15% to it! If you find it has already been added, leave only small change as an extra tip to indicate your pleasure with the service. If service has been bad, leave nothing—they've already been tipped at least 10%.

pink Italian-inspired accents. A balcony jutting out over the street has a limited number of tables popular in fine weather. Specialties include chateaubriand and young lamb with an apricot sauce, as well as poultry and veal dishes. Fresh swordfish in garlic-and-white-wine sauce is a standard, as are broiled veal chops with a mushroom sauce, vermicelli with lobster, and an array of other seafood dishes. The chef's specialty is called "The Bermuda Triangle," which is three different varieties of the best available fresh fish arranged on a platter. It can be either broiled or grilled and is served with three different sauces.

**ONCE UPON A TABLE, 49 Serpentine Rd., west of City Hall. Tel. 809/295-8585.**
   **Cuisine:** FRENCH **Reservations:** Required. **Bus:** No. 1, 2, 10, or 11.
**$ Prices:** Appetizers $6–$17.50; main courses $19.50–$39; fixed-price menus $44–$51.50. AE, DC, MC, V.
   **Open:** Dinner daily 6:30–9 or 9:30pm. **Closed:** Jan.

I think I'd come here just because of the charming name, but fortunately, it has a lot more going for it than that. If Bermuda ever had a belle-époque period, it's here in a restored and richly decorated 18th-century island home, furnished in part with antiques. An old island buggy in the front yard sets the tone of the place. Inside, you are shown to a table in one of the intimate rooms, with delicate lace curtains at the windows.

Hospitable Bermudians operate this place and serve candle-lit dinners. You can order hot or cold hors d'oeuvres, such as baked French snails, or locally caught wahoo marinated with herbs and juniperberries. Soups include Bermuda fish chowder flavored with black rum and sherry peppers. When it's available, you are given a main

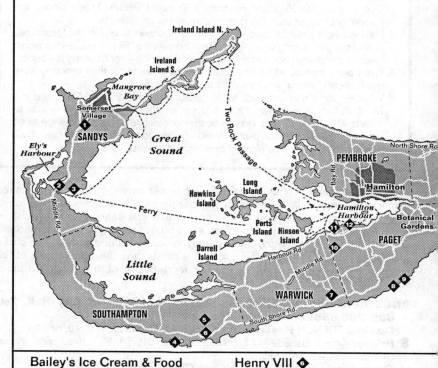

0 — 2 km
N — 1.5 m

*Atlantic Ocean*

Ireland Island N.

Ireland Island S.

*Mangrove Bay*

Somerset Village

**SANDYS**

*Ely's Harbour*

*Great Sound*

Two Rock Passage

North Shore Rd.

**PEMBROKE**

Bay Rd.

Hamilton

Ferry

Hawkins Island

Long Island

Hamilton Harbour

Botanical Gardens

Ports Island

Hinson Island

**PAGET**

Darrell Island

Harbour Rd.

*Little Sound*

Middle Rd.

Middle Rd.

**WARWICK**

**SOUTHAMPTON**

South Shore Rd.

| Bailey's Ice Cream & Food | Henry VIII ⑥ |
| D'Lites Restaurant ⑮ | Il Palio ❶ |
| Black Horse Tavern ⑳ | Inlet Restaurant ⑬ |
| Blue Foam Restaurant ❷ | La Plage ❸ |
| Carriage House ⑲ | Lantana Colony Club Restaurant ❸ |
| Clyde's Café & Bar ⑲ | Lillian's ❹ |
| Dennis's Hideaway ㉑ | Loyalty Inn ❶ |
| Fourways Inn ⑩ | Margaret Rose ⑱ |
| Glencoe Harbour Club ⑪ | Mikado ⑰ |

# BERMUDA DINING

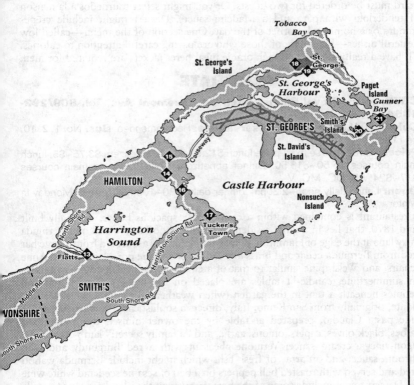

Newport Room **⑤**
Norwood Room **⑨**
O'Malley's Pub on the Square **⑲**
Ondine's **⑧**
Paraquet Restaurant **⑧**
Paw Paws **⑦**
Pickwick Room **⑫**
Plantation **⑯**
Rib Room Steak House **⑤**

San Giorgio **⑲**
Somerset Country Squire Tavern **❶**
Swizzle Inn **⑮**
Tom Moore's Tavern **⑭**
Village Inn **❶**
Waterlot Inn **⑤**
Whaler Inn **⑤**
Wharf Tavern **⑲**
White Horse Tavern **⑲**

dish choice of fresh Bermuda fish—broiled, grilled, or pan-fried with banana, champagne, or lemon butter sauce. Rack of lamb coated with herbs and Dijon mustard must be ordered for two guests. Or you might select tournedos à la maison (beef tenderloin with pâté and a Madeira sauce). Dessert might include crêpes Alexandra or a homemade sorbet of the day. One section of the menu—called low cholesterol dishes—takes care of those who are paying careful attention to calories. You'll have a really superb and memorable meal here. Jackets are required for men.

# MODERATE

**ASCOTS, in the Royal Palms Hotel, 24 Rosemont Ave. Tel. 809/292-1854.**

**Cuisine:** ITALIAN/FRENCH **Reservations:** Recommended. **Bus:** No. 1, 2, 10, or 11.

**$ Prices:** Three-course fixed-price lunch $12.50; lunch appetizers $3.75–$5, lunch main courses $5.50–$13.50. Dinner appetizers $7–$12; dinner main courses $17–$24. AE, DC, MC, V.

**Open:** Lunch daily noon–2:30pm; dinner daily 6:30–10pm. **Closed:** Monday in winter.

This restaurant is contained within a comfortably spacious house, originally built around 1870, that lies in a quiet residential neighborhood at the end of a Bermuda country lane at the edge of Hamilton. Before-dinner drinks are served from a large bar crafted from Bermuda cedar and brass in a setting of antique porcelain, Queen Anne armchairs, and Welsh pine similar to that of a chintz-filled English country house.

In summertime, candle-lit tables are placed on the house's front porch and sometimes beneath a tent in the garden (when weather warrants). Owner Claudio Vigilante, originally from San Remo, Italy, directs a sophisticated cuisine that might include pasta Claudio, prepared at table by the owner himself using sun-dried tomatoes, black olives, capers, onions, garlic, and "a family secret;" lamb cutlets in a tarragon-vinegar-cream sauce; Vermont pheasant with a red Burgundy and wild mushroom sauce; and an array of fresh fish, which might include Bermuda wahoo roasted and served with roasted bell peppers on a bed of sesame seed and white wine sauce. Dessert might include some of the best tiramisu on the island, or any of a wide array of sweet concoctions flambéed at tableside. The extensive selection is reasonably priced.

**CHANCERY WINE BAR, Chancery Lane between Reid and Front Streets. Tel. 809/295-5058.**

**Cuisine:** CONTINENTAL **Reservations:** Recommended. **Bus:** No. 1, 2, 10, or 11.

**$ Prices:** Lunch appetizers $4–$9.50; lunch main courses $7.50–$15; dinner appetizers $4.50–$12.50; dinner main courses $15.50–$26.50. AE, MC, V.

**Open:** Lunch Mon–Fri noon–2:30pm; dinner daily 6–10pm; bar daily 6pm–1am.

Contained within a street-level building whose vaulted ceiling and thick stone walls date from the early 1900s, this cozy and warmly textured wine bar offers a candle-lit ambience very much like that of a European wine cellar. A trellis-covered courtyard in back contains a handful of carefully decorated tables for al fresco dining. No one will mind if you show up just for a glass of wine, priced at from $4 a glass. Oenophiles appreciate the tasteful selection of vintages compiled by German-born Thomas Mayer—more than a hundred vintages, some very impressive—from around the world. Despite its European antecedents, dress here is casual and the atmosphere relaxed.

Lunch might include portions of fresh Bermuda fish, ratatouille, and grilled steaks.

Dinners are more elaborate, featuring seasonal game dishes, English lamb, and shellfish. Naturally, suitable vintages are available for every course.

**FISHERMAN'S REEF, 5 Burnaby Hill. Tel. 809/292-1609.**
    **Cuisine:** SEAFOOD/BERMUDIAN **Reservations:** Recommended. **Bus:** No. 1, 2, 10, or 11.
    **$ Prices:** Appetizers $4–$9; main courses $13–$22; fixed-price lunch $13; fixed-price dinner $19. AE, DC, MC, V.
    **Open:** Lunch Mon–Fri noon–3pm; dinner daily 6–10:30pm.

Fisherman's Reef lies above the Hog Penny Pub in the heart of Hamilton and is a good choice for fine local seafood and typically Bermudian dishes. Its setting is nautical setting, with a separate bar and cocktail lounge. You can order wahoo, one of Bermuda's most popular game fish, cut into steaks and topped with banana and bacon strips. Bermuda rockfish is also served. When available, a whole Bermuda fish is seasoned, stuffed, and baked in the typical island way. Also, in season, Bermuda guinea chicks—that is, small lobsters—are broiled on the half shell. Ask the waiter about the daily catch—snapper, grouper, shark, or yellowtail—which can be pan-fried, broiled, or poached. Although most people come here for fish, the chef is also adept at preparing meat courses. He does an excellent peppersteak flambé and a number of classic veal specials, including Oscar, marsala, and français. Banana fritters laced with black rum are a favorite dessert. Dress is informal.

**HARLEY'S, in The Princess, 76 Pitts Bay Rd., Hamilton. Tel. 809/295-3000.**
    **Cuisine:** SEAFOOD/GRILLS **Reservations:** Recommended at dinner. **Bus:** No. 7 or 8.
    **$ Prices:** Lunch appetizers $4–$5; lunch main courses $7–$14; dinner appetizers $4.50–$11; dinner main courses $25–$35. AE, DC, MC, V.
    **Open:** High season (usually May–Oct) lunch daily noon–4:30pm; dinner Mon–Sat 6–10pm. **Closed:** Off-season (usually Nov–Apr).

The popular Harley's is named after the bearded bon vivant who established the Princess a century ago. In warm weather, tables are extended outside to the edge of the swimming pool, creating the effect of a flowering terrace on the Italian Riviera.

    At lunch, you might want to dine on a thick sandwich, a fresh-tasting salad such as a Greek version of chicken with cashews and oranges, or one of the low-calorie and vegetarian selections. Full dinners include an array of beef, lamb, and poultry dishes, while the chef also prepares a number of fish dishes, including fresh imported Pacific salmon. Try the catch of the day, veal marsala, or Asian-style chicken with peppers and teriyaki. Fresh Bermuda chowder, laced with black rum, usually begins most meals. There is also a selection of familiar pasta dishes, such as cannelloni or fettuccine Alfredo.

**LITTLE VENICE, Bermudiana Rd., between Par-la-Ville Road and Woodbourne Avenue. Tel. 809/295-3503.**
    **Cuisine:** ITALIAN/CONTINENTAL **Reservations:** Recommended. **Bus:** No. 1, 2, 10, or 11.
    **$ Prices:** 2-course fixed-price lunch $12.75; lunch appetizers $6–$8; lunch main courses $13–$16; dinner appetizers $8.75–$9.50; dinner main courses $14–$26.75. AE, DC, MC, V.
    **Open:** Lunch Mon–Fri 11:45am–2:30pm; dinner daily 6:30–10:30pm.

This is one of the best-established and most visible Italian restaurants in Bermuda, a staple placed here as long ago as almost anyone can remember. The owner (originally from Capri) is proud of his specialties, one of which is casseruola di pesce dello chef.

This consists of a medley of Bermuda-derived products, including lobster, shrimp, mussels, clams, and several kinds of fish cooked together with white wine, herbs, and tomatoes. Other choices include fish chowder, tournedos Rossini, several different veal dishes, and an array of pastas that include homemade ravioli stuffed with spinach and ricotta cheese. If you have room for dessert, you might try the zabaglione. Italian wines are featured, either in bottles or (less expensively) in carafes. An abbreviated menu is offered at lunchtime. Dress is "smart casual."

### LOBSTER POT & BOAT HOUSE BAR, 6 Bermudiana Rd. Tel. 809/292-6898.

**Cuisine:** SEAFOOD **Reservations:** Recommended. **Bus:** No. 1, 2, 10, or 11.
**$ Prices:** Appetizers $4.50–$14.75; main courses $11.75–$54; fixed-price lunch $11.75; fixed-price dinner $22.75. AE, DC, MC, V.
**Open:** Lunch Mon–Sat 11:30am–5pm; dinner Mon–Sat 6–11pm.

**⑤** Dating from 1973, this popular fish eatery located off Front Street specializes in local seafood cooked just right and with flair. Not surprisingly, the decor is nautical. Although the Bermuda fish chowder is laced with black rum and sherry peppers and is very good, you can get that elsewhere. A unique appetizer here is the curried Bermuda rockfish (delicately seasoned and rolled in a thin crêpe). Fresh oysters are available all year and are priced according to the season. I suggest the baked Bermuda fish for two—fresh fish that has been seasoned and stuffed. You can also try the lobster potpourri, the deep-fried tiger shrimp and scallops, or the wahoo steak (a game fish). Bermuda lobster (the so-called guinea chick) is available in season (that is, from mid-September until the end of March). The typical Bermuda banana fritter is a popular finish to a meal. Dress is casual.

### LOQUATS, Bermuda House, 95 Front St. Tel. 809/292-4705.

**Cuisine:** INTERNATIONAL **Reservations:** Required. **Bus:** No. 1, 2, 10, or 11.
**$ Prices:** Appetizers $3.75–$12.50; main courses $7.95–$26. AE, DC, MC, V.
**Open:** Lunch Mon–Fri 11:30am–4pm; dinner daily 5:30–10:30pm.

Some visitors to Bermuda immediately claim Loquats as their preferred dining and drinking hangout. The entrance to the long, narrow second-story room is off an alleyway a few paces from the main artery of Front Street. You dine beneath a high sloping ceiling whose widely spaced rafters reveal slabs of Bermuda limestone laid in layers like roofing shingles. A narrow veranda overlooks the harbor, and a long and well-used bar is designed a bit like a Victorian antique.

Lunches include a large selection of flame-broiled burgers, broiled Bermuda fish, and salads. Dinner features English-style fish and chips and Bermuda fish en papillote. Spit-roasted specialties include duckling Indonesia with mango slices and green peppercorns, along with a mixed grill from the skewer. Charbroiled main dishes feature everything from veal Dutch style to meaty barbecued pork ribs. Several dishes are combination platters, such as a rack of barbecued baby back ribs with jumbo shrimp. A variety of seasonal fruit and cake desserts are available from the chef's special menu; otherwise, you can settle happily for Apple Brown Betty. Drinks are generously poured and seem to be the appropriate accompaniment to the live music featured here on most evenings.

### PRIMAVERA, 69 Pitts Bay Rd. Tel. 809/295-2167.

**Cuisine:** ITALIAN **Reservations:** Required. **Bus:** No. 7 or 8.
**$ Prices:** Appetizers $7.75–$9.75; main courses $15.75–$21; fixed-price lunch $12.75. AE, DC, MC, V.
**Open:** Lunch Tues–Fri 11:45am–2:30pm; dinner Tues–Sun 6:30–10:30pm.

Primavera, in Hamilton West between Front Street and the Hamilton Princess, is one of the finest classic Italian restaurants in town and is often viewed as an alternative to the more traditional fare served in many of the island's restaurants. You might begin with a selection of either hot or cold antipasti, including a cold seafood salad or hot baked clams served in a marinara sauce. You can follow with a soup, perhaps minestrone, or a salad, most likely a Caesar. The array of pasta dishes features tortellini Primavera (the chef's surprise), or chicken cacciatora or sautéed veal with fresh vegetables. To finish your satisfying meal, order an Italian espresso or a cappuccino.

**RED CARPET BAR AND RESTAURANT, in the Armoury Building, 37 Reid St. Tel. 809/292-6195.**

    **Cuisine:** ITALIAN **Reservations:** Recommended. **Bus:** No. 1, 2, 10, or 11.

    **$ Prices:** Lunch appetizers $4–$8; lunch main courses $9.50–$17; dinner appetizers $8–$10; dinner main courses $12–$20. AE, MC, V.

    **Open:** Lunch Mon–Sat 11:30am–2:30pm; dinner Mon–Sat 6:30–10pm.

The Red Carpet serves many Italian dishes even though the atmosphere is evocative of an English pub. This place does a thriving lunch business thanks to the many office workers who fill the buildings nearby. Later, after work, its wood-trimmed bar is popular as a place to relax with a beer amid a decor of dark-red carpeting, dim lights, and darkly stained trim. Lunches include sandwiches, cold platters, and a few hot dishes such as pan-fried fish. Dinners feature a wider selection, including veal scaloppine, veal marsala, chicken cacciatore, filet mignon, and New York-strip sirloin. Many different pasta dishes are also featured.

**SHOW BIZZ, 68 Reid St. at King St. Tel. 809/292-0676.**

    **Cuisine:** INTERNATIONAL **Reservations:** Recommended. **Bus:** No. 1, 2, 10, or 11.

    **$ Prices:** Lunch appetizers $3.50–$6; lunch main courses $7.50–$12; dinner appetizers $3.50–$8; dinner main courses $8–$18. AE, MC, V.

    **Open:** Mon–Fri noon–1am, Sat–Sun 5pm–1am.

Show Bizz is a small restaurant on the street level of a downtown office building. Inside, you'll find a black, white, and pink decor and the accessories you might have expected in a jazzy pub in England. Photographs of musical stars of the 1960s adorn the walls, and a pair of guitarists keep things lively after dark.

    The kitchen turns out savory pasta dishes, salads, hamburgers, soups, Atlantic seafood, sandwiches, steaks, and steaming platters of barbecued ribs. The establishment's bar is especially popular with the after-work crowd.

# INEXPENSIVE

**BOMBAY BICYCLE CLUB, in the Rago Furniture Building, 75 Reid St. Tel. 809/292-0048.**

    **Cuisine:** INDIAN/CONTINENTAL **Reservations:** Required. **Bus:** No. 1, 2, 10, or 11.

    **$ Prices:** Appetizers $4.75–$7.50; main courses $13.95–$21.25; fixed-price lunch $10.95. AE, MC, V.

    **Open:** Lunch Mon–Fri noon–2:30pm; dinner Mon–Sat 6:30–11pm.

Indian haute cuisine is expertly cooked and served in this third-floor upstairs hideaway where you can enjoy lunch or dinner in a relaxed atmosphere. For lunch, they offer "A Taste of India" selection daily, and a variety of dishes ranging from mulligatawny soup to chicken, beef, lamb, and seafood served with a choice of sauces, in a spicy curry, or roasted in the tandoori oven. Indian vegetarian dishes and continental selections are also available. Dress is "smart casual."

## CHOPSTICKS RESTAURANT, 88 Reid St. East. Tel. 809/292-0791.

**Cuisine:** CHINESE **Reservations:** Required. **Bus:** No. 1, 2, 10, or 11.
**$ Prices:** Appetizers $2.25–$6.95; main courses $9.95–$27.95.
**Open:** Lunch daily noon–2:30pm; dinner daily 6–11pm.

Although off the beaten track, Chopsticks offers some of Bermuda's best Chinese cuisine, including spicy soup, tangy pork ribs, and seafood. The chef specializes in Szechuan and Cantonese dishes, with an accent on fresh vegetables and delicate sauces. The fine food is served by a Bermudian staff.

Chicken dishes, including jade chicken with spears of broccoli and mushrooms and water chestnuts in a mild Peking wine sauce, are also a specialty. Peking duck is only served for two, and the staff must be informed 24 hours in advance. Seafood also figures heavily on the menu, as reflected by such dishes as shrimp in lobster sauce. Vegetarians will find solace here, as there are many vegetable combinations made to be shared.

## HOG PENNY, 5 Burnaby Hill. Tel. 809/292-2534.

**Cuisine:** ENGLISH/BERMUDIAN **Reservations:** Recommended. **Bus:** No. 1, 2, 10, or 11.
**$ Prices:** Appetizers $3.50–$8; main courses $10–$20; fixed-price lunch $9.95; fixed-price dinner $15.95.
**Open:** Lunch daily 11:30am–4:30pm; dinner daily 6–11pm.

Bermuda's most famous pub, built and decorated in the British style with dark paneled rooms, offers draft beer and ale. Old fishing and farm tools make up part of the decor, along with bentwood chairs and antique mirrors. At lunch you can order pub specials, including shepherd's pie and seafood crêpes, or a tuna salad. The kitchen prepares a number of curries, including chicken and lamb. Fish and chips and steak-and-kidney pie are the perennial favorites. Dinner is more elaborate. You can always order a fresh fish of the day, perhaps Bermuda yellowfin tuna. The Angus beef is excellent, and you may want to precede your meals with Bermuda onion soup. There is nightly entertainment from 9:30pm to 1am; dress is casual.

## M. R. ONIONS, Par-la-Ville Road North. Tel. 809/292-5012.

**Cuisine:** AMERICAN/BERMUDIAN **Reservations:** Not required. **Bus:** No. 1, 2, 10, or 11.
**$ Prices:** Appetizers $3.95–$8.95; main courses $9.95–$21.95. AE, DC, MC, V.
**Open:** Lunch Mon–Fri noon–3pm; dinner daily 5–10pm; bar daily 11:30am–1am.
**Closed:** Mon in Jan–Feb.

The name of this enormously popular restaurant and bar is a colloquialism. Bermudians are known as onions, and the "M. R." stands for "em are," or "they are"; hence the name means "they are Bermudians." Designed like an Edwardian-era bar, it's done up with lots of brass, potted palms, leaf-green walls, and miles of oak trim. Many caricatures of Bermudians hang on the walls, with a different portrait picked each month. If you go early, have a drink at the large rectangular bar that fills most of the establishment's front room. It's especially popular during happy hour (daily 5 to 7pm), when it is a favorite rendezvous for office workers in the neighborhood. Snacks are available in the bar until 10pm.

Well-prepared meals are served in a rear dining room, with specialties including house onion soup and fresh fish that includes tuna, wahoo, rockfish, and mahi-mahi. Fish can be charbroiled, pan-fried, or served with almandine or spicy Cajun blackened style. Barbecued chicken, ribs, and steak are also served. You can also order an array of burgers, and beer by the pitcher or the glass. The dessert specialties are mud pie and cheesecake, or you can choose from the elaborate sweet trolley. A bakery features onion bread. A nonsmoking dining room is available.

**PORTOFINO, Bermudiana Rd. Tel. 809/292-2375.**
 **Cuisine:** ITALIAN **Reservations:** Recommended. **Bus:** No. 1, 2, 10, or 11.
**$ Prices:** Appetizers $3.50–$9.25; main courses $9.25–$18.75. No credit cards.
 **Open:** Lunch Mon–Fri noon–3pm; dinner daily 6pm–midnight. **Closed:** Dec 25.
The decor of this Italian trattoria is typical tavern, with Chianti bottles hanging from the ceiling. It offers well-prepared and reasonably priced specialties, including four kinds of spaghetti and all the famous pastas, such as lasagne, ravioli, and cannelloni. A classic minestrone, and 13 kinds of 9-inch pizza are offered. Standard and familiar Italian dishes include Venetian-style liver, veal parmigiana, chicken cacciatore, and beefsteak pizzaiola. Snails are prepared with "a secret recipe."

**THE COLONY PUB, in the Princess, 75 Pitts Bay Rd. Tel. 809/295-3000.**
 **Cuisine:** INTERNATIONAL **Reservations:** Not required. **Bus:** No. 7 or 8.
**$ Prices:** Lunch buffet $14.75; lunch sandwiches $7 each; dinner appetizers $4–$6; dinner main courses $15–$20; pint of lager $5.20. AE, DC, MC, V.
 **Open:** Lunch daily noon–2:30pm; dinner daily 6:30–10pm.
The Colony Pub is a pleasantly informal eatery off the lobby of this famous Princess hotel. The Black Watch plaid carpets and the dark paneling give you a feeling of a Scottish pub. One of Hamilton's better bargains is the pub's buffet lunch, a tempting array of salads and platters. The roast prime rib of beef is well flavored and served with the classic Yorkshire pudding. Always ask about the fish du jour. The familiar food is good and hearty: roast country chicken, English fish and chips, and pork chops. The salads are fresh, and you might begin your meal with a French onion soup. It also offers fragrant tropical drinks whose colors include the full spectrum of a sunset.

**ROSA'S CANTINA, 86 Reid St. Tel. 809/295-1912.**

---

 **FROMMER'S COOL FOR KIDS:
RESTAURANTS**

**M. R. Onions,** in the city of Hamilton (see p. 112). Taking its name from the colloquial name for Bermudians, this is one of the best family restaurants in the city of Hamilton. Kids go for the barbecue chicken, ribs, and steak. There's also an array of burgers.

**Rosa's Cantina,** in the city of Hamilton (see p. 113). For Tex-Mex fare, this house of chili, burritos, fajitas, nachos, tacos, and enchiladas has no equal on the island. Children are given balloons to make the atmosphere most festive, and they're also offered coloring and crayons when seated.

**Paw Paws,** in Warwick Parish (see p. 116). For lunch or dinner, this is a favorite with Bermudian families, and visitors like it too. Just three miles west of Hamilton, it has good home-style cooking. Next door are both a pastry shop and an ice-cream parlor.

**Clyde's Café & Bar,** in St. George's Parish (see p. 123). This family-style dining room in St. George's is known for its good prices and informal atmosphere. Take your kid here for well-stuffed sandwiches at lunch or else familiar fare such as pork chops or roast beef in the evening.

**Cuisine:** MEXICAN **Reservations:** Required only on Fri and Sat. **Bus:** No. 1, 2, 10, or 11.
$ **Prices:** Appetizers $2.25–$6.95; main courses $12.95–$22.50. AE, MC, V.
**Open:** Lunch Mon–Sat noon–2:30pm; dinner daily 6pm–midnight.

⑤ For your Tex-Mex fix, come to this place where you can fill up on such bounty as beef and chicken fajitas, zesty chili, nachos, tacos, and enchiladas, along with frozen margaritas to put the fire out. To the sound of the music of mariachi bands, you might begin with a hearty black bean soup, and then move on to *carne asado* (mezquite grilled rib eye steak), another chef's specialty. The restaurant is reasonable in price and serves the largest burritos on the island.

## BUDGET

**BOTANIC GARDEN, in Trimingham's, 17 Front St., between Reid and Queen Streets. Tel. 809/295-1183.**
**Cuisine:** INTERNATIONAL **Reservations:** Not accepted. **Bus:** No. 1, 2, 10, or 11.
$ **Prices:** Soups and quiches $3.25; seafood salads $7.25–$8; sandwiches $6; tea 65¢; pastries $1.75–$2.75. No credit cards.
**Open:** Mon–Sat 9:30am–4:30pm.

Housed on the third floor of the most famous department store in Hamilton, this place is filled with shoppers who know good value when they see it. This self-service place is informal and ideal for morning coffee or a British afternoon tea. The pastries, pies, and cakes are excellent, especially the banana bread and the gingerbread. There is an array of sandwiches as well. No heavy foods are served, since the cooking odors would permeate the items in the adjacent furniture department.

# 2. PAGET PARISH

## VERY EXPENSIVE

**FOURWAYS INN, 1 Middle Rd. Tel. 809/236-6517.**
**Cuisine:** FRENCH/BERMUDIAN **Reservations:** In summer only 1–2 days in advance. **Bus:** No. 8.
$ **Prices:** Appetizers $6–$22; main courses $28–$78; fixed-price dinner $35; Sun buffet brunch from $32. AE, MC, V.
**Open:** Lunch daily noon–3pm; dinner daily 6:30–10:30pm.

✪ The Fourways Inn is considered by many to be the best restaurant in Bermuda. Once an 18th-century Georgian house built of coral stone and cedar, it has been tastefully converted into a dining room while maintaining the traditional Bermudian character and the old mahogany beams. Guests have a choice of dining inside or out, depending on the season. On most nights a pianist plays, and the atmosphere is graceful and relaxed, the service good. The old kitchen has been turned into the Peg Leg Bar with a whitewashed fireplace. Sunday brunch is an elaborate buffet.

An ambitious menu is featured at night, beginning with the special cold smoked-salmon soup with dill. Main-dish chef's specialties are tender filet of beef wrapped in light pastry and offered with a truffle-and-foie-gras sauce, filet of lamb in a raspberry-vinegar sauce, and roast prime rib of beef carved to order and served with the traditional Yorkshire pudding. An unusual dish is *le tartare de poissons,* fresh raw

Bermuda fish that is prepared at your table. A superb selection is the roast duck in its own gravy accompanied by fresh pear poached in red wine. For dessert, the chef is known for his soufflés (which should be ordered in advance). Try the black-rum soufflé. I find the chocolate the most delectable, but you may prefer the strawberry or Grand Marnier. The wine cellar is among the finest on the island.

The Fourways Inn is a quality place, as reflected by its prices. Men should wear jackets and ties in the evening.

# EXPENSIVE

**PICKWICK ROOM, in Newstead, 25 Harbour Rd. Tel. 809/236-6060.**
   **Cuisine:** CONTINENTAL/AMERICAN **Reservations:** Required. **Transportation:** Ferry from Hamilton.
   **$ Prices:** Fixed-price dinner $42.50. AE, MC, V.
   **Open:** Dinner daily 7:30–9pm.
Contained in one of the most quietly elegant manor-house hotels in Bermuda, this attractively dignified dining room facing Hamilton Harbour welcomes nonresidents who make a reservation. Guests dine beneath a beamed tray-style ceiling in a conservative dining room whose chintz-filled decor could have been transported from Britain. Between May and October, an outdoor barbecue is held every Tuesday and Thursday, accompanied by live dance music and by water splashing from a dolphin-shaped fountain above the swimming pool. The chefs offer a frequently changing array, including roast leg of lamb with mint sauce, grilled sirloin steak with savory butter, and roast chicken grand' mère.

**NORWOOD ROOM, in the Stonington Beach Hotel, South Shore Rd., Paget. Tel. 809/236-5416.**
   **Cuisine:** CONTINENTAL **Reservations:** Required. **Bus:** No. 7.
   **$ Prices:** Lunch appetizers $3–$5; lunch main courses $5–$17; fixed-price dinner $44.50. AE, DC, MC, V.
   **Open:** Lunch daily noon–2pm; dinner daily at 7–8:15pm.
The Norwood Room offers stately dining in a large sun-washed room with tartan carpets, spidery iron chandeliers, Spanish-style stucco arches, and fan-shaped windows looking out over the foliage and the water. The restaurant is contained within a state-run hotel training school (see "Small Hotels" in Chapter 4, "Where to Stay in Bermuda"). The service and attitude among the youthful employees are most attractive. A pianist or harpist provides music in the evening, when men should wear jackets and ties.

Lunch is served in the dining room or on the patio, and at dinner there is a fixed-price menu. The last order is taken at 8:15pm.

Appetizers might include scallops in lobster sauce or a cold plate of marinated beef with onions, perhaps mushrooms stuffed with crabmeat or Bermuda fish chowder. Main courses feature fresh filets of Bermuda fish with prawns and mushrooms, and grilled sirloin with herb butter, the all-time favorite. The cooks have a deft continental flair, as reflected in their veal steak with duxelles of mushrooms and melted cheese, and their duck with raspberry sauce. The restaurant adjoins the Overplus Bar, where you may want to stop for a before-dinner drink.

# MODERATE

**ONDINE'S, in the Elbow Beach Hotel, 60 South Shore Rd., Paget. Tel. 809/236-3535.**
   **Cuisine:** INTERNATIONAL **Reservations:** Recommended. **Bus:** No. 1, 2, or 7

**$ Prices:** Appetizers $6.50–$10.50; main courses $17.50–$26. AE, MC, V.
**Open:** Dinner daily 6:30–9:30pm.

Gracefully decorated in tones of beige, green, and pink, this 350-seat restaurant is considered the largest, finest, and most formal within the Elbow Beach Hotel. Set on the ground floor, its large windows overlook the sea. Service personnel, dressed in black and white, add a friendly but formal ritual to the experience of dining here. Menu specialties include baked snails, salads, spinach and cream tartlets, jumbo grilled scampi, veal cutlets, lamb chops, roast duckling, spicy Cajun chicken, and a succulent array of desserts.

## INEXPENSIVE

**PARAQUET RESTAURANT, South Shore Rd., P.O. Box 173, Paget. Tel. 809/236-5842.**
   **Cuisine:** BERMUDIAN **Reservations:** Not required.
**$ Prices:** Appetizers $2.50–$4.40; main courses $9–$23.75; menu of the day $9.10. No credit cards.
   **Open:** Daily 9:30am–1:30am. **Closed:** Feb.

Set near an important traffic junction on the South Shore near the Elbow Beach Hotel, this unpretentious restaurant is the center of a previously recommended apartment cluster of the same name. As you dine, you overlook a circular formal flower garden, which the Portuguese owners created. Although the lime-colored Formica, tiles, metal chairs, and plants is definitely coffee shop decor, some of the menu items are substantial restaurant fare. The chef specializes in home-style Bermudian fare. The establishment has one of the largest sandwich menus on the island, both hot and cold, as well as omelets, homemade soups (which always include a fish chowder of the day), and salads. You can order mixed platters, such as turkey breast and crabmeat, or such grilled dishes as T-bone steak, fried liver and onions, and roast half spring chicken.

# 3. WARWICK PARISH

## INEXPENSIVE

**PAW PAWS, 87 South Shore Rd., Warwick Tel. 809/236-7459.**
   **Cuisine:** FRENCH/INTERNATIONAL **Reservations:** Recommended. **Bus:** No. 7.
**$ Prices:** Lunch appetizers $4.50–$6.50; lunch main courses $6–$15.25; dinner appetizers $7.50–$8; dinner main courses $18–$22. MC, V.
   **Open:** Lunch daily 10:30am–5pm; dinner daily 7–10pm. Bar daily noon–1am.
   **Closed:** Tues in winter.

About three miles west of Hamilton, the restaurant contains dozens of paintings and photographs of Bermuda landscapes, and murals showing the Bermuda forest underbrush. Although its menu includes several dishes inspired by the cuisine of France, this restaurant is less formal and more oriented toward the family trade than its menu might imply. Lunches feature club sandwiches, grilled chicken, salads, and the restaurant's trademark dish, a baked casserole with green paw paws (papaya), ground beef, and herbs known as paw-paw montespan. In the evening, the staff happily cooks hamburgers for young children who might be dining with parents eating frog's legs, duck with orange sauce, ravioli stuffed with lobster and shellfish, and chicken layered with ham in puff pastry.

Under the same management, and immediately adjacent, are a pastry shop and an ice cream parlor.

---

# 4. SOUTHAMPTON PARISH

---

## VERY EXPENSIVE

**NEWPORT ROOM, in the Southampton Princess, 101 South Shore Rd. Tel. 809/238-8000.**
**Cuisine:** FRENCH **Reservations:** Recommended. **Transportation:** Private hotel ferry boats from Hamilton.
**$ Prices:** Appetizers $9–$21; main courses $30–$75. AE, DC, MC, V.
**Open:** Dinner daily 6:30–9:15pm (when the last orders are taken). **Closed:** Usually Jan–Feb.

★ There is no restaurant in Bermuda in which the decor is as sumptuously understated as it is in the Newport Room, and the French cuisine rates among the best in Bermuda as well. Everything about the place re-creates the expensive interior of a well-maintained yacht. A pair of exact miniature replicas of two of the winning sailing craft in the Newport to Bermuda race (reportedly costing $15,000 each) act as the illuminated centerpieces of a room that is entirely paneled in teak and rosewood, with appropriate nautical brass. Large illuminated paintings of the windblown regattas add a touch of vibrant color to an otherwise austere yet appealing room.

You'll be greeted at the entrance by a formally polite maître d'hôtel stationed beside a gleaming ship's compass. Settle into plush leather armchairs as you peruse the menu, which might include gourmet variations of *cuisine moderne,* such as venison medallions with orange sauce. The menu changes frequently. A wide array of international wines, served in Irish crystal, complements each dinner. Men are required to wear jackets and ties.

## EXPENSIVE

**HENRY VIII, South Shore Rd. Tel. 809/238-1977.**
**Cuisine:** ENGLISH/CONTINENTAL **Reservations:** Required for dinner. **Bus:** No. 7 or 8.
**$ Prices:** Appetizers $8–$12; main courses $18–$27; Sunday brunch $19.75. AE, DC, MC, V.
**Open:** Lunch Mon–Sat noon–2:30pm (sandwiches served until 3:30pm); dinner daily 6:45–10:30pm; Sun brunch noon–3pm.

This pub restaurant, located below Gibb's Hill Lighthouse between the Southampton Princess and the Sonesta Beach Hotel, has been given the royal treatment. The Tudor atmosphere is enhanced by solid oak furnishings, brass railings, ornaments, and period-style lighting fixtures throughout. You might want to drop in at the split-level Oak Room Bar for some English beer on draft.

Hot pub lunches include steak-and-kidney pie, mussel pie, and plain old hamburgers. Sandwiches are available from 2:30 to 3:30pm. The Sunday brunch is popular. In the evening, the chef gets more elegant and turns out such whimsically named dishes as "Court Jester" (broiled seafood combination) and "Steak Anne Boleyn" (flavored with cognac and simmered in a madeira sauce). The chef also prepares an English mixed grill, peppersteak, and a chateaubriand. There is entertainment in the evenings.

**WATERLOT INN, in the Southampton Princess, Middle Rd., Southampton. Tel. 809/238-0501.**

**Cuisine:** FRENCH/BERMUDIAN **Reservations:** Required. **Transportation:** Guests are transported from the hotel to this waterside inn in a shuttle.

**$ Prices:** Appetizers $6–$20; main courses $23–$55; dinner from $55; Sun brunch $30 adults; children under 12, $17. AE, DC, MC, V.

**Open:** Dinner daily 6:30–9:15pm; Sun brunch noon–1:30pm.

Some 300 years ago, merchant sailors unloaded their cargoes directly into the basement of this historic inn and warehouse. Today the best way to approach it is still by water, and that's precisely what many Bermudians do, mooring their sailing craft in its sheltered cove. At one time the Darrell family owned this house and all the land stretching from Jew's Bay to the Atlantic on the other side of Bermuda. The land's most famous occupant, Claudia Darrell, ran one of the island's best-known eateries from the house until she died. Over the years the inn has attracted such patrons as Mark Twain, James Thurber, Eleanor Roosevelt, and Eugene O'Neill. After the landmark building was devastated by a gas explosion in 1976, the Southampton Princess had it renovated and today it's one of their gourmet restaurants.

Diners enjoy a drink in an upstairs bar, entertained by the resident classical pianist. After descending a colonial staircase with white balustrades, they can sit in one of a trio of conservatively nautical dining rooms. Each is filled with captain's or Windsor chairs, oil paintings of old clipper ships, and lots of exposed wood. From the outdoor terrace, you can view the movement of pleasure craft in the bay. Main courses are likely to include filet of pan-fried Bermuda rockfish, roast duck with black-currant sauce, lamb roasted with herbs and butter, and a *pavé* of beef with freshly cracked pepper, cognac, and a cream sauce. Jackets and ties are required for men at dinner.

**WHALER INN, in the Southampton Princess, 101 South Shore Rd. Tel. 809/238-0076.**

**Cuisine:** SEAFOOD **Reservations:** Recommended. **Transportation:** Private hotel ferryboats from Hamilton.

**$ Prices:** Fixed-price dinner $36.

**Open:** Dinner daily 6:30–9:15. **Closed:** Nov–Mar.

Famous for its seafood, this restaurant is perched at the top of a low cliff overlooking the rocks and pink sands that border the Atlantic near the Southampton Princess Hotel. Its landscaped terraces sprout with carefully planned clusters of sea grape, Norfolk Island pine, and comfortably padded iron armchairs. From here you can enjoy the sunsets that redden the lapping waves of one of the island's most secluded beaches. If you want to dine on the terrace, someone will bring you a whale-shaped menu. If you prefer indoor dining, the interior's huge windows provide an airy setting where the panoramic view is the main decor.

Fixed-price items are chosen from a four-course table d'hôte menu with a wide selection of choices. To "bait your appetite," you can begin your repast with tiger prawns in a cocktail sauce, shrimp bisque, or oysters on the half shell. The chef's special main courses will be well-seasoned portions of whatever game fish the local fisherpeople brought in that day, including yellowfin tuna, barracuda, shark, wahoo, or dolphin (the fish). Main courses not dependent on the whims of the tides or ocean currents include a kettle of seafood St. David's style, mussels marinière, and a deep-fried fisherman's platter, along with pan-fried local fish with almonds and bananas. You'll get a full array of Bermuda fish, either broiled or sautéed in butter. Your "happy ending" could include banana fritters with black-rum sauce, or Armagnac ice cream with prunes. Dress is casual.

# 5. SANDYS PARISH

The following recommended eating places, of varied price and menu, are all located on Somerset Island.

## EXPENSIVE

**LANTANA COLONY CLUB RESTAURANT, Somerset Bridge. Tel. 809/ 234-0141.**
   **Cuisine:** CONTINENTAL **Reservations:** Required. **Transportation:** Hamilton ferry to Somerset Bridge.
   **$ Prices:** Fixed-price dinner $40, plus 15% service. No credit cards.
   **Open:** Dinner daily 7:30-9pm. **Closed:** Jan 5-Feb 11.
This is the elegant restaurant contained within this exclusive hotel. Guests sometimes prefer a drink near the fireplace of the huge salon before climbing the short flight of steps into the pastel-colored dining room. Ceiling trusses have been painted a pastel shade of spring green, and the neobaroque floral stencils were applied between garlands of Italian-style ornamentation. If you prefer a greenhouse effect, a second room has been glassed over with a solarium-style roof and surrounded with plants. A uniformed staff member will usher you to a table where a hibiscus has been placed at each place setting.
   The frequently changing menu might include fresh salmon steak with dill sauce, prosciutto with melon, fish terrine, fish soup Lantana, grilled sirloin Delmonico style, breast of chicken with a whisky cream sauce, Bermuda fish meunière, veal Cordon Bleu, and grilled jumbo shrimp, any of which might be accompanied by grilled tomatoes provençale. There is a large choice under each heading (appetizers, main courses, desserts, and so on). Jackets and ties are required for men. Live music is offered for dancing on certain nights of the week; call for information.

## MODERATE

**BLUE FOAM RESTAURANT, in the Somerset Bridge Hotel, 162 Somerset Rd., Somerset Bridge, Sandys. Tel. 809/234-2892.**
   **Cuisine:** BERMUDIAN **Reservations:** Not required. **Bus:** No. 7 or 8, or Hamilton ferryboat.
   **$ Prices:** Appetizers $4-$9; main courses $14-$22. AE, DC, MC, V.
   **Open:** Breakfast daily 8-10am; lunch daily 11:30am-2:30pm; dinner daily 6:30-9:30pm. **Closed:** Feb.
The Blue Foam Restaurant sits about 100 yards from the entrance to the motel-like Somerset Bridge Hotel down the road. The entrance path, indicated by a sign, winds down the hillside until you reach the panoramic restaurant, whose view encompasses bobbing moorings of Ely's Harbour. Lunches are pleasantly informal, with a full array of burgers, salads (including one of pasta and a chef's salad), chicken, fish, and shrimp

with chips. Such sandwiches as roast beef with onions and horseradish are offered, and the pizzas are 12 inches wide. At dinner, a more expensive menu includes fresh wahoo steak, filet mignon in a mushroom sauce, homemade fish chowder, and other uncomplicated yet savory fare. The grilled, baked, or sautéed fresh fish dishes here are among the best on the island.

**IL PALIO, 64 Main Rd. Tel. 809/234-1049.**
**Cuisine:** ITALIAN **Reservations:** Required. **Bus:** No. 8.
**$ Prices:** Appetizers $4–$10; main courses $12–$22; early-bird dinner special (6–7pm) $16. DC, MC, V.
**Open:** Dinner Tues–Sun 6–10pm.
Named after the famous horse race in Siena, Italy, Il Palio lies in the center of Somerset in the west end of Bermuda, near several outstanding attractions that I'll document later. Currently, it's the only restaurant in the western sector that specializes in the rich Italian cuisine, and it does so exceedingly well. If you arrive early, you can enjoy a drink in the bar downstairs before going upstairs to your well-set table. In a cozy, intimate decor, you might order fettuccine Alfredo, sautéed veal, scaloppine, roast duckling with green pepper corn sauce, or steak Diana. A selection of 9-inch pizzas is also presented nightly.

**LA PLAGE, in the Lantana Colony Club, Somerset Bridge. Tel. 809/234-0141.**
**Cuisine:** INTERNATIONAL **Reservations:** Recommended. **Transportation:** Hamilton ferry to Somerset Bridge.
**$ Prices:** Appetizers $1.50–$4; main courses $7.50–$14. No credit cards.
**Open:** Lunch daily 12:30–2:30pm. **Closed:** Jan 5–Feb 11.
Walking toward this charming restaurant will give you a chance to admire the sculpture scattered throughout the gardens of the most exclusive hotel in Sandys Parish. In many ways, it's the perfect luncheon stopover during a tour of Bermuda's west end. The urn-shaped balustrades that separate the terrace from the cove, fresh flowers, and impeccable service are much like something you might find at the edge of a lake in northern Italy. An endearing statue of an elfin girl gleefully experimenting with her mother's necklaces and lipstick stands guard beside the Roman-style pool where a stone cherub spurts water high into the air. A pier and a dock area a few steps away from the restaurant create the impression that a yacht might pull up at any moment. You'll be able to choose a table near the flowers of the sun deck, or one inside the pink-and-white summertime interior. You might begin with a Bermuda fish chowder, then follow with something from an array of offerings, which range from ordinary sandwiches (peanut butter and bacon) to elaborate fantasies such as salmon mousse, crêpes stuffed with beef and cheese, Bermuda mussel stew, and coquilles St. Jacques. Several salads are also offered, including a traditional chef's salad or one made with tropical fruit.

**LOYALTY INN, Mangrove Bay, Somerset Village. Tel. 809/234-0125.**
**Cuisine:** INTERNATIONAL **Reservations:** Recommended. **Bus:** No. 7 or 8, or ferry from Hamilton.
**$ Prices:** Lunch appetizers $3.50–$3.75; lunch main courses $5.25–$6.75; dinner appetizers $4–$12.50; dinner main courses $16.25–$22.75. Sun brunch, $18. AE, MC, V.
**Open:** Bar daily 11am–1am; restaurant, lunch Mon–Sat 11:30am–4pm; Sun brunch noon–3pm; dinner daily 6:30–10:30pm.
This 250-year-old converted home, which overlooks Mangrove Bay, is a white building that looks vaguely like a church. The bar, in a separate building, is filled with

captain's chairs and a mock fireplace. The restaurant with its decor of cedar paneling and small-paned windows attracts both visitors and locals who prefer its uncluttered atmosphere. The menu of steak, chicken, sandwiches, and seafood is not elaborate, but the dishes are well prepared and the portions are generous. The fish chowder is superb, followed by either the fish plate or tasty scallops and a salad. In the evening, if you have the appetite, you can ask for a seafood dinner. The restaurant is about a five-minute walk east of the Watford Bridge ferry landing.

**VILLAGE INN, Watford Bridge, Somerset Village. Tel. 809/238-9401.**
**Cuisine:** BERMUDIAN/EUROPEAN **Reservations:** Recommended. **Bus:** No. 7 or 8.
**$ Prices:** Lunch appetizers $3.50–$4; lunch main courses $4.75–$15; dinner appetizers $6–$8; dinner main courses $13–$28. DC, MC, V.
**Open:** Lunch Tues–Sun noon–6pm; dinner Tues–Sun 6:30–10pm.

What looks like a private vacation house sitting a few feet above a boat dock dates from the early 1700s, when it was constructed as a private home at the eastern edge of Somerset Village. Turned into a restaurant in the 1950s, it has an unpretentious paneled interior. The bar at one end of the room is a good place to share a drink with the local residents. Many diners prefer a table on one of a series of terraces that have been cut or inserted into the slope of the terrain leading down to the harbor. Specialties include both Bermudian and European cuisine, as well as a "native" barbecue. The polite staff will recommend Bermuda seafood, such as fish chowder, rockfish, and, when available, lobster. The fine food represents good value for the money.

## INEXPENSIVE

**SOMERSET COUNTRY SQUIRE TAVERN, 10 Mangrove Bay Rd. Tel. 809/234-0105.**
**Cuisine:** BRITISH/SEAFOOD **Reservations:** Not required. **Bus:** No. 7 or 8.
**$ Prices:** Appetizers $3.25–$8.75; main courses $7.25–$24. AE, MC, V.
**Open:** Lunch daily 11:30am–4pm; dinner daily 6–10pm.

You pass through a moon gate arch to reach the raised terrace of this waterside restaurant, located in the center of the village. (This restaurant can be visited on a trip to the Old Royal Naval Dockyard on Ireland Island.) If you don't want to eat within the confines of the limestone blocks and hedges that ring the terrace, go to the interior dining room downstairs. The bill of fare ranges from British "pub grub" to fresh fish caught in local waters, or the traditional roast beef with Yorkshire pudding. Local Bermudian favorites include curried mussel pie and fresh Bermuda tuna or wahoo. Look for the specialties of the day, but count on charbroiled and barbecued meals. There is light entertainment six evenings a week, and barbecues from Sunday through Tuesday.

# 6. ST. GEORGE'S PARISH

## EXPENSIVE

**MARGARET ROSE, St. George's Club, Rose Hill, St. George's. Tel. 809/297-1200.**
**Cuisine:** INTERNATIONAL **Reservations:** Required. **Bus:** No. 8, 10, or 11.

**$ Prices:** Appetizers $6–$18; main courses $22–$35. AE, DC, MC, V.
**Open:** Dinner Thurs–Tues 6–10pm.

The stylishly designed Margaret Rose is one of the most appealing restaurants in the east end of Bermuda. Named after both Princess Margaret and Rose Hill (on which it sits), the fashionably decorated restaurant overlooks the harbor and the old part of town. Candlelight adds to the romantic ambience. You might begin with the award-winning Bermuda fish chowder or else enjoy an endive-and-rose-petal salad with a pine-nut-and-raspberry dressing. The wild-mushroom ravioli served in a thyme butter sauce is also an excellent appetizer. For your main selection, you might choose Bermuda fish Picasso (with a mosaic of fresh fruit and ginger), loin of lamb with an herb-and-garlic stuffing, or breast of Barbarie duckling, pink-roasted. Several pasta specialties are also featured.

# MODERATE

**CARRIAGE HOUSE, 22 Water St., Somers Wharf. Tel. 809/297-1730.**
**Cuisine:** BEEF/SEAFOOD **Reservations:** Recommended. **Bus:** No. 3, 10, or 11.
**$ Prices:** Lunch appetizers $4.75–$12.50; lunch main courses $7.25–$12.50; dinner appetizers $7.25–$12.50; dinner main courses $18.50–$36. Fixed-price lunch $11.50. Early bird dinner (6–6:45pm) $19.50. AE, DC, MC, V.
**Open:** Lunch daily noon–2:30pm; dinner daily 6–9:30pm; Sun buffet brunch noon–2:30pm.

Housed in an old waterfront storehouse in the same building as the Carriage Museum in St. George's, the carefully restored Carriage House specializes in beef as well as seafood. It keeps its 18th-century-warehouse look with two rows of bare brick arches, the effect softened by hanging baskets of greenery. After placing your order for dinner, you can help yourself at a large salad bar in the rear of the restaurant. Or you may want to enjoy an unusually good selection of hot and cold hors d'oeuvres. The chef specializes in prime rib, the cost depending on the size of your beef, which is always cut to order and served with a ramekin of creamed horseradish in the British tradition. English roast spring lamb is also a specialty. A different soup is offered every day. At lunch, a large selection of hamburgers is offered, along with sandwich platters and Bermuda fish chowder. A choice of excellent desserts is always available. Casual dress is accepted.

**SAN GIORGIO, Water St. Tel. 809/297-1307.**
**Cuisine:** ITALIAN **Reservations:** Recommended. **Bus:** No. 3, 10, or 11.
**$ Prices:** Appetizers $2.50–$8; main courses $7.50–$15. MC, V.
**Open:** Lunch Mon–Sat noon–3pm; dinner Mon–Sat 6–11pm.

To reach this charming little Italian restaurant next to the Tucker House Museum, guests climb a short flight of steps from a point opposite Somers Wharf. The 150-year-old building was originally a private house and later served as the local telephone exchange for St. George's. Most guests begin with a selection of antipasto. Several well-prepared pasta dishes tempt diners, including tortellini and lasagna. For your main course, you can select from such elegant dishes as breast of chicken sautéed with black-cherry-and-rum sauce. The chef also does a good veal marsala. Fresh broiled wahoo with lemon butter sauce is regularly featured.

**WHARF TAVERN, Somers Wharf. Tel. 809/297-1515.**
**Cuisine:** SEAFOOD. **Reservations:** Recommended. **Bus:** No. 3, 10, or 11.

**$ Prices:** Appetizers $3.50–$8.25; main courses $6.75–$22. DC, MC, V.
**Open:** Lunch Mon–Sat 11:30am–5pm; dinner Mon–Sat 6–10pm; bar Mon–Sat 11am–1am; Sun noon–1am.

The Wharf Tavern, situated among the cluster of buildings that make up Somers Wharf, is a nautically minded, modern restaurant built on the ground floor of a building with a veranda. Only pedestrians are allowed nearby, which might account for the popularity of the porch and the window seats, and the darkly paneled bar area inside. Dinners could include curried mussels, Bermuda fish cakes with peas and rice, pan-fried or broiled rockfish, broiled wahoo, oysters on the half shell, steak-and-kidney pie, and steamed oysters or clams.

**WHITE HORSE TAVERN, King's Square. Tel. 809/297-1838.**
**Cuisine:** BERMUDIAN **Reservations:** Required for dinner. **Bus:** No. 3, 10, or 11.
**$ Prices:** Appetizers $3.75–$12; main courses $10.25–$18.75. AE, MC, V.
**Open:** Lunch daily 11am–5pm; dinner daily 6–10pm.

St. George's oldest tavern is a restaurant and cedar bar with a terrace jutting into St. George's Harbour. This white building with green shutters is one of the most popular taverns in all of Bermuda, and its location is so central you can't miss it. In fair weather (which is most of the time), guests prefer to sit on the terrace. The most ordered item here is fish and chips, cooked in the manner of St. David's Island. The Bermuda fish chowder is also good. Or you can order mussel pie, codfish cakes, or grilled wahoo with tartar sauce. St. George's fish pot is the chef's specialty. At lunch, Tavern burgers, fresh salads, and open-faced sandwiches are served. Finish off with the White Horse chocolate cake. Dress is casual.

# INEXPENSIVE

**CLYDE'S CAFE & BAR, Duke of York St. Tel. 809/297-0158.**
**Cuisine:** INTERNATIONAL **Reservations:** Recommended. **Bus:** No. 3, 10, or 11.
**$ Prices:** Appetizers $3.50–$8.50; main courses $5.50–$13.50. No credit cards.
**Open:** Mon and Wed–Sat 11am–1am, Sun noon–1am.

**Ⓢ** Rarely visited by the cruise-ship crowd, Clyde's is more known among local residents who come here for some of the best home cooking in the east end. You enter through a bar, then head past a blaring jukebox toward the family dining room in the rear. If you visit at lunch, you might want one of their well-stuffed sandwiches served with homemade cole slaw. But you can also order from an array of hot dishes at both lunch and dinner. Clyde's is known for its pork chops, Bermuda fish, shrimp, scallops, roast beef, and lobster (the price of which varies but is always more costly than the most expensive main courses on the menu). Clyde's is located opposite the entrance to Somers Garden, in a house of chiseled stone originally constructed by Bermudian slaves; it has a cement veranda in front. The same family has owned it for generations.

**O'MALLEY'S PUB ON THE SQUARE, King's Square. Tel. 809/297-1522.**
**Cuisine:** AMERICAN/BERMUDIAN **Reservations:** Not required. **Bus:** No. 3, 10, or 11.
**$ Prices:** Appetizers $5–$6; main courses $11–$16; fixed-price menu $12. AE, MC, V.
**Open:** Breakfast daily 8–11am; lunch daily noon–3pm; dinner daily 6–10pm.

**⑤** Here you'll find a two-level British pub, with a rustic atmosphere, in a building dating from 1785. On a good evening, the fun here has been compared to that of a prewar English music hall; the sing-alongs keep St. George's rocking. After a mug of beer at the downstairs pub level, guests can climb a spiral staircase to the upper-level tavern dining room, which has a veranda bar overlooking the square. Usually washed down with draft beer, the fish and chips is the most popular item; sandwiches are also available. Other good dishes include Bermuda fish chowder laced with rum and sherry peppers, pub-style chicken, and steak-and-kidney pie.

# ST. DAVID'S ISLAND

**BLACK HORSE TAVERN, 34 Great Bay Rd., St. David's Island. Tel. 809/293-9742.**

   **Cuisine:** INTERNATIONAL **Reservations:** Recommended. **Bus:** No. 3.

**$ Prices:** Appetizers $5–$8.75; main dishes $12.25–$27.50. AE, MC, V.

   **Open:** Tues–Sat 10am–1am; Sun noon–1am.

If you should land here, in a section of the island that Bermudians call "the country," you won't be disappointed. The exterior looks like a dusty-rose-colored version of a private home, complete with green shutters and a rear glassed-in porch that looks over Smith's Sound. Over the years the tavern has been host to many celebrities, including Robert Stigwood, the Australian movie producer. Many of the guests show up in yachts, but others, by far the majority, come from the nearby U.S. naval base, especially on payday.

   You might begin your meal with curried conch stew, shark hash, fish chowder, or curried mussels. This could be followed by a sandwich, a burger, or perhaps a platter of fish and chips or chicken and chips. The chef also prepares a good sirloin steak and a chicken dinner. The house drink, a "honeymoon special," combines rum apricot brandy and tequila in one potent drink.

**DENNIS'S HIDEAWAY, Cashew City Rd. Tel. 809/297-0044.**

   **Cuisine:** SEAFOOD **Reservations:** Required. **Bus:** No. 3.

**$ Prices:** Fixed-price dinners $20–$30. No credit cards.

   **Open:** Dinner daily 7–10pm.

Dennis Lamb, a burly St. David's Islander, is one of the treasures of Bermuda. So is his quaint little eatery, located in the easternmost parish of St. George's. As you approach it, you're likely to see Dennis (part Irish, part Mohawk) working in his garden in front (he even grows the cabbage he uses in his coleslaw and the beets he pickles). He'll show you into his fisherman's cottage by one of the island's little coves. Once inside, you'll feel you've left Bermuda and are visiting some little pocket-size country with a distinctive personality.

   The descendant of whalers and pilots—"wooden ships and iron men"—Dennis and his son will offer you a cuisine that has virtually disappeared in Bermuda's restaurants, one that is practiced only in private homes these days. For $30, he'll give you "the works," an array of dishes, including conch stew, dolphin (the fish), herb-flavored shark hash, shrimp, conch fritters—you name it (but please don't order the turtle, an endangered species). You bring your own wine. If you don't want to eat so much, request the fish dinner for $20. The fisherman's cottage is accessible by land or sea, and don't dress up.

   (*Warning:* This Pa Kettle ambience is not for everyone, it must be pointed out. Reactions of readers have varied tremendously. Some repeat visitors give it high marks, claiming they've made at least 20 pilgrimages here during their annual visits to Bermuda. Some first-time visitors, however, claim that travel writers who send diners here should be tarred and feathered. So go only if you're a bit adventurous!)

# 7. HAMILTON PARISH

## EXPENSIVE

**MIKADO, in Marriott's Castle Harbour Resort, Paynters Town Rd., Tucker's Town. Tel. 809/293-2040.**
   **Cuisine:** JAPANESE **Reservations:** Required. **Bus:** No. 2 from St. George's.
$ **Prices:** Appetizers $4.50–$5.75; main courses $24.95–$43.95. AE, DC, MC, V.
   **Open:** Dinner daily 6:30–10pm. **Closed:** Mon during Dec–Mar.
Contained in the lower level of the previously recommended Marriot, this is one of the most imaginative and stylish rooms in Bermuda. You pass through lacquered gateways to reach a whimsically art deco version of a Japanese tea garden. An experienced chef is assigned to each group of eight diners and prepares his cuisine much like an actor would prepare a theater offering. Grills placed near each table permit diners to view whatever is cooking. Rare imported fish mixed with very fresh Bermuda fish, such as wahoo, are used for the sushi bar. All the traditional Japanese specialties, along with an aromatic saké, are available. Dress is "smart casual."

**PLANTATION, 46 Harrington Sound Rd., Bailey's Bay. Tel. 809/293-1188.**
   **Cuisine:** BERMUDIAN **Reservations:** Recommended for dinner. **Bus:** Nos. 1 and 3.
$ **Prices:** Appetizers $4.75–$12.75; main courses $20.25–$32. AE, DC, MC, V.
   **Open:** Lunch daily noon–2:30pm; dinner Mon–Sat 6:45–9:30pm; bar service from 10am. **Closed:** Mid-Dec to mid-Feb.
⭐ The Plantation, a yellow colonial-style building with fireplaces and steep white roofs, is a charming oasis on the site of Leamington Caves. The three rooms inside, with their plush carpeting, ceiling fans, and rattan furniture, have a warm, inviting ambience. In fair weather, guests dine al fresco in the tropical garden shaded by a giant marquee. The bar with its Bermuda cedar base is ideal for a drink.
   At night, the chef shows his excellence by turning out a seafood Walsingham (wahoo, shrimp, and fresh scallops), or one of the special hors d'oeuvres that are based on the availability of fresh filet with bananas and almonds, another gently coated with Pommery mustard and topped with sliced tomatoes. One of the specialties is pan-fried noisettes of lamb. Men should wear a jacket and a tie.

**TOM MOORE'S TAVERN, Washington Lane, Bailey's Bay. Tel. 809/293-8020.**
   **Cuisine:** FRENCH/CONTINENTAL **Reservations:** Required. **Bus:** No. 1 or 3.
$ **Prices:** Appetizers $5.50–$18; main dishes $24–$29.75. AE, MC, V.
   **Open:** Dinner Mon–Sat 7–9:30pm. **Closed:** Jan 5–Feb 14.
Bermuda's oldest eating house, built in 1652 and once a private home, is located on Walsingham Bay, near the Crystal Caves, in Hamilton Parish. It was visited in 1804 by the Irish romantic poet Thomas (Tom) Moore, who wrote some of his verses here; he made reference to a calabash tree that still stands, some 200 yards from the tavern.
   The tavern is also the most famous dining room in Bermuda, having known many incarnations. In 1985 two Italians, Bologna-born Bruno Fiocca and his Venetian partner, Franco Bortoli, opened it for dinner and quickly established it as one of the most popular upmarket restaurants in Bermuda. Fortunately, they have maintained the old character of this landmark place, which has four fireplaces. A bar and lounge

are upstairs. The darkened cedar walls are a backdrop for the classical French and Italian cuisine served here.

Seafood, impeccably prepared, is the specialty. A Bermuda-lobster tank for Bermuda lobster is found outside during the season. The Bermuda fish from local waters is likely to be rockfish or yellowtail. Try quails in puff pastry or duck with a raspberry-vinegar dressing. The setting, the English silver, German crystal, Luxembourg china, and the general ambience can help make a memorable visit. Men should wear a jacket.

## INEXPENSIVE

**SWIZZLE INN, Blue Hole Hill, Bailey's Bay. Tel. 809/293-9300.**
  **Cuisine:** BERMUDIAN/ENGLISH **Reservations:** Not accepted. **Bus:** No. 3 or 11.
  **$ Prices:** Lunch appetizers $2.50–$6; lunch main courses $5–$12; dinner appetizers $3.50–$7.50; dinner main courses $7.50–$21. AE, MC, V.
  **Open:** Daily 11am–1am. **Closed:** Mon in Jan and Feb.
The home of the Bermuda rum swizzle lies west of the airport, near the Crystal Caves and the Bermuda Perfume Factory. This is one of the most venerable bars in Bermuda, some 300 years old. In the food department the meaty Swizzleburger is the most popular here. Soups are offered, and fish and chips with coleslaw is a standard. Of course, you can have the traditional English bangers and mash, and sirloin and tenderloin steaks are a feature. The inn makes an ideal "watering spot" if you're touring the island and want a drink, a lunch, even a game of darts. Every visitor to Bermuda, famous and not so famous, is likely to show up here at some point. Sports personalities are especially fond of the place, as well as visiting celebrities. Meals are served continuously throughout the day.

# 8. SMITH'S PARISH

## MODERATE

**INLET RESTAURANT, in the Palmetto Hotel, Harrington Sound Rd., at Flatts Village. Tel. 809/293-2323.**
  **Cuisine:** INTERNATIONAL **Reservations:** Not required. **Bus:** No. 10 or 11.
  **$ Prices:** Appetizers $4–$9.75; main courses $17–$28; lunch $12. AE, MC, V.
  **Open:** Lunch daily noon–2:30pm; dinner daily 7–10pm; light snacks served in pub until 10pm.
In creating this attractive restaurant, the owners added a slope-roofed modern addition onto what had been a lushly paneled lounge lined with Bermuda cedar. You can select a seat near the big windows, which look over the moon gate, the swimming pool, and the harbor, or you can relax in the darker and more intimate recesses of the back.

A good selection of sandwiches and burgers are available for lunch, and light snacks can be taken outside on the patio in fine weather. Dinners are more elaborate, with a more detailed menu and a wider selection of dishes. You might start with spinach or Caesar salad, or Bermuda fish chowder. Seafood courses include a casserole of shrimp and scallops, or perhaps fresh Bermuda fish, broiled or pan-fried. Meat dishes include grilled beef tenderloin, Bermuda chicken, breast stuffed with pâté, and grilled medallions of pork in an apple brandy sauce.

# 9. SPECIALTY DINING

## HOTEL DINING

**LILLIAN'S in the Sonesta Beach Hotel and Spa, South Shore Rd. Tel. 809/238-8122.**
   **Cuisine:** ITALIAN **Reservations:** Recommended. **Bus:** No. 7.
$ **Prices:** Appetizers $7–$12; main courses $13–$24. AE, DC, MC, V.
   **Open:** Dinner daily 6–9:30pm.

Set within the lower level of the Sonesta Beach Hotel (previously recommended), this hotel offers the cuisine of northern Italy amidst a modernized art nouveau decor of pale blues and pinks. An international brigade of waiters serves many of the classic dishes of Italy, including saltimbocca, several kinds of pastas, rollatinis, and the array of veal, pork, and beef dishes you'd expect.

**RIB ROOM STEAK HOUSE, in the Southampton Princess, 101 South Shore Rd. Tel. 809/238-8000.**
   **Cuisine:** STEAKS/SEAFOOD **Reservations:** Recommended. **Transportation:** Private hotel ferryboat from Hamilton.
$ **Prices:** Four-course fixed menu $36. AE, DC, MC, V.
   **Open:** Dinner daily 6:30–9:15pm (when the last orders are taken).

The Rib Room Steak House, styled after an American steakhouse, sits atop the golf pro shop, near the tee-off point for the first hole. As you sit in the midst of panoramic windows and upholstered armchairs, you might start your evening with a "Dark and Stormy" (black rum with ginger beer). Follow that with a main course such as baby pork spareribs, several kinds of beef broiled over charcoal, or roast prime rib of beef with Yorkshire pudding. There is also a catch of the day or ten other choices, such as chicken with short ribs or broiled lamb chops.

**TIARA ROOM, in the Princess, 76 Pitts Bay Rd. Tel. 809/295-3000.**
   **Cuisine:** FRENCH **Reservations:** Required. **Bus:** No. 7 or 8.
$ **Prices:** Appetizers $5–$13; main courses $25–$38. AE, DC, MC, V.
   **Open:** Dinner daily 6:30–9:30pm.

The gourmet choice of the posh Hamilton Princess, this modernized restaurant focuses its decor around elaborate tiara-shaped chandeliers and a sweeping panoramic view of Hamilton Harbour. Dozens of flickering candles seem to set fire to the fine crystal and heavy silver. Flambé dishes are a specialty here, adding a touch of theatricality to the decor.

The cuisine is classic French, and the menu often changes. For an appetizer, you might choose terrine du chef or antipasto. Among the soup selections are chilled soup of the day and Bermuda fish soup. The chef prepares superb fish dishes and is said to search the eastern seaboard for unique aquatic catches. From this Atlantic bounty, try the scampi provençale or a brochette of scallops broiled with cherry tomatoes and mushrooms. Among the main poultry and meat dishes, you are likely to find roast quail served with a cherry sauce, roast rack of lamb with herbs of Provence, and filet mignon with a béarnaise sauce. Men are requested to wear jackets and ties.

## DINING WITH A VIEW

**GLENCOE HARBOUR CLUB, Salt Kettle Lane, Paget. Tel. 809/236-5274.**

**Cuisine:** CONTINENTAL **Reservations:** Required. **Transportation:** The ferryboat from Hamilton every 30 minutes.

**$ Prices:** Lunch appetizers $3.50–$7.50; lunch main courses $7–$14; five-course fixed-price dinner $42.

**Open:** Lunch Mon–Fri noon–2:30pm; dinner seatings daily at 7pm and 8:30pm.

**Closed:** Lunch Dec 1–21 and Jan.

This restaurant lies within the architectural centerpiece of the Glencoe Harbour Club (previously recommended in Chapter 4, "Where to Stay in Bermuda"). Tables overlook the harbor. Originally built in the 18th century as a manor house, the building retains its original low-slung proportions, thick stone walls, and stucco facade. Meals are served either within the formal pink and green dining room or on a flowering terrace facing the sea. Crystal and silver services add touches of colonial elegance.

Lunches usually consist of burgers, salads, grilled steaks, and shrimp cocktails. Dinners are more elaborate, and might include appetizers of deep-fried camembert with apricot sauce, Bermuda fish chowder, rockfish grenobloise (with capers, butter, and wine sauce), veal piccata carbonara, and entrecôte Don Quixote, served with mushrooms, onions, and watercress. A tempting array of desserts are wheeled around the dining room on a trolley. Jackets and ties for men are recommended at dinner time.

# LOCAL FAVORITES

**RUM RUNNERS, 93 Front St., between Burnaby and Parliament Sts. Tel. 809/292-4737.**

**Cuisine:** INTERNATIONAL **Reservations:** Recommended. **Bus:** No. 1, 2, 10, or 11.

**$ Prices:** Lunch appetizers $3.75–$7.50; lunch main courses $5–$14.50; dinner appetizers $4–$7.50; dinner main courses $9.50–$18.50. AE, DC, MC, V.

**Open:** Lunch daily 11:30am–5pm; dinner daily 6:30-10pm.

Lined with bricks and aged paneling, this warmly decorated restaurant contains a pub that is a popular hangout in its own right. Both establishments are at the top of a steep flight of steps. The main dining room, the Nonsuch Room, is filled with antique rifles and bowsprits. The menu offers standard fare, with beef and veal dishes predominating. You may want to try the prime sirloin steak (10 ounces) or the prime roast rib of beef with Yorkshire pudding, or perhaps the chicken Cordon Bleu or the seafood brochette. Lunch includes sandwiches, salads, fresh fish, crab cakes, burgers, and oysters.

The same menu is served in the nearby Load of Mischief Pub. The pub has cedar trim, a beamed tray ceiling, and a somewhat less formal ambience than its neighbor. Meals tend to be less expensive, and no one minds if you order pub grub to supplement your tankard of English ale. Live music is a special event almost every night from 10pm to 1am. A pint of lager costs $4.50, and there is no cover charge.

**MACWILLIAMS, 75 Pitts Bay Rd. Tel. 809/295-5759.**

**Cuisine:** INTERNATIONAL **Reservations:** Not required. **Bus:** No. 1, 2, 10, or 11.

**$ Prices:** Appetizers $2.75–$3.25; main courses $8.75–$16.50. AE, MC, V.

**Open:** Apr–Oct daily 7:30am–10:30pm; Nov–Mar daily 8am–10pm.

Set on the western waterfront road leading to the most congested part of Hamilton, this informal restaurant is sheathed in light-colored brick and neutral-colored paneling. Designed in a coffee-shop decor but clean and bright, it serves breakfast, lunch, and dinner, as well as coffee and snacks. Lunch includes an array of sandwiches, hamburgers, soups, and salads. The evening meal features such dishes as Bermuda fish dinners, fisherman's platter, sirloin steak, liver with onions, spaghetti with meatballs, and barbecued ribs.

# FAST FOOD

**BAILEY'S ICE CREAM & FOOD D'LITES RESTAURANT, the corner of Wilkinson Ave. and Blue Hole Hill. Tel. 809/293-9333.**
    **Cuisine:** ICE CREAM **Reservations:** Not required. **Bus:** No. 3 or 11. No credit cards.
    **Open:** June–Sept daily 11am–7pm; hours vary the rest of the year. **Closed:** Jan–Feb.
At Bailey's Bay, this stands across from the also-recommended Swizzle Inn. For all-natural ice cream, there is no comparable place in Bermuda—40 different flavors are made in the 40-quart ice-cream maker. The parlor is in a small Bermuda cottage, and there is a convenient parking lot. You can eat your butterscotch crunch, almond delight, piña colada, or some exotic ice cream flavor, at one of the outdoor tables or take it away. A sandwich nook, which uses fresh-baked breads, is a popular attraction. Also featured are fresh-fruit ices, frozen yogurts, and natural juices.

**FOURWAYS PASTRY SHOP, in the Washington Mall, Reid St., at Queen St. Tel. 809/295-3263.**
    **Cuisine:** PASTRIES/SANDWICHES **Reservations:** Not accepted. **Bus:** No. 1, 2, 10, or 11.
    **$ Prices:** Tea or coffee $1.25; sandwiches $3–$5. No credit cards.
    **Open:** Mon–Sat 8am–4:30pm.
Although the bustling crowds at this shop on the ground floor of a shopping/office complex remind visitors of London, the array of very fresh pastries, tartlets, petit fours, quiches, and croissant sandwiches evokes a Viennese or Milanese coffeehouse. You can order a steaming cup of coffee or else one of ten different kinds of tea.

# AFTERNOON TEA

Bermuda still practices the British tradition of afternoon tea. (Ironically, in Britain itself, the tradition had been on the wane until it began to come back in the 1980s.) Many guests prefer to have afternoon tea at their hotels, which is a good opportunity to meet fellow guests. Others like to visit other hotels and have afternoon tea there. You should check first, however, as some hotels and resorts prefer to serve afternoon tea only to registered guests.

    Among the previously recommended restaurants and cafés, the two most outstanding ones for a traditional afternoon tea are the **Botanic Garden** (see "City of Hamilton," above) and **Fourways Pastry Shop** (see "Specialty Dining," above).

# SUNDAY BRUNCH

Sunday brunch is a real tradition in Bermuda. A fortunate few visitors manage an invitation to a private Bermudian home for this meal. If their luck continues, they'll be served the traditional "Sabbath fare" of new potatoes with boiled salt cod, which is most often accompanied by slices of banana and avocado topped with an egg-enriched cream sauce. Many Bermudian housewives also make a codfish dish flavored with tomatoes.

    Nearly all hotels serve a traditional Sunday brunch. Many guests prefer to relax on Sunday morning and not leave their hotels; others like to visit one of the popular restaurants on the island featuring Sunday brunch, including the previously recommended **Henry VIII** or the **Loyalty Inn.** The most popular place in Bermuda for Sunday lunch? See below.

**WATERLOT INN, in the Southampton Princess, Middle Rd., Southampton. Tel. 809/238-0510.**

   **Cuisine:** SUNDAY BRUNCH **Reservations:** Required. **Transportation:** Guests are transported from the hotel to this waterside inn in a shuttle.

**$ Prices:** $30 adults, children under 12, $17. AE, DC, MC, V

   **Open:** Sun brunch two seatings: 11:30am and 1pm.

⭐ This previously recommended restaurant is the most popular place on the island for Sunday brunch, attracting both visitors and Bermudians. It is imperative to reserve as far in advance as possible, because of the great popularity of this place. Brunch is buffet-style with all the classic dishes spread before you, including eggs Benedict, hot and cold meats, turkey platters, lamb dishes, and an array of seafood. Men might arrive in a smart blue blazer with tailored Bermuda shorts—it's all the fashion here.

# PICNIC FARE & WHERE TO FIND IT

Those who have a penchant for picnics can indulge it while enjoying a bicycle ride through Sandys Parish. Start by going over Somerset Bridge, the smallest drawbridge in the world, and pedal along Somerset Road to Fort Scaur Park, where you can enjoy a panoramic view of Ely's Harbour.

There are many other desirable locations as well, including Spanish Point Park in Pembroke, a series of little coves and beaches. For here you don't need to go to the trouble of packing a picnic basket, since a lunch wagon rolls around (except in winter). Private picnicking is also available at one of the island's best beaches, Warwick Long Bay. There are restrooms at the western end if you'd like to wash up before you bite down.

Many kitchens of major hotels will prepare a picnic lunch for you, but you should make the request a day in advance. Or you can walk along Front Street in Hamilton, selecting sandwiches at the various cafés or a bottle of wine and some mineral water at a local shop. If it's a weekday, the best place to obtain supplies is the following.

**THE HICKORY STICK, 2 Church St. at Bermudiana Rd. Tel. 809/292-1781.**

   **Cuisine:** DELI **Reservations:** Not accepted. **Bus:** No. 1, 2, 10, or 11.

**$ Prices:** Salads $2.60–$5; sandwiches $3.10–$6; hot takeaway platters $4.25–$6.50. No credit cards.

   **Open:** Mon–Fri 6:30am–4pm.

Set close to the rose-colored walls of the Princess Hotel in Hamilton, this might be one of the most popular delicatessens and take-out restaurants in the capital. Although one section might remind visitors of a popular coffee shop (scones, doughnuts, and morning coffee provide doses of caffeine for the neighborhood residents), most clients prefer it for its overstuffed sandwiches and takeaway portions of food. Offerings include steaming portions of chicken parmesan, barbecued spare ribs, and fish cakes, although even more popular are the salads, sandwiches, and hot dogs, all of which employees will wrap as picnic food for open-air enthusiasts. Advance telephone orders are accepted, and often are a wise idea if you don't want to wait for your order to be prepared. Paper napkins and plastic knives, forks, and spoons are provided on request.

# CHAPTER 6

# WHAT TO SEE & DO IN BERMUDA

**B**ermuda is for fun! Even the major attractions are "lightweight," designed not to tax one. Because of the island's small size, it's easy to get to know Bermuda parish by parish. After 20 miles or so, you'll run into the sea—so don't rush anywhere.

Even though a lot of people have been fitted into a tiny landmass, it doesn't look that way, mainly because houses have been fitted quite naturally into the landscape. There are no jarring billboards or neon signs to spoil the countryside, and because there are no car-rental companies, you'll encounter no traffic jams and no polluted air.

In Bermuda something is going on all the time. Sports are always a star attraction, especially golf and tennis. Sailing, horseback riding, and the pink-sand beaches are also potent lures. (See Chapter 8, "Sports & Recreation.")

As for the sights, from the western tip of Somerset to the eastern end of St. George's, there is much to see in Bermuda, either by bike, ferry, bus, or taxi. You'll need plenty of time, though—the pace is slow. Cars can only travel 15 mph in Hamilton and St. George's, 20 mph outside the towns. This speed limit is rigidly enforced, and penalties for violation are severe.

Bermuda is divided into nine parishes (or counties): Sandys Parish (in the far-western end of the island), Southampton Parish, Warwick Parish, Paget Parish (in which is the greatest concentration of hotels), Pembroke Parish (seat of the government at Hamilton), Devonshire Parish, Smith's Parish, Hamilton Parish (not to be confused with the city of Hamilton), and St. George's Parish (at the far eastern extremity; also takes in the U.S. naval air base and the little island of St. David's).

## ❓ DID YOU KNOW . . . ?

- More than 23,000 couples honeymoon here each year.
- Bermudians imported the idea of moon gates, large rings of stone used as garden ornaments, from the Orient centuries ago. Walking through a moon gate is supposed to bring good luck.
- William Shakespeare's 1610 play, *The Tempest*, was inspired by the mysterious island.
- The British ship *Sea Venture*, headed for Virginia, was wrecked on Bermuda's reefs in July 1609.
- Somerset Bridge is the world's smallest drawbridge. Only 22 inches wide, the opening was built just big enough for a ship's mast to pass through.
- Bermuda has more golf courses per square mile than any other country in the world; there are eight of them on the island's approximate 21 square miles.
- The first game of tennis in the Western Hemisphere was played in Bermuda by Sir Brownlow Gray, the island's chief justice, in 1873.
- Shallow-water wreck diving is a popular island activity. More than 120 shipwrecks have been reported in the waters around Bermuda since the island was discovered.
- With Bermuda's springtime comes the blossoming of the Easter lilies, first brought to the island from Japan in the 18th century.
- The famous pink sand of Bermuda's beaches is actually millions of crushed tiny pink coral shells.
- Bermuda has no pollution and no illiteracy. And outdoor advertising and neon signs are banned.
- Bermuda's cruise-ship policy permits only four ships at a time in its harbors.
- Automobile rentals are banned in Bermuda. Only one person per household is permitted to own an automobile.
- Once believed to be extinct, the cahow bird was rediscovered in Bermuda, where today it nests in the late fall and winter months.

In the early days these districts, which encompass about 21 square miles, were called "tribes." By the beginning of the 17th century the term "Tribe Road" was used to describe the boundaries between parishes. Pembroke, because it encloses the city of Hamilton, is the largest parish in population; St. George's has the most land area.

Many local guidebooks are fond of pointing out that "you can't get lost in Bermuda." Don't you believe them! Along narrow, winding roads—originally designed for the horse and carriage—you *can* get lost, several times, especially if you're looking for an obscure guesthouse along some long-forgotten lane. I've been with taxi drivers of 25 years' experience who have gotten lost in Bermuda.

You won't stay lost for long, though. Bermuda is so narrow that if you keep going in either an easterly or westerly direction, you'll eventually come to a main road. At its broadest point Bermuda is only about 2 miles wide. The principal arteries are the North Shore Road, the Middle Road, and the South Shore Road, so you'll at least have some indication as to what part of the island you're in.

Sometimes it starts raining almost without warning. Never attempt to stay on your vehicle in drizzly or rainy weather. Pull off the road and wait. Skies usually clear rapidly and the road dries quickly, but it is easy to have an accident on Bermuda's slippery roads after a rain, especially if you're not accustomed to using a motor scooter.

Gasoline stations—called "petrol stations" here—appear fairly frequently in Bermuda. But once you "tank up," chances are you'll have plenty of energy to get you to your destination; for example, one tank of gas in a motorbike will take you from Somerset in the west to St. George's in the east.

In this chapter we'll go on a do-it-yourself tour, taking in Bermuda parish by parish. You could also take one of the walking tours described in Chapter 7.

## SUGGESTED ITINERARIES

After you've landed in Bermuda, you may be eager to explore the island, especially if your time is short. Below is a suggested itinerary for the first five days. A week's visit will let you

# IMPRESSIONS

*[Many Britons in Bermuda, to their dislike,] find that while the colony is supposedly and unquestionably British—notionally, legally, officially—it is in very many senses dominated by the United States, is utterly dependent on the United States and can well be regarded, and not by cynics alone, as the only British colony which is more like an American colony, run by Bermudians, on Britain's behalf, for America's ultimate benefit.*
—SIMON WINCHESTER, *THE SUN NEVER SETS: TRAVELS TO THE REMAINING OUTPOSTS OF THE BRITISH EMPIRE* (1985)

---

break up your sightseeing trips with time to relax, or enjoy the beach, or to go boating or engage in some of the other sports activities offered.

For those with more time to explore in a more leisurely fashion, see "Suggested Itineraries" in Chapter 3, "Arriving in Bermuda."

## IF YOU HAVE ONE DAY

If you've only got one day to devote to sightseeing attractions, I suggest you spend it in the historic capital of **St. George's.** It has everything from a ducking stool to narrow, alleyway-like streets with quaint names: Featherbed Alley, Duke of York Street, Petticoat Lane, Old Maids' Lane, Duke of Kent Street. You can spend a day exploring British-style pubs, seafood restaurants, shops (several major Hamilton stores have branches here), old forts, museums, and churches. You'll even see stocks and a pillory once used to humiliate wrongdoers.

## IF YOU HAVE TWO DAYS

**Day 1:** Spend Day 1 as above.
**Day 2:** Devote this day to sightseeing and shopping in the city of **Hamilton.** Since it's likely that you'll be staying in one of the hotels in Paget or Warwick, a ferry from either parish will take you right into the city.

In Hamilton, you can always blend sights with shops, although for many visitors, the shops are more compelling. Try to time your visit to avoid the arrival of cruise ships. On those days, facilities in Hamilton can get cramped.

## IF YOU HAVE THREE DAYS

**Days 1–2:** Spend Days 1–2 as above.
**Day 3:** For a third day of sightseeing, I suggest you take the ferry from Hamilton across Great Sound to **Somerset.** (Your cycle can be carried on the boat—you'll need it later.) You'll be let off at the western end of Somerset Island in Sandys Parish, where you'll find the smallest drawbridge in the world. It's easy to spend an hour walking around Somerset Village. Then head east until you reach a beach on Long Bay along the northern rim of the island. There are several places for lunch in Sandys Parish (see Chapter 5, "Where to Dine in Bermuda"). The Somerset Country Squire Tavern, a typical village inn, is one of the best. It's near the Watford Bridge ferry stop at the western end of the island.

After lunch you can go across Watford Bridge to Ireland Island, home of the important Maritime Museum. On your way back to Somerset Bridge and the ferry back to Hamilton, you might take the turnoff to Fort Scaur. From Scaur Hill you'll have a commanding view of Ely's Harbour and an excellent view over Great Sound. If you don't want to traverse Somerset again, the ferry at Watford Bridge will take you back to Hamilton.

### IF YOU HAVE FIVE DAYS

**Days 1–3:** Spend Days 1–3 as above.

**Day 4:** Make the most of this beach day, heading for Horseshoe Bay Beach in the morning. Spending most of your time there, exploring hidden coves in all directions. You can have lunch right on the beach at a concession. In the afternoon visit Gibbs Hill Lighthouse. After a rest at your hotel, sample some Bermudian night life.

**Day 5:** To conclude your stay, head for Flatts Village, lying in the eastern sector of Smith's Parish. Explore the Bermuda Aquarium, Zoological Garden, and Natural History Museum, and consider an undersea walk offered by the Hartley family (see "Organized Tours," below). Have lunch at the Palmetto Hotel & Cottages, then visit Elbow Beach. Make sure you've purchased your duty-free liquor to take back with you. After having afternoon tea at one of the hotels, take in an island show that evening.

# 1. THE TOP ATTRACTIONS

Although Bermuda is a small island, you really can't see much of it in a day or two. So, if you have more time, you may want to explore it methodically, parish by parish, as most visitors tend to do and as we shall do here, visiting the sights and attractions of each parish as we head from east to west. If your time is limited, however, you may want to consider only the highlights. They are:

- Walking tour of St. George's (explored in this chapter and in Chapter 7, "Bermuda Walking Tours").

- Walking and shopping tour of City of Hamilton. Attractions are documented in this chapter and in Chapter 7, "Bermuda Walking Tours". If you want to combine shopping and sightseeing, read also Chapter 9, "Savvy Shopping."

- Maritime Museum at the Royal Dockyard in the West End.

- Bermuda Aquarium, Zoological Garden, and Natural History Museum, along North Shore Road across Flatts Bridge.

- Crystal Caves, on Crystal Caves Road, a cave discovered in 1907.

- Leamington Caves, Harrington Sound Road, with its underground lakes.

- Verdmont, Verdmont Lane, in Smith's Parish. This 18th-century mansion stands on property once owned by the founder of South Carolina.

- Fort Hamilton, Happy Valley Road, a massive Victorian fortification overlooking the city of Hamilton and its harbor.

- Botanical Gardens, South Shore Road, a Shangri-La in the mid-Atlantic.

- Gibbs Hill Lighthouse, the oldest cast-iron lighthouse in the world.

- Horseshoe Bay Beach in Southampton, most photographed of the pink sandy beaches of Bermuda.

- Elbow Beach at Paget, Bermuda's top sun and swim stretch of sand.

# 2. ST. GEORGE'S PARISH

Settled in 1612, the town of St. George's was once the capital of Bermuda, losing that position to Hamilton in 1815. The town was settled three years after Admiral Sir George Somers and his shipwrecked party of English sailors came ashore in 1609. The town was founded by Richard Moore, of the newly created Bermuda Company, and a band of 60 colonists. It was the second English settlement in the New World (Jamestown, Virginia, was the first). Named after England's patron saint, its coat-of-arms depicts St. George and the dragon. Sir George Somers died in Bermuda in 1610, and his heart was buried in the St. George's area (the rest of his body was taken home to England for burial).

Almost four centuries of history come alive here, and generations upon generations of sailors have set forth from its sheltered harbor. St. George's even played a role in the American Revolutionary War. Bermuda depended on the American colonies for food, and when war came, food ran dangerously short. Although a British colony, loyalties were divided, as many Bermudians had kinsmen living on the American mainland. A delegation headed by Col. Henry Tucker went to Philadelphia to petition the Continental Congress for food and supplies, for which the Bermudians were willing to trade salt. George Washington had a different idea, however. He needed gunpowder, and a number of kegs of it were stored at St. George's. Without the approval of the British/Bermudian governor, a deal was consummated that resulted in the gunpowder's being trundled aboard American warships waiting in the harbor of Tobacco Bay under cover of darkness. In return, the grateful colonies supplied Bermuda with food.

## IN TOWN

**King's Square,** also called Market Square or King's Parade, is the center of life in St. George's. The square contains the colorful Pub on the Square and White Horse Tavern, where you may want to stop for a drink after your tour. Also on the square you'll see a pillory and stock. Honeymooners like to have themselves photographed in them today, but they were used in deadly earnest in earlier times. Victims were sometimes placed in the pillory for a certain number of hours—sometimes with one ear nailed to the post! "Criminals" were burned on the hand or branded, fined in tobacco, nailed to the post, or declared "infamous." Often they had their ears cut off or were made to "stand in a sheet on the church porch."

Offenses for which Bermudians were punished in the early days offer an illuminating glimpse of the social life of the time. Along with such "usual" acts as treason, robbery, arson, murder, and "scandal," records of the assizes (courts) of the early 1600s include concealing finds of ambergris, exporting cedarwood, railing against the governor's authority, hiding tobacco, being "notorious cursers and swearers," leading an "uncivil life and calling her neighbor an old Bawd and the like," neglecting to receive Holy Communion, the acting of any stage play of any kind whatsoever, and playing at unlawful games such as dice, cards, ninepins.

The street names in St. George's also evoke days of yore. **Petticoat Lane** (sometimes called Silk Alley) got its name when two recently emancipated slave girls were said to have paraded up and down the lane rustling their new and flamboyantly colored silk petticoats. **Barber's Lane** is also named for a former slave. It honors Joseph Hayne Rainey (mentioned in Chapter 1, "Getting to Know Bermuda"), a freedman from the Carolinas who fled to Bermuda aboard a blockade runner during

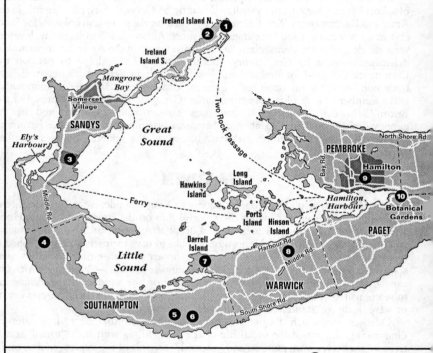

Scale bar: 0 — 2 km / 1.5 m

**Atlantic Ocean**

Ireland Island N. ①
②
Ireland Island S.

Mangrove Bay

Somerset Village

SANDYS

Ely's Harbour ③

Great Sound

Two Rock Passage

North Shore Rd

PEMBROKE

Hamilton ⑨

Bay Rd.

Hawkins Island

Long Island

Ferry

Ports Island

Hinson Island

Hamilton Harbour

⑩ Botanical Gardens

PAGET

Middle Rd

④

Darrell Island

Little Sound

⑦

Harbour Rd

⑧

Middle Rd

WARWICK

SOUTHAMPTON

⑤ ⑥

South Shore Rd

---

**DEVONSHIRE PARISH:**
Palm Grove ⑬
**HAMILTON PARISH:**
Bermuda Aquarium, Museum
& Zoo ⑮
Bermuda Perfumery ⑲
Crystal Caves ⑱
Leamington Caves ⑰

**PAGET PARISH:**
Botanical Gardens ⑪

Waterville (House) ⑩
**PEMBROKE PARISH
(Hamilton City):**
Bermuda Historical Society Museum ⑨
Bermuda National Gallery ⑨
Sessions House (Parliament Building) ⑨
**ST. GEORGE'S PARISH:**
Confederate Museum ⑳
Fort St. Catherine ㉒
Ocean View Golf Course ⑫

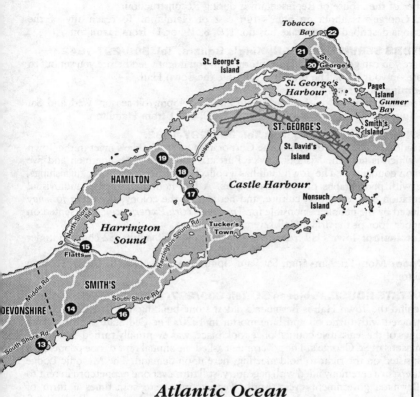

St. George's Island

Tobacco Bay **22**

**21**

**20** St. George's

*St. George's Harbour*

**ST. GEORGE'S**

Paget Island

Gunner Bay

Smith's Island

St. David's Island

*Castle Harbour*

Nonsuch Island

**19**

**18**

HAMILTON

Causeway

**17**

*Harrington Sound*

Tucker's Town

North Shore Rd

Harrington Sound Rd

**15**

Flatts

SMITH'S

Middle Rd

**14**

South Shore Rd

**16**

DEVONSHIRE

**13**

South Shore Rd

*Atlantic Ocean*

the Civil War. He was a barber in Bermuda for the rest of the war. Upon its conclusion he returned to the United States and was elected to Congress, becoming the first black member of the House of Representatives during Reconstruction.

St. George's is about an hour's run east of Hamilton. To reach any of the attractions described below, take bus no. 1, 3, 8, 10, or 11 from Hamilton.

**VISITORS SERVICE BUREAU, King's Square. Tel. 809/297-1642.**
Here you can get a map and any information you might need before you set out to explore on your own. The bureau is opposite the Town Hall.
**Admission:** Free.
**Open:** Summer Mon–Sat 9am–1pm and 2–4:45pm; off-season Wed and Sat 9am–1pm and 2–4:45pm. **Bus:** No. 1, 3, 8, 10, or 11 from Hamilton.

**TOWN HALL, 7 King's Square. Tel. 809/297-1532.**
Headed by a mayor, officers of the Corporation of St. George's meet in the Town Hall, which is near the Visitors Service Bureau. There are three aldermen and five common councillors. The Town Hall has a collection of Bermuda cedar furnishings, along with photographs of previous mayors. A half-hour multimedia, audiovisual presentation on the history, culture, and heritage of the colony, *Bermuda Journey* (produced by the people responsible for *The New York Experience*), is presented on the upper floor of the Town Hall several times a day.
**Admission:** Town Hall free; *Bermuda Journey* $3.50 adults, $2 children under 12.
**Open:** Mon–Fri 9am–5pm, Sat 9am–4pm. **Bus:** No. 1, 3, 8, 10, or 11 from Hamilton.

**OLD STATE HOUSE, Princess St. Tel. 809/297-1260.**
Behind the Town Hall is Bermuda's oldest stone building, the Old State House, constructed with turtle oil and lime mortar in 1620. The Old State House, where meetings of the legislative council once took place, was eventually turned over to the Freemasons of St. George's. The government asked the annual rent of one peppercorn and insisted on the right to hold meetings here upon demand. The Masonic Lodge members, in a ceremony filled with pageantry, still turn over one peppercorn in rent to the Bermuda government every April. (Peppercorns were sometimes a form of payment in the old days. In the late 18th century, for example, two small islands off King's Square were sold for a peppercorn apiece. In 1782 Henry Tucker bought Ducking Stool Island, and in 1785 Nathaniel Butterfield bought Gallows Island; several years later Simon Fraser purchased both for 100 peppercorns and combined them into one, making what is today Ordnance Island.)

For those who have never witnessed the 45-minute spectacle of the annual rent payment, it begins around 11am with the gathering of the Bermuda Regiment on King's Square and the subsequent arrival of the premier, mayor, and other dignitaries, all amid the bellowing introductions of the town crier. As soon as all the principals have taken their places, a 17-gun salute is fired as the governor and his wife make a grand entrance in their open horse-drawn landau. His Excellency inspects a military guard of honor, while the Bermuda Regiment Band plays. The stage is, of course, now set for the center of attention: presentation of *a* peppercorn, which sits on a silver plate atop a velvet cushion. Payment is made in a grand and formal manner, after which the Old State House is immediately used for a meeting of Her Majesty's Council.
**Admission:** Free.
**Open:** Wed 10am–4pm. **Bus:** No. 1, 3, 8, 10, or 11 from Hamilton.

**DELIVERANCE II, Ordnance Island. Tel. 809/297-1459.**
Across from St. George's town square and over a bridge is Ordnance Island, where

visitors see a full-scale replica of *Deliverance I,* a pinnace (small sailing ship) constructed in 1609 by the shipwrecked survivors of the *Sea Venture* to carry them on to Virginia.

A tape recording guides visitors through the ship. Alongside *Deliverance II* is the ducking stool, a replica of a horrible contraption used in 17th-century witch trials. Its use is demonstrated on Wednesday only.

**Admission:** $2 adults, 50¢ children.
**Open:** Daily 10am–4pm. **Bus:** No. 1, 3, 8, 10, or 11 from Hamilton.

### ST. PETER'S CHURCH, Duke of York St. Tel. 809/297-8359.

Back on King's Square, head east to the Duke of York Street, where St. Peter's Church, believed to be the oldest Anglican place of worship in the Western Hemisphere, is located. The original church on this spot, built by colonists in 1612 almost entirely of cedar with a palmetto-leaf thatch roof, was almost destroyed by a hurricane in 1712. Some of the interior, including the original altar from 1615 (still in daily use) was salvaged, and the church was rebuilt in 1713. It has been restored many times since and provides excellent examples of architectural work of the 17th to the 20th centuries. The tower was added in 1814. On display in the vestry is a silver communion service given to the church by King William III in 1697. Before the Old State House was constructed, the colony held public meetings in the church. The first assize convened here in 1616, and the first meeting of Parliament was in 1620. Sunday and weekday services are conducted here.

**Admission:** Free, but donations appreciated.
**Open:** Daily 10am–4:30pm (guide available Mon–Sat). **Bus:** No. 1, 3, 8, 10, or 11 from Hamilton.

### GRAVEYARD OF ST. PETER'S, entrance opposite Broad Alley.

Some of the tombstones in this graveyard are more than three centuries old; many tombs mark the graves of slaves. Here you'll also find the grave of Midshipman Richard Dale, an American, who was the last victim of the War of 1812. The churchyard also contains the tombs of Gov. Sir Richard Sharples and his aide, Capt. Hugh Sayers, who were murdered while walking the grounds of Government House in 1973.

**Bus:** No. 1, 3, 8, 10, or 11 from Hamilton.

### CONFEDERATE MUSEUM, King's Square. Tel. 809/297-1423.

This was once the Globe Hotel, headquarters of Maj. Norman Walker, the Confederate representative in Bermuda, and contains relics from the island's involvement in the American Civil War. St. George's was the port from which ships carrying arms and munitions ran the Union blockade. A replica of the Great Seal of the Confederacy is fitted to a Victorian press so that visitors can emboss copies as souvenirs.

**Admission:** $3 adults, free for children under 12.
**Open:** Mon–Sat 10am–5pm. **Closed:** Public holidays. **Bus:** No. 1, 3, 8, 10, or 11 from Hamilton.

### TUCKER HOUSE MUSEUM, 5 Water St. Tel. 809/297-0545.

This was the home of the well-known Tucker family of England, Bermuda, and Virginia. It displays a notable collection of Bermudian furniture, portraits, and silver. Also in the Tucker House is the Joseph Rainey Memorial Room, where this African American refugee (mentioned above) of the Civil War practiced barbering.

**Admission:** $3 adults, free for children under 12 years.
**Open:** Mon–Sat 10am–5pm. **Closed:** Public holidays. **Bus:** No. 1, 3, 8, 10, or 11 from Hamilton.

### CARRIAGE MUSEUM, 22 Water St. Tel. 809/297-1367.

Transportation in Bermuda was only by carriage until 1946, when the "automobile age" arrived. Many of these old conveyances have been preserved to delight present-day visitors to Hamilton. The museum is in a renovated old Royal Engineers warehouse, located next to Somers Wharf.

**Admission:** "By donation."

**Open:** Mon–Fri 10am–5pm. **Closed:** Public holidays. **Bus:** No. 1, 3, 8, 10, or 11 from Hamilton.

### SOMERS GARDEN, Duke of York St. Tel. 809/297-1532.

The heart of Sir George Somers was buried here in 1610; a stone column perpetuates the memory of Bermuda's founder. The garden was opened in 1920 by the Prince of Wales (later King of England and subsequently Duke of Windsor).

**Admission:** Free.

**Open:** Daily 8am–4pm. **Bus:** No. 1, 3, 8, 10, or 11 from Hamilton.

### UNFINISHED CATHEDRAL, Blockade Alley.

After leaving Somers Garden, head up the steps to the North Gate, which opens onto Blockade Alley. The structure here is known as the "folly of St. George's." The plan was that this cathedral, begun in 1874, would replace St. Peter's. But the planners ran into money troubles, then a schism developed, and, as if that weren't enough, a storm swept over the island and caused considerable damage to the structure. Result: the Unfinished Cathedral.

**Bus:** No. 1, 3, 8, 10, or 11 from Hamilton.

### ST. GEORGE'S HISTORICAL SOCIETY MUSEUM, 3 Featherbed Alley. Tel. 809/297-0423.

Housed in a home built around 1700, this museum contains an original 18th-century Bermuda kitchen complete with utensils from that period. Exhibits include a 300-year-old Bible, a letter from George Washington, and American Indian ax heads. (Some early settlers on St. David's Island were Native Americans, mainly Pequot.)

**Admission:** $2 adults, 50¢ children 16 and under.

**Open:** Sun–Fri 10am–4pm. **Bus:** No. 1, 3, 8, 10, or 11 from Hamilton.

### FEATHERBED ALLEY PRINTERY, in Featherbed Alley. Tel. 809/297-0009.

Here you'll find a working press—the kind invented by Gutenberg in the 1450s—that was in use for some 350 years. The alley gets its name because featherbeds were placed here for drunks to sleep on until they could sober up.

**Admission:** Free.

**Open:** Mon–Sat 10am–4pm. **Bus:** No. 1, 3, 8, 10, or 11 from Hamilton.

### OLD RECTORY, at the head of Broad Alley, behind St. Peter's Church. Tel. 809/297-0879.

Built by a reformed pirate in 1705, this charming old Bermuda cottage was later inhabited by Parson Richardson, who was nicknamed the "Little Bishop." Now a private home, it's administrated by the Bermuda National Trust.

**Admission:** Free, but donations are appreciated.

**Open:** Wed 10am–5pm. **Bus:** No. 1, 3, 8, 10, or 11 from Hamilton.

### ST. GEORGE'S LIBRARY, 5 Queen St. Tel. 809/297-1912.

St. George's Library is in an 18th-century Bermuda home, Stuart Hall. Cedar-

beamed rooms and Bermuda furniture provide a cozy atmosphere in this circulation library, a branch of the Bermuda Public Library.
**Admission:** Free.
**Open:** Mon and Wed 10am–1pm and 2–6pm, Sat 10am–1pm and 2–5pm. **Bus:** No. 1, 3, 8, 10, or 11 from Hamilton.

**BRIDGE HOUSE, 1 Bridge St. Tel. 809/297-8211.**
One of the best known galleries in Bermuda, this displays only works by Bermudian artists, including Alfred Birdsey. Owned by the National Trust, the house was constructed in the very early years of the 18th century. It was home to several of the colony's governors. Perhaps its most colorful owner was Bridger Goodrich, a Loyalist from Virginia, whose privateers once blockaded Chesapeake Bay. So devoted was he to the king that he also sabotaged Bahamian vessels trading with the American colonies. The house is called Bridge because a bridge used to stand over a muddy creek (filled in now).
**Admission:** Free.
**Open:** Mon, Thurs, Fri, Sat 10am–5pm; Tues–Wed 10am–9pm; Sun 11am–3pm. Mid-Jan to mid-Feb Wed and Sat only, 10am–5pm. **Bus:** No. 1, 3, 8, 10, or 11.

## ON THE OUTSKIRTS OF TOWN

From its earliest days St. George's has been fortified, and although it never saw much military action, the reminders of those former days are interesting to explore. On the outskirts of the town, the forts are reached by Circular Drive.
Nearby, along the coast, is **Building Bay,** where the shipwrecked victims of the *Sea Venture* built their vessel, the *Deliverance,* in 1610.

**GATES FORT, Cut Rd. No phone.**
Gates Fort was built by Sir Thomas Gates, one of the original band of settlers on the *Sea Venture.* The fort dates from 1609. Gates was governor-designate for the colony of Virginia.
**Open:** Daily 10am–4:30pm. **Bus:** No. 1, 3, 8, 10, or 11.

**FORT ST. CATHERINE, Barry Rd. Tel. 809/297-1920.**
Towering above the beach where the shipwrecked crew of the *Sea Venture* came ashore in 1609 is Fort St. Catherine, first completed in 1614 and named for the patron saint of wheelwrights and carpenters. The fortifications were upgraded over the years. The last major reconstruction occurred from 1865 to 1878, so the fort's appearance today is largely the result of work done in the 19th century.
Now a museum, visitors begin their visits by seeing a series of dioramas, "Highlights in Bermuda's History." Museum figures are used to show various activities taking place in the Magazine of the fort, restored and refurnished as it was in the 1880s. Large Victorian muzzle-loading cannons can be seen on their original carriages. In the Keep, which served as the living quarters of the fort, you can see information on local and overseas regiments that served in Bermuda, a fine small-arms exhibit, a cooking-area display, and an exhibition of replicas of the crown jewels of England. A short audiovisual show on the St. George's defense systems and the forts of St. George's can be seen here.
**Admission:** $2.50 adults, free for children under 12.
**Open:** Daily 10am–4:30pm. **Closed:** Christmas Day.
**Bus:** No. 1, 3, 8, 10, or 11 from Hamilton.

# 3. HAMILTON PARISH

Around Harrington Sound, the sights differ greatly from those of St. George's—more action, less history. Public buses 1 or 3 from Hamilton get you here in about an hour. Hamilton Parish is bordered on the east by St. George's and on the southwest by Smith's Parish. The parish encloses **Harrington Sound,** a landlocked saltwater lake that is 1½ miles at its widest and 2⅛ miles long. It was named for John, first Lord Harrington of Rutland, England.

Some experts believe that way back in unrecorded time Harrington Sound was a cave that fell in. Its gateway to the ocean is through an inlet at Flatts Village. However, it is believed that there are underwater gateways as well. Several deep-sea fish have been caught in the sound.

For the best sightseeing view of the parish, visitors head for **Crawl Hill,** right before they come to Bailey's Bay. At this point, the highest place in Hamilton Parish, you can enjoy a view of the North Shore. Crawl is a corruption of the word "kraal," where turtles were kept before slaughter. Shelly Bay, named for one of the passengers of the *Sea Venture,* is the longest beach along the North Shore.

The **Hamilton Parish Church,** reached by going down Trinity Church Road, stands on Church Bay and dates from 1623, when it was just a one-room structure. It has been much altered over three and a half centuries.

**BERMUDA PERFUMERY, 212 North Shore Rd., Bailey's Bay. Tel. 809/ 293-0627.**
Lili Perfumes are made here. Visitors are given guided tours showing the perfume-making process, including the old method of extracting scents from native flowers. Among the fragrances produced are passion flower, Bermuda Easter lily, and oleander jasmine. A small botanic garden with a seating area and walkways provides an attractive resting place. You can also visit the orchid house, with its more than 500 orchids, and the nature trail, which passes through a large area of the property that is planted with tropical flowers, shrubs, and trees. The perfumery has a gift shop, the Calabash.

**Admission:** Free.
**Open:** Mon–Sat 9am–5pm, Sun 10am–4pm. **Bus:** No. 1 or 3. **Closed:** Sun in winter.

**BERMUDA AQUARIUM, ZOOLOGICAL GARDEN, AND NATURAL HISTO-RY MUSEUM, North Shore Rd., Flatts Village. Tel. 809/298-2727.**
Across Flatts Bridge, this complex is home to an amazing collection of tropical marine fish, turtles, harbor seals, and other forms of sea life. In the museum you can see exhibits on the geological development of Bermuda, deep-sea exploration, and humpback whales. The complex also has a zoo with Galapagos tortoises, alligators, and monkeys, along with an outstanding collection of birds, including parrots and flamingos.

You can bring a picnic lunch or choose from one of several restaurants in Flatts Village. There is parking for cycles and cars across the street from the Aquarium.
**Admission:** $5 adults, $2 children ages 5–12, free for children under 5.
**Open:** Daily 9am–5pm. **Closed:** Christmas Day. **Bus:** Take no. 10 or 11 from Hamilton, or no. 10 or 11 from St. George's. **Directions:** From Hamilton, follow Middle Road or North Shore Road east to Flatts Village; from St. George's, once over the causeway, follow North Shore Road or Harrington Sound Road west to Flatts Village.

**CRYSTAL CAVES, 8 Crystal Caves Rd., off Wilkinson Ave., Bailey's Bay. Tel. 809/293-0640.**

⭐ This cave is composed of translucent formations of stalagmites and stalactites, a setting including the crystal-clear Cahow Lake. Discovered in 1907, the cave is reached by a gently sloping path and a few steps. At the bottom, some 120 feet below the surface, is a floating causeway that follows the winding cavern, where hidden lights illuminate the glistening interior. All tours through Crystal Caves are guided.

**Admission:** $3 adults, $1.50 children ages 5–11.

**Open:** Feb–Mar and Nov–Dec Sun–Fri 10am–4pm; Apr–Oct daily 9:30am–4:30pm. **Closed:** Jan. **Bus:** No. 1 or 3.

**LEAMINGTON CAVES, 46 Harrington Sound Rd., Bailey's Bay. Tel. 809/293-1188.**

⭐ This grotto, which is attached to the Plantation Club, has stunning crystal formations and underground lakes. It was first discovered by a young boy, who noticed a small opening on the rocky hillside that he and his father were clearing for plowing in 1908. He slipped through the hole with a rope and candles and found a wonderland of natural cave splendors some 1.5 million years old. Guided tours take you along lighted walkways with hand rails, through the high-vaulted, amber-tinted grotto.

*Note:* Also at Bailey's Bay, **Tom Moore's Jungle** consists of wild woods. The poet Tom Moore is said to have spent many hours writing poetry under a still-standing calabash tree. Since the jungle is held in private trust, permission has to be obtained to enter it. It's much easier to pay your respects to the Romantic poet by calling at the Tom Moore Tavern (see "Hamilton Parish" in Chapter 5, "Where to Dine in Bermuda").

**Admission:** $3 adults, $1 children ages 4–12, free for children under 4.

**Open:** Mon–Sat 9:30am–4pm. **Closed:** Dec–Feb. **Bus:** No. 1 or 3.

**DEVIL'S HOLE AQUARIUM, 92 Harrington Sound Rd. Tel. 809/293-2072.**

The pool of this former cave is fed by the sea through half a mile of subterranean passages. A natural aquarium, it's stocked with some 400 individual fish, including moray eels, sharks, giant groupers, and massive green turtles. Visitors can tempt the pond's inhabitants with baited but hookless lines. It has been open to the public since 1834.

**Admission:** $5 adults, $3 children ages 6–12, $1.50 children under 5.

**Open:** Apr–Aug daily 9am–5pm; Sept–Mar 10am–4:15pm. **Bus:** No. 1 or 3.

# 4. SMITH'S PARISH

Smith's Parish, named for Sir Thomas Smith, a member of the Bermuda Company, faces the open sea on both its northern and southern borders. To the east is Harrington Sound, and to the west, bucolic Devonshire Parish.

The parish takes in **Flatts Village,** one of the most charming little parish towns of Bermuda, reached by bus 10 or 11 from Hamilton. This was a smugglers' port for about 200 years. The origin of the name is lost to history. Once it was the center of power for a coterie of successful "planter politicians" and landowners. Their government ranked in importance second only to that of St. George's, then the capital. People gathered at the rickety Flatts Bridge to "enjoy" such public entertainment as a hanging on the gallows. A so-called blasphemer in 1718 had his tongue bored through with a fire-hot poker. If the offense was serious enough, victims were drawn and quartered here. From Flatts Village you'll have good views of both the inlet and Harrington Sound.

At the top of McGall's Hill, which you can visit after seeing the Verdmont mansion (see below), is **St. Mark's Church.** A church built in 1746 once stood near the site of St. Mark's. When it became unsafe, a local family, the Trotts, donated land for the construction of St. Mark's, on which construction began in 1846, with the first services conducted on Easter Sunday in 1848. Work on the church continued, however, and subsequent additions—such as the chancel—were made until the closing years of the 19th century. St. Mark's Church was based on the same designs as the Old Devonshire Parish Church.

**VERDMONT, 6 Verdmont Lane, Smith's Parish (tel. 809/236-7369).**

This is an 18th-century mansion that holds a special significance to U.S. citizens interested in colonial and Revolutionary War history. It stands on property owned in the 17th century by William Sayle, who left Bermuda to found South Carolina on the American mainland and then became its first governor. The house was built before 1710 by John Dickinson, a prosperous ship owner who was also Speaker of the House of Assembly in Bermuda from 1707 to 1710. Verdmont passed to Mr. Dickinson's granddaughter, Elizabeth, who married the Hon. Thomas Smith, Collector of Customs. Their oldest daughter, Mary, married Judge John Green, a Loyalist who came to Bermuda in 1765 from Philadelphia. During and after the American Revolution, Green was judge of the Vice-Admirality Court and had the final say on prizes brought in by privateers. Many American shipowners lost their vessels through his decisions. The house is now administrated by the National Trust. It contains many antiques, china, and portraits, along with the finest cedar stair balustrade in Bermuda.

**Admission:** $3 adults, children under 12 free.

**Open:** Apr–Oct Mon–Sat 9:30am–4:30pm; Nov–Mar Mon–Fri 10am–4pm. **Closed:** One week in either Jan or Feb (dates vary). **Bus:** No. 1 from Hamilton or St. George's.

**SPITTAL POND, South Shore Rd. No phone.**

Follow the rather steep Knapton Hill Road west to South Shore Road, turning at the sign for Spittal Pond, Bermuda's largest wildlife sanctuary. The most important of the National Trust's open spaces, it is 60 acres in extent and contains about 25 species of waterfowl, which can be seen annually from November to May. Visitors are asked to keep to the scenic trails and footpaths provided. Bird-watchers, in particular, visit in January, when as many as 500 species of birds can be observed wintering on the pond.

Spittal Pond also shelters **Spanish Rock,** on a cliff facing the sea. It contains a cipher dating from 1543, probably carved by an Iberian mariner who may have been shipwrecked here.

**Admission:** Free.

**Open:** Daily sunrise to sunset. **Bus:** No. 1 or 3.

# 5. DEVONSHIRE PARISH

As you wander its narrow lanes, with some imagination you can picture yourself in the original Devon in England. The parish takes its name from the first Earl of Devonshire. It is a lush, hilly parish, rarely spoiled by commercial intrusions.

Along the North Shore Road is **Devonshire Dock,** long a seafarer's haven, near the border to Pembroke Parish. Fishermen still bring in such catches as grouper and rockfish, so you can shop for dinner if you've been fortunate enough to get a nearby cottage with a kitchen. British soldiers in the War of 1812 came here to be entertained by local women.

At the **Arboretum** on Middle Road, you'll discover one of the most tranquil oases in Bermuda, an open space with a wide range of Bermudian plant and tree life. It was created by the Department of Agriculture and Fisheries.

Along the South Shore Road, you can visit the **Edmund Gibbons Nature Reserve,** west of the junction with Collector's Hill. This portion of marshland, owned by the National Trust, provides living space for a number of birds and rare species of Bermuda flora. It's open daily at no charge. Visitors must keep out of the marshy area.

## OLD DEVONSHIRE CHURCH, Middle Rd. Tel. 809/236-3671.

On Middle Road stands the Old Devonshire Parish Church, a house of worship said to have been built on the site in 1624, although the present foundation is from 1716. This is the major attraction of the parish. An explosion virtually destroyed the church on Easter in 1970, but it was reconstructed. Today the church is very tiny, looking almost more like a vicarage than a church. Some of the church relics survived the blast, including silver from 1590, said to be the oldest on the island. The church is built of limestone, with a high pitched roof constructed in the early English style. It was designed by Sir George Grove. The Old Devonshire Parish Church stands northwest of the "new" Devonshire Parish Church which dates from 1846.

**Admission:** Free.

**Open:** Daily 9am–5:30pm. **Bus:** No. 2.

## PALM GROVE, 38 South Shore Rd. No phone.

One of the delights of Devonshire Parish, this private estate lies 2½ miles east of Hamilton. Its famous for the pond that has a relief map of Bermuda in the middle of it. Each parish is an immaculately manicured grassy division. A much-photographed Desmond Fountain stands at the edge of the pond. The site, which has some stunning flower gardens, opens onto a view of the sea.

**Admission:** Free.

**Open:** Mon–Fri 9am–5pm. **Bus:** No. 1.

# 6. PEMBROKE PARISH (CITY OF HAMILTON)

The city of Hamilton is not in Hamilton Parish but in Pembroke Parish, which is a peninsula that opens at its northern rim onto the vast Atlantic Ocean and on its southern side onto the beautiful Hamilton Harbour. Its western border edges Great Sound. The parish is named after the third Earl of Pembroke, who was a power in the Bermuda Company of 1616. Nearly one-fourth of Bermuda's population lives in Pembroke Parish, most of them in the capital of Hamilton.

The ideal way to see Hamilton, or the parish itself, for the first time is to sail in through Hamilton Harbour, past the offshore cays. You'll join fishermen and the yachting set and cruise ships.

The Irish poet Tom Moore and the American humorist Mark Twain publicized the glories of Bermuda, but, for the British at least, the woman who put Bermuda on the tourist map was Princess Louise. The daughter of Queen Victoria, she spent several months in Bermuda in 1883. Her husband was the governor-general of Canada, so she traveled to Bermuda to escape the fierce cold up north. Although in the 20th century Bermuda was to play host to a string of royal visitors, including Queen Elizabeth II, Princess Louise was the first royal personage to set foot in the colony. And once she was here she turned up all over the island, visiting and chatting with its friendly people and winning their respect and admiration. Upon reaching Canada, she told reporters that she'd found the Shangri-La of tourist destinations.

In the early days there was only one hotel, the Hamilton Hotel on Church Street, which was destroyed by fire in 1955. The Hamilton Princess hotel, still in existence and named in honor of Princess Louise, opened in 1884. Over the years it has had a colorful history, none more dramatic than when it was taken over by Allied agents in World War II.

If Princess Louise were to visit today, she would most likely be housed at **Government House,** which stands on North Shore Road and Langton Hill. Not open to the public, it is the magnificent residence of the governor of the island. The large and beautiful grounds may be viewed on application to the governor's aide-de-camp. A Victorian residence, it has sheltered many notable guests, including Queen Elizabeth II and her husband, Prince Philip, as well as Prince Charles, Sir Winston Churchill, and President John F. Kennedy. The saddest moment for Government House was in 1973, when Gov. Sir Richard Sharples and his aide, Capt. Hugh Sayers, along with the governor's dog, Horsa, were assassinated while walking on the grounds. This led to a state of emergency in Bermuda.

While touring Pembroke Parish, visitors are fond of looking at **Black Watch Well** at the junction of North Shore Road and Black Watch Pass. Excavated by a detachment of the Black Watch Regiment, the well was ordered dug in 1894, when Bermudians suffered through a long drought.

# CITY OF HAMILTON

Since 1815 Hamilton has been the capital of Bermuda. Hamilton was once known as the "Show Window of the British Empire." Both Mark Twain and Eugene O'Neill, who lived in places opening onto Hamilton Harbour, cited the beauty of the place. On little islands in the harbor, prisoners-of-war and victims of plague were held in prison or in quarantine, respectively.

A stroll along Front Street will take you by some of Hamilton's most elegant stores, but you'll want to branch off into the little alleyways to check the shops and boutiques to be found there. If you get tired of walking or shopping (or both), you can also go down to the docks and take one of the boats or catamarans waiting to show you the treasures of Little Sound and Great Sound.

On some days you may get to see locals buying their fresh fish—that is, that part of the catch not earmarked for restaurants—right from the fisherpeople who sell the "catch of the day" at Front Street docks. Although rockfish seems to turn up more often than any other fish, you'll also see snapper, grouper, and many other species. In the 1930s, seaplanes would land passengers right in Hamilton Harbour.

Most Bermudians consider the winter months too cold to wear Bermuda shorts, but come May, all the businesspeople along Front Street seem to don a pair. The British military introduced these shorts to Bermuda in the early part of the 20th century. By the 1920s and 1930s the garment had become very fashionable, although they were not worn to dinner parties or to church services. Originally worn with a white shirt, a tie, a jacket, and knee stockings, it was considered "daring" to wear the shorts five inches above the knee. And to go beyond that and wear Bermuda short-shorts could have gotten you ticketed by the police in the years after World War II. For some, Bermuda shorts, at least at summer cocktail parties, remain de rigueur.

Most people come to Hamilton to shop, but the city also contains a number of sightseeing attractions. Named for a former governor, Henry Hamilton, it was incorporated as a town in 1793. In 1815, because of its central location and its large, protected harbor, it was chosen as the island's new capital, replacing St. George's. Since Hamilton occupies only 182 acres of land in its entirety, it is most often explored on foot.

Today Hamilton is the hub of the island's economy, but long before it got such fancy labels as "showcase of the Atlantic," it was a modest outlet for the export of Bermuda cedar and fresh vegetables.

Hamilton boasts the largest number of eating and drinking establishments in Bermuda, especially on or near Front Street. These restaurants charge a wide range of prices, and there are many English-style pubs if you'd like to go on a pub crawl. Although there is a huge conglomeration of bars, religion isn't neglected—there are 12 churches within the city limits, one or two of which merit a sightseeing visit.

Hamilton should be seen not only on land but also from the water, and there are frequent boating tours of the harbor and its coral reefs to enable you to do so. If you're visiting from other parishes, the ferry will let you off at the western end of Front Street, which is ideal if you'd like to pay a call to the **Visitors Service Bureau** and pick up a map. The location is near the Ferry Terminal. The staff here also provides information and helpful brochures. Hours are 9am to 4:45pm Monday through Saturday.

To return to the parishes of Paget, Warwick, and Sandys, ferries leave daily between 6:50am and 11:20pm. On Saturday and Sunday, there are fewer departures.

Opposite the Visitors Service Bureau stands the much-photographed **"Bird Cage,"** where it used to be possible to see a police officer directing traffic. Such a sight is now rare. Visitors wondered for years if the traffic director was for real or placed there for tourist photographs.

Nearby is **Albuoy's Point,** site of the Royal Bermuda Yacht Club, founded in 1844. The point, named after a 17th-century professor of "physick," is a public park overlooking Hamilton Harbour.

## PUBLIC LIBRARY AND BERMUDA HISTORICAL SOCIETY MUSEUM, 13 Queen St., Par-la-Ville Park. Tel. 809/295-2487.

After leaving the harbor, proceed up Queen Street to the Public Library and the Bermuda Historical Society Museum, which has a collection of old cedar furniture, antique silver, early Bermuda coins (hog money), and costumes, plus the sea chest and navigating lodestone of Sir George Somers, whose flagship, *Sea Venture,* was stranded on Bermuda's reefs in 1609. You will also find portraits of Sir George and Lady Somers as well as models of the ill-fated *Sea Venture,* along with models of *Patience* and *Deliverance.*

The library and museum lie in **Par-la-Ville Park** on Queen Street, which still dwells in the 19th century. It was designed by William Bennett Perot, Hamilton's first postmaster—from 1818–1862—and an eccentric one at that. As he delivered mail around the town, he is said to have placed letters in the crown of his top hat, so as to preserve his dignity. You enter the park by the landmark rubber tree, planted in 1847.

**Admission** (library and museum): Free.

**Open** (library and museum): Mon–Tues and Thurs–Sat 9:30am–12:30pm and 1:45–4:30pm. **Bus:** No. 1, 2, 10, or 11.

**PEROT POST OFFICE, Queen St., at the entrance to Par-la-Ville Park. Tel. 809/295-5151.**

Bermuda's first stamp was printed in this landmark building. Beloved by collectors from all over the world, the stamps, signed by Perot, are considered priceless. It is said that Perot and his friend, Heyl, who ran an apothecary shop, conceived the first postage stamp to protect the post office from cheaters. People used to stop off at the post office and leave letters but not enough pennies to send them. The postage stamps were printed in either black or carmine.

Philatelists can purchase Bermuda stamps of today in this same post office. For its 375th anniversary, Bermuda issued stamps honoring its 1609 discovery. One stamp portrays the admiral of the fleet, Sir George Somers, along with Sir Thomas Gates, the captain of the *Sea Venture*. Another depicts a building in the settlement of Jamestown, Virginia, which was on the verge of extinction when Sir George and the survivors of the Bermuda shipwreck finally arrived with supplies in late 1610. A third shows the *Sea Venture* stranded on the coral reefs of Bermuda. Yet another shows the entire fleet, originally bound for Jamestown, leaving Plymouth, England, on June 2, 1609.

**Admission:** Free.
**Open:** Mon–Fri 9am–5pm. **Bus:** No. 1, 2, 10, or 11.

**HAMILTON CITY HALL, 17 Church St. Tel. 809/292-1234.**

The city hall is an imposing white structure with a giant weather vane and wind clock to tell maritime-minded Bermudians which way the wind is blowing. Completed in 1960, the building is headquarters for Hamilton's municipal government. The theater on the first floor is the scene for stage, music, and dance productions throughout the year, and is also the main site of the Bermuda Festival. City Hall is also the venue for **The Bermuda National Gallery** (see below).

**Admission:** Free.
**Open:** Mon–Fri 9am–5pm. **Bus:** No. 1, 2, 10, or 11.

**BERMUDA NATIONAL GALLERY, City Hall, 17 Church St. Tel. 809/295-9428.**

Located in the East Wing of City Hall, the Bermuda National Gallery is the home of The Masterworks Bermudiana Collection, with artwork from artists such as Georgia O'Keefe, Winslow Homer, Charles Demuth, Albert Gleizes, Ogden Pleissner, and Jack Bush. The Masterworks Foundation was established in 1987 to return to the island works of art that depict Bermuda and to exhibit them.

The Bermuda National Gallery is also home to the Hereward T. Watlington collection, which includes paintings from the 15th to 19th centuries of artists such as Reynolds, Gainsborough, and deHooch. The gallery also has displays of smaller paintings and watercolors collected by the Bermuda Archives and National Trust, as well as a room for changing exhibits.

While a National Gallery for Bermuda has been long overdue, Bermuda's humid climate and damaging sunlight made it necessary to build a gallery with proper climate control and lighting. As a result, The **Bermuda Fine Art Trust** was developed and was incorporated by an Act of Parliament in 1982. In 1988, the Hon. Hereward T. Watlington bequeathed his collection of European paintings to the people of Bermuda on condition that they be housed in a European-standard climate-controlled environment. The Corporation of Hamilton offered the use of the East Exhibition Room of City Hall and gave a financial donation to begin construction of a proper facility.

**Admission:** $3 adults; children under 16 admitted free.
**Open:** Mon–Fri 10am–4pm; Sat 10am–noon. **Bus:** No. 1, 2, 10, or 11.

### CATHEDRAL OF THE MOST HOLY TRINITY, Church St. Tel. 809/292-4033.

A short distance away, the Bermuda Cathedral on Church Street is the so-called mother church of the Anglican diocese. It was given status as a cathedral in 1894 and formally consecrated in 1911. A comprehensive restoration and enhancement program has just been carried out. Features of the building are a splendid reredos, magnificent stained glass windows, and the carvings of the choir stalls.

**Admission:** Free.

**Open:** Daily 7:15am–5pm. **Bus:** No. 1, 2, 10, or 11.

### SESSIONS HOUSE, 21 Parliament St. Tel. 809/292-7408.

Built in the 1820s, this is an Italian Renaissance–style structure with the Jubilee Clock Tower, constructed in the jubilee year of Queen Victoria. The House of Assembly meets on the second floor, and visitors are allowed in the gallery (call 809/292-1350 to learn the time of assemblies). On the lower floor, the chief justice presides over the Supreme Court.

**Admission:** Free.

**Open:** Mon–Fri 9am–5pm. **Bus:** No. 1, 2, 10, or 11.

# 7. PAGET PARISH

Visitors flock to Paget for its beautiful South Shore beaches, the best on the chain of islands. Named after the fourth Lord Paget, the parish has a lot of historic homes and gardens, but most of them are not open to public view, except on special occasions. During the springtime College Weeks, the Elbow Beach Hotel is the center of most activities.

Most visitors who stay here in one of the section's many hotels use the ferry service, with landing docks at Salt Kettle, Hodson's, and Lower Ferry. It's also possible to "commute" by ferry to Warwick Parish or Sandys Parish to the west.

Paget Parish is the setting of **Chelston,** on Grape Bay Drive, the official residence of the U.S. consul-general (which is open only during the Garden Club of Bermuda's open-houses-and-gardens program in the spring). It stands on 14½ acres of land-scaped grounds overlooking South Shore Rd.

### BOTANICAL GARDENS, Point Finger Rd., South Shore Rd. Tel. 809/236-4201.

This 36-acre landscaped park is one of the major attractions of the island, with hundreds of flowers, shrubs, and trees all clearly identified; it is also riddled with pathways. Attractions include a garden of hibiscus (more than a hundred species of this flower alone), an aviary, and a miniature forest. It's best to take one of the 90-minute walking tours that depart at 10:30am on Tuesday, Wednesday, and Friday, in season, from the Visitor Centre. From mid-November through March, tours are only on Tuesday and Friday. You can always visit on your own, however.

**Admission:** Free.

**Open:** Daily, sunrise to sunset. **Bus:** No. 1, 2, or 7. If you're on a bike or moped, turn left off Middle Road onto Tee Street. At Berry Hill Road, go right. About a mile farther on to the left is the signposted turnoff to the gardens on Point Finger Road.

### WATERVILLE 5 The Lane (Harbour Rd.), corner of Pomander Rd. Tel. 809/236-6483.

This is one of the oldest (built prior to 1735) houses in Bermuda, and was the home of seven generations of the prominent Trimingham family. It was from the cellar storage rooms of this house that James Harvey Trimingham started, in 1842, the business that was to become Trimingham Brothers, Ltd., one of Bermuda's finest Front Street shops. Waterville is now the headquarters of the Bermuda National Trust and houses its office, reception rooms, and shop Trustworthy. Major renovations were carried out in 1811, and the house has been restored in this period. The two main rooms have also been furnished in this period, mainly with Trimingham family heirlooms specifically bequeathed for use in the house. Waterville is just west of the Trimingham roundabout very near the city of Hamilton.

**Admission:** Free.
**Open:** Mon–Fri 9am–5pm. **Shop:** Tues–Sat 10am–4pm. **Bus:** No. 8 from Hamilton.

**PAGET MARSH, Middle Rd. Tel. 809/236-6483.**

Paget Marsh is 18 acres of unspoiled woods and marshland, with vegetation and birdlife of ecological interest. It can be visited only when special arrangements are made with the National Trust (tel. 809/236-6483).

**Admission:** Free.
**Open:** Mon–Fri 9am–5pm by special arrangement. **Bus:** No. 8 from Hamilton.

**BIRDSEY STUDIO, Stowe Hill. Tel. 809/236-6658.**

One of Bermuda's best-known painters, Alfred Birdsey, invites visitors to his gallery. His son-in-law, Tony Davis, will probably be there to answer questions and quote prices for original works in watercolor and oils by the painter who has exhibited around the world. Birdsey is known for sun-washed landscapes and seascapes with Bermuda settings.

Birdsey's daughter, Antoinette, exhibits some of her flower paintings, while another daughter, Joanne, displays whimsical and amusing versions of animals for children.

**Open:** Mon–Fri 9am–4pm. **Bus:** No. 8 from Hamilton.

# 8. WARWICK PARISH

Famed for its two golf courses, this western parish of Bermuda was named after the second Earl of Warwick, a shareholder in the Bermuda Company of 1610.

**Warwick Long Bay,** on South Shore Road, with public conveniences, is one of the finest beaches of Bermuda and forms the major attraction of the parish. In the vicinity, you can go inside **Christ Church,** across from the Belmont Hotel on Middle Road, daily from 9am to 4pm. Built in 1719, it is one of the oldest Scottish Presbyterian churches in the New World.

If you're in the parish on a Sunday morning, it seems that nearly everyone heads for Paw Paws Restaurant, a popular place serving local Bermudian food (see "Warwick Parish" in Chapter 5, "Where to Dine in Bermuda").

# 9. SOUTHAMPTON PARISH

This parish is a narrow strip of land opening at its northern rim onto Little Sound and on its southern shore onto the wide Atlantic Ocean. It is bordered by Warwick Parish in the east and Sandys Parish in the west. The U.S. Naval Air Station Annex is also here. If you see red flags hoisted in the area, take care. They're there to warn of aerial firing.

Celebrated for its beaches, the parish was named after the third Earl of Southampton. **Horseshoe Bay** is one of Bermuda's most attractive public beaches, with changing rooms, a snackbar, and space for parking.

**GIBBS HILL LIGHTHOUSE, Gibbs Hill, Lighthouse Road between South Shore Rd. and Middle Rd. Tel. 809/238-0524.**

The main attraction of this parish is the Gibbs Hill Lighthouse, built in 1846. It is the oldest cast-iron lighthouse in the world. The magnificent view of the Bermuda islands and its sweeping shoreline from the outlook balcony at the top is worth the 185-step climb. The workings of the machinery are explained by the lighthouse keeper. In spring, visitors may see migrating whales beyond the South Shore reefs. You can see a collection of shipwreck artifacts recovered by Teddy Tucker.

**Admission:** $2 (free for children under 5).

**Open:** Daily 9am–4:30pm. **Bus:** No. 7 or 8 from Hamilton.

# 10. SANDYS PARISH

There are those who on arrival in Bermuda head directly for Sandys Parish and never leave until it's time to go home. For many, the far-western tip of Bermuda is that special, with its rolling hills, lush countryside, and pleasant bays. The parish is actually made up of a group of islands, and was named in honor of Sir Edwin Sandys, one of the shareholders of the original Somers Island (Bermuda) Company, as well as a director of the Virginia Company and the East India Company.

**Somerset Island,** the largest of the Sandys group, where the village of Somerset lies, pays tribute to Sir George Somers of *Sea Venture* fame; Sandys Parish is often called Somerset. Somehow it has always stood apart from the rest of Bermuda. For example, during the U.S. Civil War, when most of the country sympathized with the Confederate cause, Sandys Parish stood firmly in the Union camp.

To explore this tip of the fishhook of Bermuda, it is best to take a ferry (fare of $3) plying the Great Sound, a 45-minute run from Hamilton to Waterford Bridge. Bikes can be taken aboard the ferry (motor-assisted cycles are assessed $3). Ferries also stop at Cavello Bay, Somerset, and the Royal Naval Dockyard. The **Visitors Service Bureau** is on Somerset Road near St. James' Church (tel. 809/234-1388). It's open Monday through Saturday from 10am to 4pm from May through November. After leaving Fort Scaur (see below), you can continue on the 17th-century **Somerset Bridge,** the world's smallest drawbridge. When open for marine traffic, the space between the spans is a mere 22 inches at road level. Much photographed, it is just big enough to allow the mast of a sailboat to pass through.

On Somerset Road is the **Scaur Lodge Property,** an open area that includes the site of Scaur Lodge, a Bermuda cottage that was severely damaged by a waterspout that moved up on land, turning into a tornado and driving across this neck of Somerset Island. This typical Bermuda steep-shoreline hillside is open daily at no charge.

Sandys Parish has areas of great natural beauty, including **Somerset Long Bay,** a public beach, which the Bermuda Audubon Society is developing into a nature preserve; and **Mangrove Bay,** a protected beach right in the heart of **Somerset**

**Village.** You can take pictures from the public wharf. Try to walk around the old village; it's filled with typically Bermudian houses and contains some interesting shops.

**FORT SCAUR, Ely's Harbour, Somerset Rd. Tel. 809/234-0908.**

✪ On the highest hill in Somerset, this fort was part of a ring of fortifications constructed in the 19th century, during the troubled relations between Britain and the United States. Built as a last-ditch defense line for the Old Royal Naval Dockyard, the fort was skillfully constructed to take advantage of the land contours in order to be well camouflaged from the sea. It has subterranean passages and a dry moat that stretches across the land from Ely's Harbour to Great Sound. Fort Scaur was opened to visitors in 1957 and has become one of Somerset's most popular tourist attractions. The fort offers views of Ely's Harbour and Great Sound, and points as far away as St. David's Lighthouse and Fort St. Catherine can be seen with the free telescope. Picnic tables, benches, and restrooms in the fort are provided. Surrounding it are 22 acres of parkland filled with interesting trails, picnic areas, a rocky shoreline for fishing, and a public dock for access from the sea.

**Admission:** Free.

**Open:** Daily 10am–4:30pm. **Closed:** Christmas. **Bus:** No. 7 or 8 from Hamilton.

**SPRINGFIELD LIBRARY AND GILBERT NATURE RESERVE, Main Rd. Tel. 809/234-1980.**

In the center of the island stands Springfield, an old plantation home restored by the National Trust that today houses Somerset Library, a branch of the Bermuda Public Library. The Gilbert Nature Reserve consists of five acres of unspoiled woodland, and bears the name of the family who owned the property from the beginning of the 18th century until it was acquired by the Bermuda National Trust in conjunction with the Bermuda Audubon Society in 1973. No admission is charged for either the nature reserve, the home (the branch library), or the outbuildings (used as a nursery school).

**Admission:** Free.

**Open:** Nature reserve sunrise to sunset. **Library:** Mon and Wed 9am–1pm and 2–5pm; Sat 10am–1pm and 2–5pm. **Bus:** No. 7 or 8 from Hamilton.

**ST. JAMES' ANGLICAN CHURCH, Main Rd. No phone.**

This is considered one of the most beautiful churches in Bermuda. It was built on the site of a structure that was destroyed by a hurricane in 1780. The present church was built nine years later, although the north and south aisles were added in 1836, the entrance gates in 1872, and the spire and chancel in 1880. The church was struck by lightning in 1939 but has been restored.

**Admission:** Free.

**Open:** Daily 8am–7pm. **Bus:** No. 7 or 8 from Hamilton.

---

# 11. IRELAND ISLAND

A multimillion-dollar cruise-ship dock and tourist village has grown up in this historic area, which was used by the British navy until 1951. The site also shelters the Bermuda Maritime Museum, the Neptune Theatre, the Crafts Market, and the Bermuda Arts Centre. Ferries from Hamilton stop at Ireland Island, in the extreme west end of

Bermuda, once per hour from 7am to 6pm. The fare is $3 each way. A bus leaves Hamilton for the Royal Naval Dockyard every 15 minutes from 8am to 8pm Monday through Saturday. The journey takes one hour and costs $2.50 for adults, half price for children.

The **Royal Naval Dockyard** has been transformed into a park, with Victorian street lighting and a Terrace Pavilion and bandstand for concerts. Vendors can be found pushing carts filled with food, dry goods, and local crafts. A full-service marina with floating docks is in operation along with a marina clubhouse and showers.

On a historical note, when this dockyard, which had been on British Admiralty land, was sold in 1953 to the Bermudian government, it marked the end of British naval might in the western Atlantic.

**BERMUDA MARITIME MUSEUM, Old Royal Navy Dockyard, Ireland Island. Tel. 809/234-1333.**

In a large 19th-century fortress, built by convict labor, the museum continues to improve exhibits about Bermuda's nautical heritage. Its most famous exhibit is in the 1837 Shifting House, which was opened in 1979. It is devoted to various exhibits consisting of such artifacts as gold bars, pottery, jewelry, silver coins, and other items recovered from 16th- and 17th-century shipwrecks, including the *Sea Venture*. But most visitors come here to gaze at the Tucker Treasure.

A well-known local diver, Teddy Tucker, is credited with making the most significant marine archaeological find of this century when, in 1955, he discovered the wreck of the *San Antonio*, a Spanish vessel that went down off the coast of Bermuda in a violent storm in 1621. One of the great treasures of this find, the Pectoral Cross, was stolen only minutes before Queen Elizabeth II opened the museum in 1975. The priceless original cross was replaced by a fake. To this day, the original cross has never been recovered, and its mysterious disappearance is still the subject of much discussion.

The fortress' massive buildings of fitted stone, with their vaulted ceilings of English brick, are alone worth a visit. So are the 30-foot defensive ramparts; the underground tunnels, gunports, and magazines; and the water gate and pond for entry by boat from the sea. Exhibits in four exhibition halls illustrate the island's long, intimate connection with the sea—from Spanish exploration to 20th-century ocean liners, from overcanvassed racing dinghies to practical fishing boats, from shipbuilding and privateering to naval exploits. The Shifting House contains shipwreck exhibits, including some earthenware and pewter belonging to the English settlers aboard the *Sea Venture*, wrecked in 1609.

As you enter the Parade Ground at the entrance to the museum, you'll notice a 10-foot-high figure of King Neptune. This is a figurehead from the HMS *Irresistible*, recovered when the ship was broken up in 1891. The **Queen's Exhibition Hall** houses general maritime exhibits, including those on navigation, whaling, cable and wireless, and "Bermuda in Five Hours," this last a reference to the advertisements touting Pan American's early "flying boats." The building was constructed in 1850 for the storage of 4,860 barrels of gunpowder.

The **Forster Cooper Building** (from 1852) of the museum illustrates the history of the Royal Navy in Bermuda, including the Bromby Bottle Collection. This exhibit was opened in 1984 by Princess Margaret. The Boatloft houses part of the museum's boat collections, including the century-old fitted dinghy *Victory*, the 17-foot *Spirit of Bermuda*, and the *Rambler*, the only surviving Bermuda pilot gig. The original dockyard clock is a working exhibit on the upper floor, and chimes the quarters and the hours.

**Admission:** $6 adults, $2 children under 12.

**Open:** Daily 10am–4:30pm. **Closed:** Christmas. **Transportation:** Ferry from Hamilton. **Bus:** No. 7 or 8.

**THE NEPTUNE CINEMA, Cooperage Building, 4 Freeport Rd., opposite the Maritime Museum entrance. Tel. 809/234-2923.**

*The Attack on Washington,* an audiovisual presentation about Bermuda's unusual role in the War of 1812 between Britain and the United States, is shown here. The film graphically re-creates the burning, in Washington, D.C., of the Executive Mansion (White House—painted white after the smoke cleared), plus the eventual British defeat at Fort McHenry.

**Admission:** $2.50 adults, $1.50 children.

**Open:** Continuous shows start every half hour daily 10am–4pm. **Transportation:** Ferry from Hamilton. **Bus:** No. 7 or 8.

**BERMUDA CRAFT MARKET, in the Cooperage Building, 4 Freeport Rd. Tel. 809/234-3208.**

The market is the place to watch local artists at work and to buy their wares. Established in 1987, it offers works in Bermuda cedarwork, candles, clothing, dolls, fabrics, hand-painted items, jewelry, metal and gem sculpture, needlework, quilts, shell art, glass panels, and woven cane goods among other items.

**Admission:** Free.

**Open:** Daily 10:30am–4pm. **Transportation:** Ferry from Hamilton. **Bus:** No. 7 or 8.

**BERMUDA ARTS CENTRE, 4 Freeport Rd.**

Works and lectures by local and international artists are featured here. New exhibits are installed every month.

**Admission:** $1 adults, 50¢ children under 12 years, suggested as donation.

**Transportation:** Ferry from Hamilton.

# 12. COOL FOR KIDS

Families with children will enjoy a wide variety of activities April through October when family fun can consist of water sports such as sailing, water skiing, snorkeling, or glass-bottom boat trips; tennis; visits to museums and caves; and a wide array of walking tours.

Most resort properties offer specific children's activities, and there are special family packages. Most of the larger properties will also provide babysitting services for minimal fees.

Here are some of the favorite activities for kids:

**Bermuda Aquarium, Zoological Garden, and Natural History Museum** (*see page 142*). This provides a learning experience about the undersea world. Hand-held tape recorders are available for listening to the history of marine life while visiting live exhibits of Bermuda's native fish.

**Bermuda Maritime Museum** (*see page 153*). Entire families take equal delight in viewing the exhibits of Bermuda's nautical history in this authentic Victorian fortress museum.

**Bermuda Railway Trail** (*see page 158*). A nature walk for the whole family, this 21-mile trail can be walked in sections, as your energy and interest dictate. There are strolls overlooking the seashore or along quiet tree-lines alleyways.

**Devil's Hole** (*see page 143*). The first established tourist attraction in Bermuda—

founded in 1834—this aquarium is located near Harrington Sound. Kids toss baited but hookless lines to feed fish and turtles in this natural marine environment.

**Crystal Caves** (*see page 143*). Two boys chasing a runaway ball in 1907 discovered this enormous cavern surrounded by an underground lake. Easy walkways take parents and children down into the caverns of the crystal caves located near Hamilton Parish.

**Undersea Walk** (see "Organized Tours," below). Explore the ocean floor with "helmet diving." Following a pre-dive educational lecture aboard the ship, children can walk along the ocean floor for face-to-face encounters with friendly native sea creatures.

**Horseback Riding** (see Chapter 8, "Sports & Recreation"). Spicelands Riding Center accepts riders over 21 years old, but the Lee Bow Riding center is well equipped for younger riders.

# 13. SPECIAL-INTEREST SIGHTSEEING

## FOR THE ARCHITECTURE LOVER

All of Bermuda holds special delight for the architecture lover. Mark Twain wrote of the whiteness of Bermuda houses and roofs: "It is exactly the white of the icing of a cake, and has the same emphasized and scarcely perceptible polish. The white of marble is modest and retiring compared with it . . . clean-cut fanciful chimneys—too pure and white for this world—that will charm one's gaze by the hour."

For more details and lore, refer to "Art, Architecture, and Literature" in Chapter 1, "Getting to Know Bermuda." The **town of St. George's**—being the oldest and most historic settlement—holds the most fascination for those interested in architecture (see Chapter 7, "Bermuda Walking Tours").

The **Old State House** is the oldest stone house in Bermuda, constructed in 1620. The governor at the time, Nathaniel Butler, believed that he was constructing the house in an Italianate style. He ordered workers to use a combination of turtle oil and lime as mortar. This set the style for subsequent buildings in Bermuda.

Many architects have wanted to finish the **Unfinished Cathedral** in St. George's, reached by going up Blockade Alley. Construction was launched in 1874, but a schism developed in the church and then there was no money to go ahead.

The **Old Rectory** in St. George's, now a private residence, dates from 1705 when it was built by a former pirate. Found on Broad Alley, it is distinguished by its Dutch doors, chimneys, shutters, and what is called a "welcoming arms" staircase.

From an architectural point of view, one of the most intriguing structures in St. George's is **St. Peter's Church,** standing on Duke of York Street. This is the oldest Anglican Church in the Western hemisphere, dating from 1620. It was constructed to replace an even older structure from 1612 that had been badly assembled from posts and palmetto leaves. A storm did that church in in 1712. The present St. Peter's was rebuilt and enlarged in 1713. In 1833, the galleries on each side of the church were added. The section around the triple-tier pulpit is believed to be the oldest part of the structure, dating from the 1600s. The first governor of the island, Richard Moore, ordered construction of the dark red Bermuda cedar altar in 1615. It is the oldest surviving piece of woodwork from the colonial days.

Also in St. George's, **Tucker House,** on Water Street, was constructed of native limestone. The house is also interestingly furnished, mostly with pieces from the mid-1700s and early 1800s.

The other architectural monument of note in Bermuda is **Verdmont,** lying on Verdmont Lane in Smith's Parish. Dating from around 1710, it was once occupied by a wealthy shipowner. It has known many owners in its long history, including an American Loyalist, John Green, who fled from Philadelphia to Bermuda at the end of the War of American Independence. Built to resemble an English manor house, the house has a striking double roof and a quartet of large chimneys. Each room has its own fireplace. The sash windows are in a style once fashionable in certain English manor houses.

## FOR THE LITERARY ENTHUSIAST

Thomas (Tom) Moore (1779–1852), the Irish poet, has left more memories—literary and romantic—than any other writer ever to visit Bermuda. He once stayed at Hillcrest Guest House in St. George's (see Chapter 4, "Where to Stay in Bermuda"). He soon became enamored of Nea Tucker, the teenage bride of one of the most prominent men in town. "Sweet Nea! Let us roam no more," he once wrote of his beloved.

It is said that the lovesick poet would gaze for hours upon Nea's veranda, hoping that she'd appear. A jealous Mr. Tucker one day could tolerate this no more, and banished the poet from his property. St. George's honors this unrequited romance by naming the street down which Tom Moore was chased Nea's Alley.

One of the most popular restaurants in Bermuda is Tom Moore's Tavern (see Chapter 5, "Where to Dine in Bermuda"). The restaurant was once the private home of Samuel Trott, who had built it in the 17th century. Unlike the jealous Tucker,

## FROMMER'S FAVORITE BERMUDA EXPERIENCES

**Strolling Bermuda's Pink Sands**   The pink sand beaches are reason enough to come to the island. Find your favorite cove (perhaps Whale Bay, Astwood Cove, or Jobson's Cove), and stroll aimlessly at dawn, at twilight, whenever your fancy dictates.

**Cycling Across the Land**   On a rented bicycle, or maybe a moped built for two, explore Bermuda from end to end. Start in St. George's in the East End and go all the way to the Royal Naval Dockyard in the West End.

**Following the Deserted Railway Trail**   As you follow this intermittent trail from one end of the island to the other, you'll see stunning seascapes, exotic flora and fauna, and hear the soothing sounds of the island's bird life.

**Touring by Horse and Buggy**   No one has ever improved on this old-fashioned method of sightseeing and shopping along Hamilton's Front Street. Or, better yet, go on a two-hour shopping tour of Somerset Village in the West End.

**Viewing Bermuda from Gibb's Hill Lighthouse**   Climb the 185 steps of one of the oldest cast-iron lighthouses in the world for one of the Atlantic Ocean's greatest views. Springtime visitors may be lucky enough to see migrating whales beyond the shore reefs.

descendants of Samuel Trott befriended Moore, and he was a frequent visitor to the house. In his writing, the bard immortalized the calabash tree on the Trott estate. He liked to sit under this tree and pen his verse.

Many famous writers, including Mark Twain, were to visit Bermuda in the years to come, following in Moore's footsteps. There are no literary shrines, however, to any of them.

The playwright Eugene O'Neill was convinced that cold weather adversely affected his writings. He also thought that Bermuda would "cure" him of alcoholism. His daughter, Oona, was born in Bermuda (she later married Charlie Chaplin). O'Neill and his family rented cottages on what is now Coral Beach Club property. Later, O'Neill bought the house Spithead, in Warwick. In 1927, however, his marriage ended, and O'Neill left his family—and Bermuda.

A different type of family, British playwright Noël Coward and his longtime companion, Graham Payn, later acquired Spithead. The house is now in private hands.

# 14. ORGANIZED & OTHER TOURS

## ORGANIZED TOURS

A major sightseeing attraction in Bermuda is a ride aboard one of the **Looking Glass Cruises,** Ferry Dock, Hamilton (tel. 809/292-8652), which leave daily at different times between 8am and 10pm. One of the most interesting cruises is the Reef & Wreck Adventure, which lasts two hours and costs $25 for adults, half price for children. Departures are daily at 10am and 1:30pm. Passengers can see the wreck of the HMS *Vixen* and can observe reef fish and coral formations. Also to be seen are 50 islands of the west end of Bermuda, and guests are provided with a lively commentary. Unlimited complimentary bar is included.

The Cruise of Lights is also popular. It lasts 1¾ hours, costs $30 for adults, $15 for children, and departs Tuesday through Saturday at 10:30pm, with a special cruise on Monday at 8:30pm. Honeymooners are especially fond of this one. The vessel goes through the islands of Great Sound as a nocturnal world unfolds, complete with the coral reef and a sunken wreck. The glass-bottom boat is specially lit for the best viewing. Music is also played, and the commentary includes talk of the constellations of the zodiac.

**BDA Water Tours Ltd.,** P.O. Box 1572, Hamilton (tel. 809/295-3727), offers two- and three-hour trips, most of which include the sea gardens; passengers board glass-bottom boats to view the wonders of coral reefs and fish. Also available are a variety of water trips, ranging from two-hour sea-garden tours to snorkeling and dinner cruises. You can call 24 hours a day for information.

The original **undersea walk** offered by Bronson Hartley can be arranged by writing or calling Mr. Hartley at 5 Northshore Rd., P.O. Box FL 281, Flatts F1 BX, Bermuda (tel. 809/292-4434). Anybody can take part in this adventure, featured twice in *Life* magazine. It's as simple as walking through a garden, and you won't even get your hair wet. A helmet is placed on your shoulders as you climb down the ladder of the boat to begin your guided walk. It is an ideal underwater experience for nonswimmers and those who must wear glasses. Safe and educational, the walk takes you to see the feeding of corals and breathing of sponges, as well as the feeding of sea anemones. The skipper and host, Mr. Hartley, personally conducts the tours. His ability to train fish in their natural habitat has been acclaimed in many publications. His 50-foot boat, *Carioca*, leaves Flatts Village daily at 10am and 2pm. The underwater wonderland walk costs $40 per adult or $30 for children under 12. Bus: No. 10 or 11.

To help find a solution for a threatening world problem, the **Bermuda Biological Station for Research, Inc.,** a U.S. nonprofit organization, has been given a grant to study the "carbon cycle," as part of an understanding of climate change and the "greenhouse effect" by the U.S. National Science Foundation. Some $500,000 will be used every year for this research. The Bermuda Biological Station has the world's longest and most continuous data on the oceanographic absorption of human-released carbon dioxide, having tracked levels of it for more than 38 years over an area 13 miles southeast of Bermuda. The station also has kept extensive data on acid rain in the North American atmosphere.

Vacationers to Bermuda can learn firsthand what Bermuda-based scientists are studying at the station by taking a free hour-long guided tour of the station's grounds and laboratory in St. George's. Tour leaders explain what scientific studies are being conducted in Bermuda and how they relate to the overall world environment. Other topics discussed include the island's natural areas, including the coral reefs, protected by strict conservation laws, and how people have caused changes in the fragile ecological environment.

The special educational tours on Wednesday at 10am are conducted by scientists involved in the station's special projects and by specially trained volunteers. Visitors should assemble in the Biological Station's main building. Coffee and snacks are served, and participants are asked to give a donation for the refreshments.

For information on the tours, contact the Bermuda Biological Station for Research, Inc., 17 Biological Lane, Ferry Reach, St. George's (tel. 809/297-1880).

# ON YOUR OWN

**BERMUDA RAILWAY TRAIL**   One of the most unusual sightseeing adventures in Bermuda is following the Bermuda Railway Trail (or parts thereof), which stretches for 21 miles along an old train right-of-way across three of the interconnected islands that make up Bermuda. Opened in 1931, the Bermuda Railway was abandoned in 1948. Once the island's main source of transportation, the train gave way to the automobile.

Before setting out on this trek, arm yourself with a copy of the *Bermuda Railway Trail Guide,* obtainable at the Bermuda Department of Tourism in Hamilton or at the Visitors' Service Bureau in Hamilton or St. George's. You're now ready to hit the trail of the old train system that was affectionately called "Rattle and Shake" (considered the most costly rail line, per mile, ever constructed). There are a variety of ways to explore the trail: horseback, bicycle, moped, or the ever-trusty feet.

Although the line covered 21 miles of the island between St. George's in the east and Somerset in the west, a three-mile stretch has been lost to roads in and around the capital city of Hamilton. For the most part, though, the trail winds along an automobile-free route, with some views of Bermuda not seen by the general public since the end of World War II.

As for some of the things you'll see en route, the trail cuts through the beautiful five-acre Springfield Library and Gilbert Nature Reserve (described above). You'll also see some of the rare Bermuda cedar, which nearly vanished in the blight that struck the island in the early 1940s. Along the trail, too, is much greenery and semitropical vegetation, such as the poinsettia, oleander, and hibiscus. Fort Scaur, the 1870s fortress in Sandys Parish, can also be seen and visited.

**BIRD-WATCHING**   There is a nucleus of bird-watching enthusiasts in Bermuda, but there are not many organized tours. Visiting bird-watchers are advised to make arrangements for tours with local enthusiasts.

Bird-watchers might contact **David Wingate,** Conservation Officer at 809/236-4201 or **Eric Amos** at 809/236-9056. They occasionally—but not always—accompany interested bird-watchers as part of their conservation work. They'll also advise by phone of the island's best retreats, walkways, and hideaways. Before calling, pick up a copy of David Wingate's *Check List and Guide to the Birds of Bermuda* or Eric Amos's *A Guide to the Birds of Bermuda,* both of which titles are available at local bookstores.

You can also contact the **Bermuda Audubon Society,** P.O. Box 1328, Hamilton HM AX, Bermuda (tel. 809/293-7394), for information about any organized field trips.

# CHAPTER 7

# BERMUDA WALKING TOURS

**1. CITY OF HAMILTON**
**2. HISTORIC ST. GEORGE'S TOWN**
**3. SANDYS PARISH**

**Y**ou can cover much of Bermuda on foot, especially the harbor city of Hamilton and the historic town of St. George's. Indeed, if you had the time you could walk—or, if you prefer, cycle—through all the parishes of the island, taking in the major attractions of each. But most visitors would rather devote their vacation time to less taxing pursuits, such as lying insouciantly on the beach or playing a leisurely game of golf.

If, however, you are among the hardy few and do not mind a little physical exertion if the reward promises to exceed the effort, then you should certainly consider taking one or perhaps all three of the walking tours suggested below. For the best way to familiarize yourself with a new place—city, town, or village—is by taking a stroll through it and experiencing its everyday activities from close up.

## WALKING TOUR 1 — CITY OF HAMILTON

**Start:** The Visitors Service Bureau/Ferry Terminal
**End:** Fort Hamilton
**Time:** 2½ hours
**Best Time:** Any sunny day.
**Worst Time:** When cruise ships are anchored in Hamilton Harbour.

Begin your tour along the harborfront at the:

1. **Visitors Service Bureau/Ferry Terminal.** (You might want to take an orientational ferry ride around the inner harbor; that way, you'll get an overview of Hamilton before concentrating on specific landmarks or monuments. Or you could take the ferry ride at the end of the tour.) Pick up some free maps and brochures of the island here.

From the bureau, you emerge onto Front Street again, the main street of Hamilton and its principal shopping artery. Before 1946, no automobiles were permitted on this street, but today its active traffic includes small automobiles (driven only by Bermuda residents), buses, mopeds, and bicycles. You'll also see horse-drawn carriages, which are the most romantic (although the most expensive) way to see Hamilton.

Observe the docks in back of the Ferry Terminal. Here is where you board

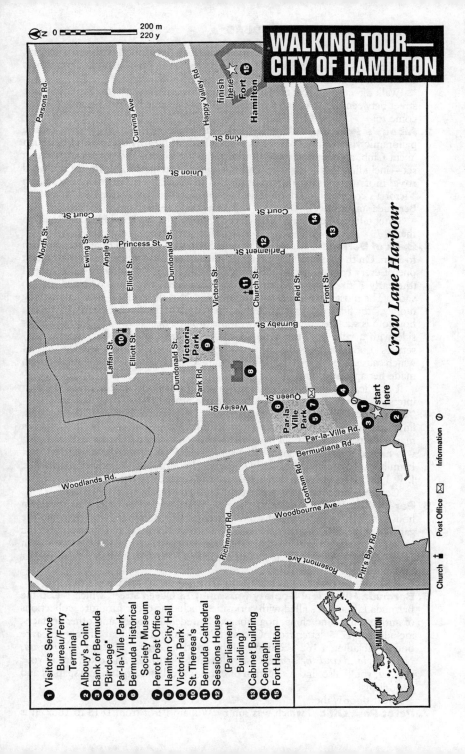

# WALKING TOUR—
# CITY OF HAMILTON

200 m
0
220 y

*Crow Lane Harbour*

finish
here
Fort
Hamilton

Parsons Rd.
Curving Ave.
Happy Valley Rd.
King St.
Union St.
Court St.
North St.
Ewing St.
Angle St.
Princess St.
Parliament St.
Court St.
Reid St.
Front St.
Elliott St.
Dundonald St.
Victoria St.
Church St.
Burnaby St.
Laffan St.
Elliott St.
Dundonald St.
Park Rd.
Victoria
Park
Wesley St.
Queen St.
Par-la-
Ville Park
Par-la-Ville Rd.
Bermudiana Rd.
Woodlands Rd.
Gorham Rd.
Woodbourne Ave.
Richmond Rd.
Rosemont Ave.
Pitt's Bay Rd.

start
here

HAMILTON

**1** Visitors Service
    Bureau/Ferry
    Terminal
**2** Albouy's Point
**3** Bank of Bermuda
    "Birdcage"
**4** Par-la-Ville Park
**5** Bermuda Historical
    Society Museum
**6** Perot Post Office
**7** Hamilton City Hall
**8** Victoria Park
**9** St. Theresa's
**10** Bermuda Cathedral
**11** Sessions House
    (Parliament
    Building)
**12** Cabinet Building
**13** Cenotaph
**14** Fort Hamilton

Church ✝   Post Office ◼   Information ❼

ferries to the parishes of Warwick and Paget (for a description of their attractions, see Chapter 6, "What to See & Do in Bermuda"). You can also take a ferry across Great Sound, going to the West End (Somerset of Sandys).

Walk directly south of the Ferry Terminal toward the water, taking a short side street between the Visitors Service Bureau and the large Bank of Bermuda. You'll come to:

**2. Albouy's Point,** a small grassy park with benches and trees opening onto a panoramic vista of the boat- or ship-filled harbor. Nearby is the Royal Bermuda Yacht Club, an elite rendezvous of both the Bermudian and American yachting set—including lots of the rich and famous—since the 1930s. To use the word *royal* in its name, special permission had to come from Prince Albert, Queen Victoria's consort, in London. The club sponsors the widely televised Newport–Bermuda Yacht Race.

After taking in the view, walk directly north, crossing Point Pleasant Road, to the:

**3. Bank of Bermuda,** which can be visited Monday through Friday from 9:30am to 3pm. On the mezzanine is Bermuda's most extensive coin collection—at least one of every coin minted in the United Kingdom since the time of King James I (the early 17th century). Many Spanish coins used in colonial days are also on show. The most famous Bermudian money—also on exhibit—was called "hog money," the first coins ever minted on the island. In use since the early 1600s, the hog coin is stamped on one side with the ill-fated *Sea Venture* and on the other side with a wild hog, the main source of food, other than fish, for the early settlers. Look for an 1887 £5 piece depicting Queen Victoria, the issuance of which caused a protest in the British Empire. Critics claimed that the small crown made her appear foolish.

Upon leaving the bank, head east along Front Street to the point where it intersects with Queen Street. This is the site of the:

**4. "Birdcage,"** the most photographed sight in Bermuda. Here you'll sometimes, find a policeman (or perhaps a policewoman) directing traffic. If the "bobbie" is a man, he's likely to be attired in regulation Bermuda shorts. The traffic box, which was named after its designer, Michael "Dickey" Bird, stands at a little bit of Hamilton geography called Heyl's Corner, honoring an American southerner, J. B. Heyl, who operated an apothecary shop nearby in the 1800s.

Continue north along Queen Street until you reach:

**5. Par-la-Ville Park,** which was once a private garden belonging to the town house of William B. Perot, the first postmaster of Bermuda, who designed the gardens in the 19th century. He collected rare and exotic plants from all over the globe, including an Indian rubber tree which was seeded in 1847. Mark Twain wrote that he found the tree "disappointing" in that it didn't bear rubber overshoes and hot water bottles.

Also opening onto Queen Street at the entrance to the park is the:

**6. Bermuda Historical Society Museum,** 13 Queen Street, which is also the Bermuda Library. It's filled with curiosities, including cedar furniture, collections of antique silver and china, hog money, Confederate money, and other artifacts, including a 1775 letter from George Washington. The library has many rare books, including a 1624 edition of John Smith's *General Histoire of Virginia, New England and the Somers Isles*. If you'd like to rest and catch up on your reading, you'll also find a selection of current local and English newspapers and periodicals.

Next door is the:

**7. Perot Post Office,** which was run by William Perot from 1818 to 1862. It is said that he'd go down to collect the mail from the clipper ships, but would put it under his top hat so as to preserve his dignity. As he proceeded through town, he'd greet his friends and acquaintances by tipping his hat—and thereby delivering their mail at the same time. He started printing stamps in 1848. A Perot stamp is extremely valuable today, as only 11 are known to exist; some are owned by Queen Elizabeth II. The last time a Perot stamp came on the market in 1986, it fetched $135,000.

Continue to the top of Queen Street, then turn right onto Church Street to reach:

8. **Hamilton City Hall,** 17 Church Street, which dates from 1960 and is crowned by a white tower. The bronze weathervane on top is a replica of the *Sea Venture*. In the main lobby are portraits of the queen and paintings of former island leaders. The Bermuda Society of Arts holds frequent exhibitions at this hall. The Benbow collection of stamps is also displayed here.

---

**REFUELING STOP** The **Fourways Pastry Shop** at Washington Mall and Reid Street was previously recommended in Chapter 5, "Where to Dine in Bermuda." It is on the ground floor of a shopping and office complex and serves the most irresistible pastries in town. You can also order ice cream, tartlets, quiches, and croissant sandwiches, along with espresso and cappuccino.

---

In back of Hamilton City Hall, opening onto Victoria Street, lies:

9. **Victoria Park,** a cool, refreshing oasis frequented by office workers on their lunch breaks. Containing a sunken garden and ornamental shrubbery, it also has a Victorian bandstand. The four-acre park was laid out in honor of Queen Victoria's Golden Jubilee in 1887. Outdoor concerts are held here in summer.

Cedar Avenue is the eastern boundary of Victoria Park. If you follow it north for two blocks, you reach:

10. **St. Theresa's,** a Roman Catholic cathedral that is open daily from 8am to 7pm. Dating from 1927, it was inspired by the Spanish Mission style of architecture. It is one of half a dozen Roman Catholic churches in Bermuda; its treasure is a gold and silver chalice given by Pope Paul VI on his visit to the island in 1986.

After a visit to the cathedral, retrace your steps south along Cedar Avenue until you return to Victoria Street. Cedar Avenue now becomes Burnaby Street. Continue south on this street until you come to Church Street where you cut left. A short walk along this street (on your left) leads to the:

11. **Bermuda Cathedral,** or the Cathedral of the Most Holy Trinity as it is sometimes called. This is the seat of the Anglican Church of Bermuda, and it towers over the city skyline. Its style is neo-Gothic, characterized by stained-glass windows and soaring arches. The lectern and pulpit duplicate those of St. Giles in Edinburgh, Scotland.

Leave the cathedral and continue east along Church Street to the:

12. **Sessions House** (Parliament Building), on Parliament Street, between Reid and Church Streets, which is open to the public Monday through Friday from 9am to 5pm. The Parliament of Bermuda is considered the third-oldest in the world, after Iceland's and England's. You can see political action, Bermuda style, from the Visitors' Gallery. The speaker is attired in full wig and flowing black robes.

Continue to walk south along Parliament Street until you approach Front Street, where you should turn left to the:

13. **Cabinet Building,** between Court and Parliament Streets. The official opening of Parliament takes place here in late October or early November. In a plumed hat and full regalia, the governor makes his "Throne Speech." If you visit on a Wednesday, you'll see the Bermuda Senate in action. The building is open Monday through Friday from 9am to 5pm.

In front of the Cabinet Building is the:

14. **Cenotaph,** a memorial to Bermuda's dead in World War I (1914–18) and in World War II (1939–45). In 1920 the Prince of Wales laid the cornerstone. (Later, in 1936, as King Edward VIII he would abdicate to marry an American divorcée, Wallis Simpson, and later still, during World War II, now the Duke of Windsor, he would serve as governor of the Bahamas.) The landmark is a replica of the Cenotaph in London.

Continue east along Front Street until you reach King Street, then head north until you come to Happy Valley Road. Go right on this road until you see the entrance (on your right) to:

15. **Fort Hamilton,** an imposing old fortress on the eastern outskirts of Hamilton. The Duke of Wellington ordered its construction to protect Hamilton Harbour. Filled with underground passageways and complete with a moat and 18-ton guns, it was considered outdated even before it was completed. The fort never fired a shot, but it makes for interesting viewing nonetheless. Go if for no other reason than to enjoy the view of the city and harbor. In summer, try to time your visit for noon when the kilted Bermuda Isles Pipe Band performs a skirling ceremony on the green, accompanied by dancers and drummers. It's a fairly good walk to the fort, so wind down with some old-fashioned tea at the Fort Hamilton Tea Shoppe, where you can also order light refreshments.

# WALKING TOUR 2 — HISTORIC ST. GEORGE'S TOWN

**Start:** King's Square.
**End:** Somers Wharf.
**Time:** 2 hours (not counting interior visits).
**Best Time:** Any sunny day except Sunday when much is closed.
**Worst Time:** When a cruise ship is anchored in harbor.

In the east end of the island, St. George's was the second English town to be established in the New World, after Jamestown in Virginia. For the history buff, it holds more interest than Hamilton. (For more detailed descriptions of its attractions, refer to "St. George's Parish," in Chapter 6, "What to See & Do in Bermuda.") We'll begin the tour at:

1. **King's Square,** also known as Market Square and King's Parade, the very center of St. George's. Only some two centuries old, it's not as historic as St. George's itself. It was once a marshy part of the harbor—at least when the shipwrecked passengers and crew of *Sea Venture* first saw it. On the water's edge stands the Visitors Service Bureau, which you may want to visit to pick up additional information. Displayed on the square is a replica of the pillory and stocks that used to be used to punish criminals, and, in many cases, the innocent.

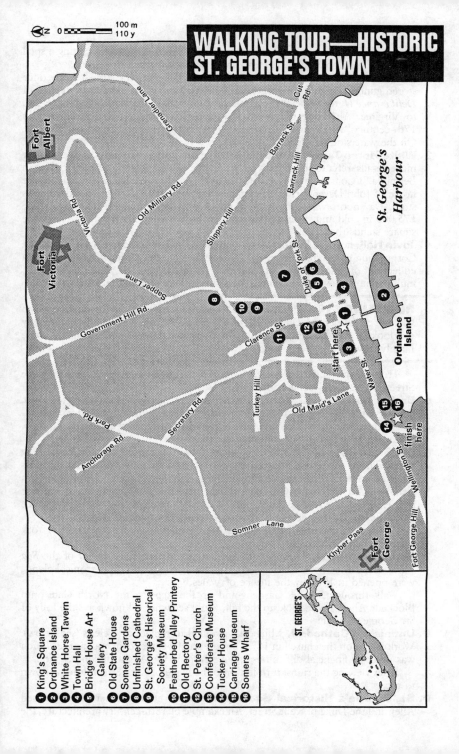

# WALKING TOUR—HISTORIC ST. GEORGE'S TOWN

100 m
0
110 y

Fort Albert

Fort Victoria

Grenadier Lane

Old Military Rd.

Victoria Rd.

Sapper Lane

Government Hill Rd.

Park Rd.

Anchorage Rd.

Secretary Rd.

Turkey Hill

Somner Lane

Khyber Pass

Fort George

Fort George Hill

Barrack St.

Cut Rd.

Barrack Hill

Slippery Hill

Duke of York St.

Clarence St.

Old Maid's Lane

Water St.

Wellington St.

St. George's Harbour

Ordnance Island

start here

finish here

**7** **6** **5** **4** **2** **8** **10** **9** **1** **12** **13** **11** **3** **15** **16** **14**

ST. GEORGE'S

1. King's Square
2. Ordnance Island
3. White Horse Tavern
4. Town Hall
5. Bridge House Art Gallery
6. Old State House
7. Somers Gardens
8. Unfinished Cathedral
9. St. George's Historical Society Museum
10. Featherbed Alley Printery
11. Old Rectory
12. St. Peter's Church
13. Confederate Museum
14. Tucker House
15. Carriage Museum
16. Somers Wharf

You could be severely punished here for such alleged "crimes" as casting a spell over your neighbor's turkeys. Head south across the small bridge to:

**2. Ordnance Island,** jutting into St. George's Harbour. The British Army once stored gunpowder and cannons here, but today the island contains a replica of *Deliverance II,* the vessel that carried the shipwrecked *Sea Venture* passengers on to Virginia. Alongside the vessel is a ducking stool, a contraption used in 17th-century "witch trials." Retrace your steps across the bridge to King's Square. On the waterside stands the:

**3. White Horse Tavern,** a restaurant jutting out into St. George's Harbour. (For more details, refer to the section on St. George's, in Chapter 5, "Where to Dine in Bermuda.") Consider the tavern for a luncheon stopover later. It was once the home of John Davenport, who came to Bermuda in 1815 to open a dry goods store. Davenport was considered a bit of a miser, but upon his death some £75,000 in gold and silver was discovered stashed away in his cellar. Across the square stands the:

**4. Town Hall,** near the Visitors Service Bureau. The hall is the meeting place of the Corporation governing St. George's. It contains antique cedar furnishings and a collection of photographs of previous Lord Mayors. *Bermuda Journey,* a multimedia audiovisual presentation, is shown here several times a day.

---

**REFUELING STOP   Pub on the Square,** King's Square (recommended in Chapter 5, "Where to Dine in Bermuda"). This British-style pub has a balcony overlooking the square. You can get a beer or a burger here, but many come mainly to watch the scene below.

---

From King's Square, head east along King Street, cutting north on Bridge Street. There you'll come to the:

**5. Bridge House Art Gallery,** 1 Bridge Street. Constructed shortly after 1700, this was once the home of several governors of Bermuda. Furnished with 18th- and 19th-century antiques, it is now home to an art gallery and souvenir shop. Return to King Street and continue east to:

**6. Old State House,** which actually opens onto Princess Street, at the top of King Street. This is the oldest stone building in Bermuda, dating from 1620, and was once the home of the Bermuda Parliament. It is the site of the ancient Peppercorn Ceremony, in which the Old State House pays the government "rent" of one peppercorn annually. (See "St. George's Parish," in Chapter 6, "What to See & Do in Bermuda," for details of this grand ceremony filled with pageantry.

Continue your stroll down Princess Street until you come to the Duke of York Street, the entrance to:

**7. Somers Gardens.** The heart of Sir George Somers, the admiral of the *Sea Venture,* is buried here. The gardens, containing palms and other tropical plants, were opened in 1920 by the Prince of Wales.

Walk through Somers Gardens and up the steps to the North Gate onto Blockade Alley. If you look up the hill, you'll see what is known as "the folly of St. George's"—the:

**8. Unfinished Cathedral,** which was planned to replace St. Peter's (see below). Work began on the church in 1874, but eventually came to an end, as the church was beset by financial difficulties and a schism in the Anglican congregation.

After viewing the ruins, turn left onto the Duke of Kent Street, leading down to the:

**9. St. George's Historical Society Museum,** at the corner of Featherbed Alley and the Duke of Kent Street. An example of 18th-century architecture, the house contains a collection of Bermudian historical artifacts and cedar furniture. Around the corner on Featherbed Alley is the:

10. **Featherbed Alley Printery,** which has a working replica of the type of printing press invented by Johann Gutenburg in Germany in the 1450s. Go up Featherbed Alley and straight onto Church Street. At the junction with Broad Lane, look to your right to see the:

11. **Old Rectory,** at the head of Broad Alley, behind St. Peter's Church. Now a private home, but administered by the National Trust, it was built in 1705 by a reformed pirate. If you'd like to go inside, it is open only on Wednesday and Friday from 10am to 4pm.

After seeing the Old Rectory, you can go through the back of the churchyard entrance, opposite Broad Alley, to reach:

12. **St. Peter's Church.** The church's main entrance is on Duke of York Street. This is believed to be the oldest Anglican place of worship in the Western Hemisphere. In the churchyard you'll see many headstones, some dating back three centuries. The assassinated governor, Sir Richard Sharples, was buried here. The present church was built in 1713, with a tower added in 1814. Across the street is the:

13. **Confederate Museum.** When it was the Globe Hotel, it was the headquarters of Major Norman Walker, the Confederate representative in Bermuda. It was once a hotbed of blockade-running.

As you continue along Duke of York Street, you reach Barber's Lane, honoring Joseph Hayne Rainey. A former slave from South Carolina, Rainey and his French wife fled to Bermuda at the outbreak of the Civil War. He became a barber in St. George's but eventually returned to South Carolina, where in 1870 he was elected to the U.S. House of Representatives—the first African American to serve in Congress.

Nearby is Petticoat Lane, also known as Silk Alley. The name dates from the 1834 emancipation, when two former slave women who'd always wanted silk petticoats like their former mistresses, finally got some and constantly paraded up and down the lane to show off their new finery.

Continue east until you reach:

14. **Tucker House,** opening onto Water Street. This was the former home of a prominent Bermudian family, whose members have included an island governor, a treasurer of the United States, and a captain in the Confederate Navy. The building houses an excellent collection of antiques, including silver, portraits, and cedar furniture. One room is devoted to relics of the previously mentioned Rainey. Diagonally across from the Tucker House is the:

15. **Carriage Museum,** 22 Water Street. Here are housed some of the more interesting carriages in use in Bermuda until 1946 when the automobile arrived After visiting the Carriage Museum, you'll be at:

16. **Somers Wharf,** a multimillion-dollar waterfront restoration project, that now includes shops, restaurants, and taverns. It's the site of the Carriage House restaurant (in case you want to make a luncheon stopover), see Chapter 5, "Where to Dine in Bermuda," for more details.

# WALKING TOUR 3 — SANDYS PARISH

**Begin:** Somerset Bridge
**End:** Springfield Library and Gilbert Nature Reserve.

**Time:** 8 hours.
**Best Time:** Any sunny day.
**Worst Time:** When the weather's bad.

Sandys (pronounce it as if there were no *y*) is the far western parish of Bermuda, consisting of Somerset Island (the largest and southernmost), Watford, Boaz, and Ireland islands. When Bermudians cross over Somerset Bridge, they say they are "up the country."

Craggy coastlines, beaches, nature reserves, fishermen's coves, old fortifications, winding lanes, and sleepy villages characterize the area. All the principal attractions lie along the main road from Somerset Bridge to the Royal Naval Dockyard, which is at the end of Ireland Island.

Although we are classifying this as a walking tour, because of the distances involved, you may want to rent a bicycle or moped to help you cover the longer stretches.

From the center of Hamilton, you can take a ferry to Somerset. Check the schedule, as some boats take 30 minutes to get there, while others take up to an hour. The longer trip gives you more time to take in the waters of Bermuda's Great Sound. You can take your cycle or moped aboard the ferry. You can also see the West End by public bus; refer to Chapter 6, "What to See & Do in Bermuda," for details on how to visit by bus.)

To begin the tour, take the ferry from Hamilton to:

1. **Somerset Bridge,** linking Somerset Island with the rest of Bermuda. It was one of the first three bridges constructed in the 1600s, and is said to be the smallest drawbridge in the world—its opening is just wide enough to accommodate a sailboat mast. Near the bridge you can take a look at the old Somerset Post Office and see an 18th-century cottage known as "Crossways."

   After viewing this, walk up Somerset Road for some 75 yards to the entrance to the:

2. **Railway Trail,** which is confined to pedestrians, cyclists, and bikers. This trail follows the path of old "Rattle and Shake," the former Bermuda Railway line that once ran across the entire length of the island. Since it is unlikely that you'll walk the whole railway track (although some hearty visitors do just that), you may like to know that this particular section of the track, lying between Somerset Bridge and Sound View Road, is considered one of the most attractive on the island. Parts of the trail open onto the coast, affording panoramic vistas of the Great Sound.

   The trail goes across the parkland of Fort Scaur, with its large moat. If you're there around noon, you might consider this as a picnic spot. If you've got all day for Somerset (highly recommended), you might also want to take time out for a swim before returning to your walking or cycling. Others prefer to take lunch at the Lantana Colony Club, one of the most exclusive cottage colonies on Bermuda (see Chapter 4, "Where to Stay in Bermuda").

   Follow the signposts to:

3. **Fort Scaur,** opening onto Somerset Road. The British, fearing an attack from the United States, constructed this fort on the highest hill in Somerset in the 1870s to protect Her Majesty's Royal Naval Dockyard. A huge dry moat was cut right across Somerset Island. Visitors wander at leisure around this fort, which proved unnecessary, since the feared U.S. invasion never materialized. If you stand on the ramparts, you'll be rewarded with a spectacular view of Great Sound. Through a free telescope, you can see such distant sights as St. David's Lighthouse and Fort

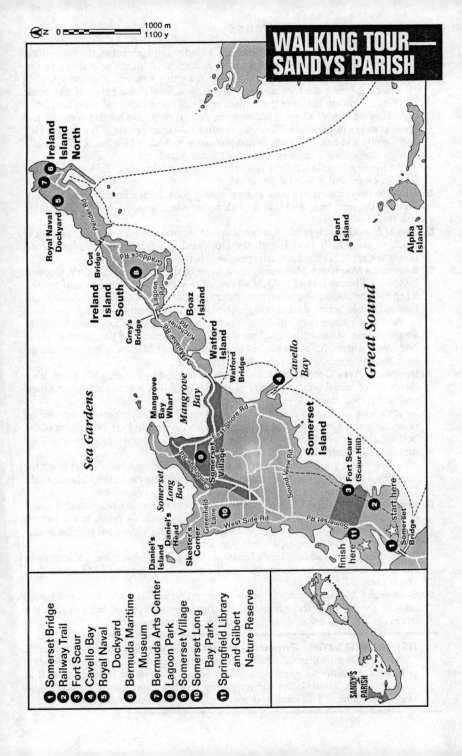

## WALKING TOUR— SANDYS PARISH

1000 m
0
1100 y

*Great Sound*

*Sea Gardens*

Ireland Island North

Royal Naval Dockyard

Pender Rd.

Cut Bridge

Craddock Rd.

Ireland Island South

Lagoon Rd.

Grey's Bridge

Boaz Island

Kitchener Rd.

Malabar Rd.

Watford Island

Watford Bridge

Mangrove Bay Wharf

*Mangrove Bay*

Somerset East Shore Rd.

*Cavello Bay*

Somerset Island

Cambridge Rd.

Somerset Village

Sound View Rd.

Fort Scaur (Scaur Hill)

Somerset Rd.

start here

Somerset Bridge

*Somerset Long Bay*

Daniel's Head

Daniel's Island

Greenfield Lane

Skeeter's Corner

West Side Rd.

finish here

Pearl Island

Alpha Island

SANDY'S PARISH

1. Somerset Bridge
2. Railway Trail
3. Fort Scaur
4. Cavello Bay
5. Royal Naval Dockyard
6. Bermuda Maritime Museum
7. Royal Naval Dockyard
8. Bermuda Arts Center
9. Lagoon Park
10. Somerset Village
11. Somerset Long Bay Park
12. Springfield Library and Gilbert Nature Reserve

St. Catherine in the East End of Bermuda. Filled with picnic areas, the fort stands on 22 acres of parkland. If you take the eastern moat all the way down to the Great Sound shore, you'll find ideal places for either swimming or fishing.

After exploring the fort grounds, resume your walk along the railway track and continue north for more than a mile until you come to Sound View Road. Go right here and stroll along this sleepy residential street containing some of the finest cottages in Bermuda. Continue around a wide arc, passing Tranquility Hill and Gwelly and Saltsea Lanes. When you come to Scott's Hill Road, take a right and go along for 85 yards or so to East Shore Road.

At the first junction, a little road branches off to the right. Take it. It's called Cavello Lane, and it will take you to:

**4. Cavello Bay,** a sheltered cove and a stopping point for the ferry from Hamilton. Wait for the next ferry and take it (with your cycle or moped) to Watford Bridge and the:

**5. Royal Naval Dockyard.** You could spend an entire afternoon here, as there is much to see. On Ireland Island, the Dockyard is a sprawling complex spread across six acres. The major attraction here is the:

**6. Bermuda Maritime Museum,** at the heart of the Dockyard complex. Opened by Queen Elizabeth II in 1975, it allows visitors to cross a moat to explore the Keep and the 30-foot-high defensive ramparts. There is an excellent exhibition of Bermuda's old boats, documenting the island's rich maritime history.

Across the street from the Maritime Museum is the Old Cooperage Building, where you can see an audiovisual presentation, *The Attack on Washington,* at the Neptune Cinema. Adjacent to the cinema is the Craft Market, where you can go on a shopping expedition. Next door, call at the:

**7. Bermuda Arts Center,** which was opened in 1984 by Princess Margaret. It's a showcase of visual arts and crafts of the island and is a nonprofit organization staffed by volunteers.

It's a long walk to Somerset Village from the Dockyard, yet many view cycling or walking along its length one of the highlights of a trip to Bermuda. Some of the best beaches in Bermuda are found here, so if you get tired along the way, take time out for a refreshing dip in the ocean.

Leave by the south entrance to the Dockyard, walking down Pender Road for about half a mile. Cross Cockburn's Cut Bridge, heading for Ireland Island South. Go straight along Cockrange Road, which will take you to:

**8. Lagoon Park.** Enter the park as you cross over Grey's Bridge onto Ireland Island South. The park, which is crisscrossed by walking trails, has a lagoon populated with ducks and other wild fowl. There are places for picnics in this park, which is always open, charging no admission.

To continue, go across Grey's Bridge, entering Boaz Island, and walk or cycle along Malabar Road. On your right you'll see the calm waters of Mangrove Bay. You'll eventually arrive at:

**9. Somerset Village,** one of the most charming in Bermuda. One road goes through the village. Although you can do some serious shopping here, most of the stores are actually branches of larger stores in Hamilton.

---

**REFUELING STOP   Somerset Country Squire Tavern** (see Chapter 5, "Where to Dine in Bermuda," for a complete description). At this English-style pub, you can order an excellent selection of sandwiches or burgers, as well as such pub grub as steak-and-kidney pie or "bangers and mash" (sausages and mashed potatoes). The kitchen is also noted for its luscious desserts.

---

Follow Cambridge Road west to:

**10. Somerset Long Bay Park,** which is always open. It often attracts families because of its good beach and shallow waters opening onto Long Bay. You can also picnic in the parkland. The nature reserve here is operated by the Bermuda Audubon Society, and the pond lures migrating birds in both spring and autumn, including the Louisiana heron, the snowy egret, and the purple gallinule.

Return to Cambridge Road (now becoming Somerset Road, also known as Main Road) until you come to the arched gateway leading to:

**11. Springfield Library and Gilbert Nature Reserve,** on five acres sprawling around an 18th-century former plantation house. The library is a branch of the Bermuda Library. You can explore the old plantation's slave quarters and various outbuildings. A trail leads through the nearby nature reserve, which is protected by the Bermuda National Trust.

After leaving the reserve, continue along Somerset Road until you reach Somerset Bridge, where you can take the ferry back to Hamilton.

# CHAPTER 8

# SPORTS & RECREATION

**1. SPORTS**
**2. RECREATION**

**B**ermuda's climate is ideal for outdoor sports activities, the most popular of which among tourists are tennis and golf. If you're an enthusiast of either game, therefore, you'll find a fair number of attractive tennis courts and professionally designed golf courses around the island where you may practice your swing, often with players of better than average ability. But if you should hesitate to pick up a racket or golf club because your game has been somewhat neglected of late, fear not: your Bermudian partner, on the court or on the links, will deem it quite improper to remark that your game is anything but superb; and if a word of friendly criticism is ever offered, be assured that it will be as gentle as the ocean breezes that sweep over the island.

## 1. SPORTS

The most often played spectator sports, in this tradition-bound British colony, are cricket, soccer, field hockey, and the not terribly genteel game of rugby. Boating, yachting, and sailing are also favorites, as there is a great deal of opportunity to participate in these water sports.

An overview of the country's sports-related options is given below. The Bermuda Department of Tourism can provide dates and venues for upcoming events.

**CRICKET**  Its arcane rules have been memorized and are understood by far more Bermudians than you might have realized before your arrival. If you arrive in midsummer (the game's seasonal high point), you'll probably see several regional teams practicing on cricket fields throughout the island. Each match includes enough pageantry to remind participants of the game's imperial antecedents, and enough conviviality (picnics, socializing, and chitchat among the spectators) to provide sociological insights into Bermuda. The year's most important cricket event, the Cup Match Cricket Festival, occurs during late July or early August. Then, playoffs between Bermuda-based and visiting teams occur at the St. George's Cricket Club, Willington Slip Rd. (tel. 809/234-0327) and at the Somerset Cricket Club, Broome St. off Somerset Rd. (tel. 809/234-0327). Over the rest of the year, these organizations keep in close touch with the various cricket-related activities throughout the island.

**FIELD HOCKEY**  One of the great games of women's athletics involves opposing teams armed with curved wooden mallets. Each side—usually clad in knee socks and either shorts or kilts—tries to drive a small white ball into the opposing team's net.

Bermuda has several different teams that play against one another on Sunday afternoons between October and April. In September, Bermuda welcomes massive throngs of field hockey enthusiasts from throughout the Atlantic basin. The venue is the Hockey Festival, held every year at the National Sports Club, Middle Road, Devonshire Parish (tel. 809/236-6994). Admission is usually free.

**GOLF**   Enthusiasts claim that Bermuda offers some of the finest all-around golfing terrain in the world. Part of this derives from the climate, which supports lush driving ranges and putting greens. In addition, the ever-present golfing enthusiasts play at surprisingly high levels. Golf tournaments are held throughout the year, culminating in the annual, much publicized Bermuda Open in early October. Both amateurs and professionals are welcome to vie for one of the most sought after golfing prizes in the world.

**RUGBY**   A blend of American-style football with European soccer, this rough 'n tumble game attracts many aficionadoes within Bermuda. Rugby players (devoid of protective padding) from several hotly competitive local teams seem to revel in this violent sport. The Easter Rugby Classic, attracting teams from throughout the British Commonwealth, is the final event in the island's rugby season, which runs between September and April. The locale for virtually every rugby game in Bermuda is within the National Sports Club, Middle Road, Devonshire (tel. 809/236-6994).

**SOCCER**   The fast-paced game of soccer is gaining increasing numbers of fans on both sides of the Atlantic. Bermudians view soccer as an important part of elementary education and therefore actively encourage this sport for children and teenagers. In early April, teams from countries around the Atlantic and Caribbean compete for the Diadora Youth Soccer Cup, with players in three different age divisions. Games are held on various fields and playing grounds throughout the island. More accessible to visitors at other times, however, are the many games between high school athletic teams, held regularly throughout the year.

**YACHTING**   Bermuda has never hesitated to draw upon its geographical position in the mid-Atlantic to lure the yachting crowd. The yacht-racing season runs every year from March to November, with most racing events taking place on weekends. Most yachting occurs within the relatively calm waters of Bermuda's Great Sound. Although watching these races from land can be confusing because of the shifting sightlines, the best land vantage points include Spanish Point, the islands northeast of Somerset, and Hamilton Harbour. Closer views are available from the decks of privately owned boats that anchor near the edge of the race course. Despite the confusion among newcomers when watching these carefully choreographed regattas, the sight of a fleet of racing craft with spinnakers and pennants aloft is always exciting.

In late June, Bermuda is the final destination in two of the most important annual races of the yachting world: the Annapolis–Bermuda Race and the even more prestigious Newport–Bermuda Race. Both provide enough visual distraction and maritime pageantry to keep even the most enthusiastic maritime devotees enthralled. Participating yachts range from 30 to 100 feet in length, and their skippers are said to be among the most dedicated in the world.

Around Halloween, the autumn winds propel dozens of less exotic racing craft through the waters of the Great Sound. These compete in a series of one-on-one playoffs for the King Edward VII Gold Cup International Match Racing Tournament.

The island's yachting options are by no means limited to the above-mentioned handful of international competitions. Bermuda's sheltered bays and windswept open seas provide year-round enticement for anyone who has ever wanted to experience the thrill of a snapping jib and taut mainsail.

# 2. RECREATION

## SAILING

Bermuda is one of the world's sailing capitals. Sail-yourself boats are available on a half-day (4-hour) or full-day (8-hour) basis.

**SALT KETTLE BOAT RENTALS, Ltd., Salt Kettle Rd., P.O. Box PG 201, Paget PG BX, Bermuda. Tel. 809/236-4863.**
Salt Kettle rents Sunfish, daysailers, and motorboats. Sunfish are rented at $50 (4 hours) or $80 (8 hours), and a 17-foot O'Day Daysailer costs $75 (4 hours) or $120 (8 hours). Sailing instruction is also given; a 2-hour beginner course for an O'Day Daysailer costs $75.
**Open:** Daily 9am–5pm. **Bus:** No. 8.

**SOUTHSIDE SCUBA WATER SPORTS, Grotto Bay Beach Hotel, 11 Blue Hole Hill, Hamilton Parish. Tel. 809/293-2915.**
Blue Hole rents Sunfish for $50 (4 hours) or $80 (8 hours). A 13-foot Boston Whaler with a Bimini top rents for $90 (4 hours) or $130 (8 hours). A wide range of other equipment is also available for rent as well, including Hobie Cats and water bikes.
**Open:** Daily 9am–5pm. **Bus:** No. 1, 3, 10, or 11.

**BERMUDA CARIBBEAN YACHT CHARTER, 2A Light House Rd., Southampton Parish. Tel. 809/238-8578.**
Yachts for charter with a licensed skipper can be rented at a number of places, including Bermuda Caribbean Yacht Charter. The 52-foot ketch *Night Wind* operates from April to November and charges $250 for a half day, $480 for a full day for six passengers. Any additional person pays an extra $15 each.
**Open:** Daily 9am–5pm. **Bus:** No. 7 or 8.

## FISHING

Bermuda is considered one of the world's finest fishing centers, especially when it comes to light tackle fishing. Blue marlin catches have increased dramatically, and Bermuda can also add bill-fishing to an already enviable reputation. Fishing is a year-round sport in Bermuda, but is best from May through November. No license is required.

Visitors to the island may obtain fishing information from the International Game Fish Association representative for Bermuda: Tom Smith (tel. 809/238-0112).

**Bermuda Game Fishing Association,** P.O. Box HM 1306, Hamilton HM FX, Bermuda, is an advisory body representing all the IGFA affiliated clubs in Bermuda and caretaker for all local records and world records held locally.

### DEEP-SEA FISHING

Wahoo, amberjack, blue marlin, white marlin, dolphin, tuna, and more can be found in these waters. In addition, Bermuda offers a wealth of equipment to help you get them.

**BERMUDA SPORTSFISHING, Creek View House, 8 Tulo Lane, Pembroke HM 02, Bermuda. Tel. 809/292-5535.**
Bermuda Sportsfishing is run by the De Silva family, who have been in business for

many years. They charge $600 for a half day of fishing and from $750 to $825 for a full day. If given enough notice, the family can compose groups of six, in which case the charge is only $100 per person for a half day and $150 per person for a full day, with all equipment included in the price. Boats include a 50-foot all-wood vessel with two bathrooms, a kitchenette, three "fighting chairs," and space for up to 20 persons. There is also a 36-foot sportsfishing boat available.

**Open:** Daily 7am–10pm. **Bus:** No. 1, 2, 10, or 11.

## REEF FISHING

Reef fishing is likely to turn up such catches as greater amberjack, almaco jack, great barracuda, little tunny, Bermuda chub, gray snapper, yellow tail snapper, and assorted bottom fish. Three major reef bands lie off Bermuda's shore. The closest one begins about ½ mile offshore, stretching for nearly 5 miles. The Challenger Bank is about 14 miles offshore, and Argus Bank is the most distant, at about 30 miles. Of course, the farther you go, the more likely you are to turn up big fish.

Several charter companies offer either half- or full-day charters. Arrangements can be made through Bermuda Sportsfishing (see "Deep Sea Fishing," above).

## SHORE FISHING

This type of fishing turns up such catches as bonefish, palometa (pompano), gray snapper, and great barracuda. Locals and most visitors prefer shore fishing at Spring Benny's Bay or West Whale Bay. Great Sound and St. George's Harbour are other promising grounds.

For most activities, directors at hotels will make arrangements for you. If they can't, go to **Four Winds Fishing Tackle,** 2 Woodlands Rd., Pembroke (tel. 809/292-7466), where you can rent rod and reels. Rates are $10 for 24 hours with a $30 deposit required. You can also go to Harbour Road Marina, Newstead, in Paget (tel. 809/234-6060), where rod, reel, and tackle can be rented at $6 for four hours or $10 for one day, with a $20 deposit.

# GOLF

Since the first course was laid out in 1922, golf has become one of Bermuda's most popular sports. It can be played year-round, but early spring, winter, and fall offer the best seaside golf conditions. You must arrange your starting time at any of the eight courses in advance through the management of your guesthouse or hotel. Women's and men's clubs, either right- or left-handed, are available at each course, and most leading stores in Bermuda sell golf balls.

Tournaments are held throughout the year, with top players participating. For information, contact the **Bermuda Golf Association,** P.O. Box HM 433, Hamilton HM BX, Bermuda (tel. 809/238-1367).

The Castle Harbour Hotel golf course is considered one of the most scenic courses on the island, while the Port Royal, designed by Robert Trent Jones, is a challenge to your golfing expertise. Two famous courses, the Mid Ocean Club at Tucker's Town and the Riddells Bay Golf and Country Club, are private, and introduction by a member is required before you can play there. One of the most photographed golf courses in Bermuda is at the Southampton Princess hotel, where rolling hills and flowering shrubs add to the players' enjoyment.

The golf courses listed below that are part of a hotel complex also allow nonguests to use their facilities. All of these golf courses have pros, and you can take lessons if you wish.

**BELMONT HOTEL, GOLF & COUNTRY CLUB, between Harbour and Middle Rds., Warwick Parish. Tel. 809/236-1301.**

This course has 18 holes, par 70, 5,777 yards. Greens fees are $30 for hotel guests, $45 for others. A full set of golf clubs rents for $20; gas golf carts rent for $32, handcarts $7. It can also be played as a 9-hole course.

**Open:** Daily 7am–5pm. **Transportation:** Ferry from Hamilton.

**PORT ROYAL GOLF COURSE, Middle Rd., Southampton Parish. Tel. 809/234-0974.**

This is a public course with 18 holes, par 71, 6,565 yards. Greens fees are $36 (reduced rates are available after 4pm). There are no caddies. A full set of clubs rents for $14, golf carts $26, handcarts $6. The clubhouse, which overlooks the ocean and the 9th and 18th greens, boasts a bar and a restaurant serving breakfast and lunch.

**Open:** Daily 7am–5pm. **Bus:** No. 7 or 8.

**SOUTHAMPTON PRINCESS GOLF CLUB, 101 South Shore Rd., Hamilton. Tel. 809/238-0446.**

This course has 18 holes, par 54, 2,684 yards. Greens fees for hotel guests are $24, $28 for visitors. There are no caddies. Rental of clubs is $13 per 18 holes and gas golf carts for $22 to $24.

**Open:** Daily 7am–5pm. **Bus:** No. 7 or 8.

**CASTLE HARBOUR GOLF CLUB, Tucker's Town, Hamilton Parish. Tel. 809/293-2040.**

This course has 18 holes, par 71, 6,440 yards. Greens fees are $75 for 18 holes. There are no caddies. A full set of clubs rents for $24; gas golf carts rent for $35 for 18 holes (mandatory use of golf carts); and shoe rental is $6.

**Open:** Daily 7:30am–6pm. **Bus:** No. 22. **Directions:** Exit off Harrington Sound Road, follow Paynters Road to Castle Harbour resort entrance.

**OCEAN VIEW GOLF COURSE, 31 Parsons Lane, Devonshire. Tel. 809/236-6758.**

This course has 9 holes, par 35, 2,956 yards. Greens fees are $22 (for 9 holes or the course played for 18 holes). There are no caddies. A full set of clubs rents for $10; gas golf carts rent for $13 for 9 holes, $26 for 18 holes; handcart rental is $5 for 9 or 18 holes.

**Open:** Daily 7:30am–6:30pm. **Bus:** No. 2.

**ST. GEORGE'S GOLF CLUB, Park Rd., St. George's Parish. Tel. 809/297-8067.**

St. George's has 18 holes, par 64, 4,504 yards. Greens fees for 9 or 18 holes are $24 (reduced rates are available after 4pm). There are no caddies. A full set of clubs rents for $12; gas golf carts rent for $26, handcarts for $5.

**Open:** Daily 7:45am–5pm. **Bus:** No. 6, 8, 10, or 11.

# HORSEBACK RIDING

**SPICELANDS RIDING CENTRE, Middle Rd., Warwick Parish. Tel. 809/238-8212.**

Here you'll find trail rides for $25 per person for 1 hour. The popular early morning ride, a 2-hour jaunt with a full breakfast following, costs $37.50 per person. From May to September, weekly evening rides and lunch rides costing $30 are offered.

**Open:** Call daily 9am to 5pm the day before to make arrangements. **Bus:** No. 7 or 8.

**LEE BOW RIDING STABLES, Tribe Rd., Devonshire Parish. Tel. 809/236-4181.**

Lee Bow is especially for children aged 6 to 18, although riders of all ages are accommodated, often in small groups of no more than four. Instruction is available. Lessons and trail rides are given for $25 per hour.

**Open:** Make reservations one day in advance; call daily 9am to 5pm. **Bus:** No. 3.

# PARASAILING

**SOUTHAMPTON PRINCESS HOTEL, 101 South Shore Rd., Southampton Parish. Tel. 809/238-2332.**

From April to November, this hotel offers parasailing from a 40-foot catamaran. Rates are $45 per person for a single parachute. If you go only for the boat ride, the cost is $10 per person if space is available.

**Open:** Daily 8:30am–5pm. **Transportation:** Private hotel ferryboat from Hamilton.

**MARRIOTT'S CASTLE HARBOUR RESORT, Paynters Town Rd., Hamilton Parish. Tel. 809/293-2915.**

Parasailing here is from a Nordic Ascender, and up to six persons are taken out in a boat at a time. Single parachute rides cost $45 per person. If space is available, you can go along for just the boat ride for $10.

**Open:** Daily 8am–5pm (until July through September). **Bus:** No. 2 from St. George's.

# SNORKELING

Marine biologists have always claimed that far more lies below the surface of the sea than usually appears above it. If you're a snorkeling enthusiast, a handful of Bermuda-based companies are ready, able, and willing to help you.

**BERMUDA WATER SPORTS, at the Grotto Bay Beach Hotel, Hamilton Parish. Tel. 809/293-2640.**

This center offers a glass-bottom snorkel cruise aboard a 60-foot motorized catamaran. Priced at around $35 for a 3½ hour cruise, the experience includes free use of snorkeling equipment, and the expertise of a crew well-versed in the marine life of Bermuda's offshore reefs. There's a cash bar and a freshwater shower on board, as well as recorded music that imbues the event with something like a private party atmosphere.

**Open:** Daily 9am–5pm. **Bus:** No. 1, 3, 10, or 11.

**BERMUDA WATER TOURS, P.O. Box HM 1572, Hamilton Parish HMGX. Tel. 809/295-3727.**

This outfit departs for snorkeling tours twice daily between April 1 and mid-November (weather permitting) from the docks near Hamilton Harbour's Ferryboat Terminal. Large glass-bottom boats, well-equipped with a cash bar, showers, and an ample assortment of free snorkeling equipment are used. On the return trip, a calypso singer helps to while away the time. A 3½-hour tour costs $40.

**Open:** Booking hours 24 hours a day. **Bus:** No. 1, 2, 10, or 11.

**SALT KETTLE BOAT RENTALS, Salt Kettle, Paget Parish. Tel. 809/236-4863.**

Salt Kettle offers snorkeling cruises on a 34-foot cruiser (without a glass bottom) every Monday through Saturday. The $33, four-hour tour includes free use of snorkeling equipment. The boat stops above offshore reefs teeming with marine life, as well as at the sites of two underwater shipwrecks whose rusted hulks are eerily evocative of the many maritime disasters that so influenced the early history of Bermuda. Rum swizzles and soft drinks are included in the price.

**Open:** May 15–Oct 15 Mon–Fri 9:30am and 1:30pm and Sat 9:30am only. **Call:** 9am–5pm Mon–Sat. **Transportation:** Ferryboat from Hamilton every 30 minutes.

# SWIMMING & BEACHES

Bermuda is one of the world's leading beach resorts, its miles of pink-sand shoreline broken now and then by cliffs to form sheltered coves. Many stretches have shallow water for some distance out and sandy bottoms, making them safe for children and nonswimmers. Hotels and private clubs often have their own private beaches, but there is no shortage of public facilities in Bermuda, which are under the supervision of the Parks Division of the Department for Agriculture and Fisheries.

At most of the public beaches you'll find public restrooms and usually a place nearby for drinks or snacks. Although dozens of spots appropriate for sunbathing, swimming, and beachcombing will present themselves to you during your circumnavigation of Bermuda, here is a listing of the island's most famous, arranged clockwise beginning with the south shore beaches closest to the city of Hamilton.

**ELBOW BEACH**  One of the most consistently popular beaches in Bermuda, Paget Parish's Elbow Beach incorporates almost a mile of (occasionally interrupted) pale pink sand and the swimming facilities of at least three hotels into its perimeter. There's usually a $3 fee imposed for visitors who are not residents of one of these hotels. The beach, because of the protective coral reefs that surround it, is usually considered one of the safest beaches on the island, and is the preferred venue for foreign college students vacationing on Bermuda during Easter break. The Elbow Beach Surf Club (tel. 809/236-3535) offers umbrellas and beach chairs for rent; toilet facilities are available. Adjacent to the paid facilities lies the free public beach. Take bus no. 7 or 8 from Hamilton.

**ASTWOOD COVE**  Set within Warwick Parish, at the bottom of a steep and winding road that intersects with South Shore Road, this beach does not have any problem with overcrowding throughout most of the year because of its remote location. Most maps will identify its location within Astwood Park, the trees and shrubbery of which seem designed as a verdant backdrop to the beach itself. Take bus no. 7 or 8 from Southampton.

**WARWICK LONG BAY**  Very different from the sheltered coves of nearby Chaplin and Horseshoe Bays (see below), this popular beach features a half-mile stretch of sand that aficionadoes claim is one of the longest on the island. Against a backdrop of scrubland and low grasses, the beach lies on the southern side of South Shore Park, in Warwick Parish. Despite the frequent winds, the waves are surprisingly small because of an offshore reef. Jutting above the water less than 200 feet offshore is a jagged coral island that, because of its contoured shape, appears to be floating above the water's foam. There are restrooms at the beach's western end.

**CHAPLIN BAY**  Straddling the boundary between Warwick and Southampton Parish, this small but secluded beach almost completely disappears during storms or particularly high tides. Geologists usually admire the open-air coral barrier that partially separates one half of the beach from the other. Chaplin Bay, like its more westerly (and more famous) neighbor, Horseshoe Bay (see below), lies at the southern extremity of South Shore Park. Take bus no. 7 or 8 from Hamilton.

**HORSESHOE BAY BEACH** Bermuda's most famous beach is the one at Horseshoe Bay, South Shore Road, Southampton Parish, where the Beach House (tel. 809/238-2651) contains lockers, changing rooms, toilets, and showers, as well as food, drink, and rental equipment for the beach or surf. You can also buy magazines, suntan lotion, and other sundries you may need. Take bus no. 7 or 8 from Hamilton.

**CHURCH BAY** Although it lies along Bermuda's southwestern edge, at the point in Southampton Parish where the island hooks off to the northeast (and where the waves pound the shore mercilessly), this beach is sheltered by rows of offshore reefs. Marine life abounds within the relatively calm waters, much to the delight of snorkelers and swimmers. Equally appreciative of this location are sunbathers, who nestle within the beach's unusually deep pink sands. Take bus no. 7 or 8 from Hamilton.

**SOMERSET LONG BAY** Whenever offshore storms trouble the waters northwest of Bermuda, the water is considered unsafe for swimming. Its bottom isn't always sandy or of a consistent depth, and many people consider the beach more suited to beachwalking than for actual bathing. Despite that, it's isolated enough from the bulk of Bermuda's population to appeal to anyone looking to escape from the madding crowd. The undeveloped parkland of Sandy's Parish shelters it from the rest of the island, and the beach's long length—about a quarter-mile of crescent-shaped sand—is considered unusual by Bermudian standards. You'll find restrooms, changing facilities, and spectacular sunsets. Reach it via Cambridge Road in Sandy's Parish, or take bus no. 7 or 8 from Hamilton.

**SHELLY BAY BEACH** Set on the north shore of Hamilton Parish within a cove whose encircling peninsula partially shelters it from the direct attack of the mid-Atlantic waves, this public beach offers abundant pink sand, changing rooms, a shop where you can buy souvenirs and film, a snack bar, facilities for the rental of beach towels and both lounging and snorkeling equipment. The Shelly Bay Beach House (tel. 809/293-1237) is open daily from 10am to 7pm. Take bus no. 10 or 11 from Hamilton.

**TOBACCO BAY BEACH** This is the most frequently visited beach on St. George's Island, and by far the most popular with day trippers who visit the historic town of St. George from their residence within more westerly Bermudian hotels. Visually, the beach probably resembles the broad open sands of Bermuda's southern shore more than anything else on the north side of the island. The beach's pale pink sand lies sheltered within a coral-sided cove a short walk west of both Fort St. Catherine and St. Catherine Beach (see below). Look for the area's Beach House, Naval Tanks Hill, St. George's (tel. 809/293-9711), which offers equipment rentals, toilets, changing rooms, showers, and a snack bar. Take bus no. 10 or 11 from Hamilton.

**ST. CATHERINE BEACH** For years, this fine beach was off-limits to anyone not residing within a nearby (recently bankrupted) hotel. At presstime, with the hotel still unoccupied, anyone could benefit from its location near the historic village of St. George's. Set close to the base of Fort St. Catherine, this beach faces the easterly winds blowing in from the central Atlantic. To reach it, take bus no. 10 or 11 from Hamilton.

**JOHN SMITH'S BAY** This is the only public beach within Smith's Parish, and as such, tends to be popular with residents of Bermuda's eastern end. Long, flat, and richly scattered with the pale pink sand for which the south shore is famous, this beach usually has a warm-weather lifeguard whose protection understandably appeals to families with children. Toilet and changing facilities are on site. Take bus no. 1 from Hamilton.

# TENNIS

Nearly all the big hotels, and many of the smaller ones, have courts, most of which are usually lit for night play. It's best to come to Bermuda with your own tennis clothing and sneakers since such an outfit may be required. Colored tennis togs, so popular in America, have now arrived in Bermuda. Before this, tennis outfits had to be white.

Each of the facilities described below has a tennis pro on duty, and lessons can be arranged. In case you didn't come prepared, you can rent rackets and buy balls at each place.

**GOVERNMENT TENNIS STADIUM, Cedar Ave., Pembroke Parish. Tel. 809/292-0105 for court reservations and to arrange lessons.**
There are six clay and two asphalt courts here. Charges for clay are $5 for adults, $3 for juniors; for asphalt $4 for adults, $2 for juniors. An extra $5 is charged for lit play at night. Tennis attire is mandatory. Rackets rent for $4 per hour; balls cost $6 per can.
**Open:** Mon–Fri 8am–10pm, Sat–Sun 8am–7pm. **Bus:** No. 1, 2, 10, or 11.

**PORT ROYAL GOLF COURSE, off Middle Rd., Southampton Parish. Tel. 809/234-0974.**
The Port Royal Golf Course also has tennis facilities. The four Plexipave courts cost $5 in daytime; night play is $5 extra to cover the lights.
**Open:** Daily 8am–10pm. **Bus:** No. 7 or 8.

**ELBOW BEACH HOTEL TENNIS COURTS, 60 South Shore Rd., Paget Parish. Tel. 809/236-3535.**
At the Elbow Beach Hotel, there are five LayKold courts (one for lessons only). Hotel guests are charged $8 (others pay $12) to play here. Two of the courts are lit for night play, when hotel guests pay an extra $2 and visitors pay $3.
**Open:** Call for bookings daily 9am–5pm. **Bus:** No. 1, 2, or 7.

**SOUTHAMPTON PRINCESS, 101 South Shore Rd., Southampton Parish. Tel. 809/238-8000.**
This has Bermuda's largest tennis court layout, with 11 True-Flex courts, 3 of them lit for night play. Hotel guests pay $10 per hour and outsiders are charged $12 per hour; there is a $2 surcharge for lights at night. Rackets rent for $6 per hour, and balls cost $6 per can.
**Open:** Call daily 9am–5pm for arrangements. **Bus:** No. 7 or 8.

# UNDERWATER SPORTS

Bermuda's waters are considered the clearest in the western Atlantic. hence they're ideal for scuba diving and snorkeling as well as for helmet diving. Many of the hotels, as mentioned, have their own water-sports equipment. If not, there are several independent establishments that rent equipment.
*Note:* Spearfishing is not allowed within 1 mile of any shore, and spearguns are not permitted in Bermuda.

**BLUE WATER DIVERS CO. LTD., Somerset Bridge, Sandys Parish. Tel. 809/234-1034.**
Bermuda's oldest and largest full-service scuba-diving operation offers introducto-

ry lessons and dives at $75 for a half-day experience. Daily one- and two-tank dive trips cost $60 and $75, respectively, with a $15 reduction if you have equipment. Snorkeling trips are $28 per half day. Full certification courses are available through PADI, NAUI, and SSI. All equipment is provided. Reservations are necessary.

**Open:** Daily 8am–6pm. **Bus:** No. 6 or 7.

**SOUTH SIDE SCUBA LTD., Sonesta Beach Hotel, Southampton (tel. 809/238-1833); and the Grotto Bay Beach Hotel, 11 Blue Hole Hill, Hamilton Parish (tel. 809/293-2915).**

South Side Scuba Ltd. is known for its daily two-tank wreck and reef dives, costing $65. A Resort Course lesson plus dive is $75. A single-tank dive goes for $50, and you can snorkel off the boat for $20. Deduct $10 if you have your own diving gear, except for Resort Courses; otherwise, the rates include all equipment. The company has two fully equipped, custom-built fiberglass dive boats, with the latest approved safety gear.

**Call:** Day before, 9am–5pm. **Bus:** No. 7 to Sonesta; no. 1, 3, 10, or 11 to Grotto Bay.

# WATERSKIING

You can waterski in the protected waters of Hamilton Harbour, Great Sound, Castle Harbour, Mangrove Bay, Spanish Point, Ferry Reach, Ely's Harbour, Riddells Bay, and Harrington Sound. May through September is the best time for this sport. Bermuda law requires that waterskiers be taken out by a licensed skipper. Only a few boat operators participate in this sport, and charges fluctuate with fuel costs. Rates include the boat, skis, safety belts, and usually an instructor. Hotels and guesthouses can assist with arrangements.

**BERMUDA WATER SKIING, Grotto Bay Beach Hotel, Hamilton Parish. Tel. 809/293-2640.**

Up to three persons are taken out for skiing on board a Ski Nautique. You pay $30 for 15 minutes, $50 per half hour.

**Open:** Mar–Nov daily 9am–5pm, weather permitting. **Closed:** Dec–Feb. **Bus:** No. 1, 3, 10, or 11.

**BERMUDA WATERSKI CENTRE, Robinson's Marina, Somerset Bridge. Tel. 809/234-3354.**

Up to four people can go waterskiing with a specially designed Mastercraft. Lessons are available. The per-person charge is $40 for a half hour of skiing, $75 for one hour.

**Open:** Apr–Oct daily 8:30am–6:30pm; periodically the rest of the year. **Bus:** No. 6 or 7.

# CHAPTER 9

# SAVVY SHOPPING

1. **THE SHOPPING SCENE**
2. **HAMILTON SHOPPING A TO Z**
3. **SHOPS AROUND THE ISLAND**

**M**ost of Bermuda's best shops are along Front Street in Hamilton. Here, where shopping is relaxed and casual, you'll come across many good buys. Among the choicest items are imports from Great Britain and Ireland, such as Shetland and cashmere sweaters, Harris tweed jackets, Scottish woolen goods and tartan kilts, and even fine china and crystal—many costing appreciably less than in their country of origin. Savvy shoppers from the United States will find that prices are at least 25% less than what they would be back home.

Other good buys are "Bermudiana"—products made in Bermuda or manufactured elsewhere exclusively for local stores. They include cedarwood gifts, carriage bells, coins commemorating the 375th anniversary of the island's settlement, flower plates by Spode, pewter tankards, handcrafted gold jewelry, traditional-line handbags with cedar or mahogany handles, miniature cottages in ceramic or limestone, shark's teeth polished and mounted in 14-karat gold, decorative kitchen items, Bermuda shorts (of course), silk scarves, and watches with Bermuda-map or longtail faces.

Liquor is also a good buy. You're allowed one quart duty free. But even with U.S. tax and duty, you can save between 35% and 50%, depending on the brand. Liqueurs offer the largest savings.

For other shopping ideas, see "What to Buy" in Chapter 3, "Arriving in Bermuda."

---

## 1. THE SHOPPING SCENE

The best and widest choice of shopping is in Hamilton (see "Hamilton Shopping A to Z," below). Although the largest array of shops are on **Front Street,** you may want to explore the back streets as well, especially if you're an adventurous shopper.

**The Emporium** on Front Street, a restored building constructed around an atrium, contains a number of shops, including jewelry stores. **Windsor Place** on Queen Street is another particularly Bermudian shopping mall.

The "second city" of **St. George's** also has many shops, stores, and boutiques, including branches of famous Front Street stores. King's Square, the center of St. George's, is filled with shops, with other major centers at **Somers Wharf** and on **Water Street.**

Don't overlook the shopping possibilities of the West End either. **Somerset Village** in Sandys Parish has many shops. But outshining them is the **Royal Naval Dockyard** area on Ireland Island. Here you can visit the Craft Market, Island Pottery, and the Bermuda Arts Centre, and you'll see local artisans at work.

**STORE HOURS** Stores in Hamilton, St. George's, and Somerset are generally open

Monday through Saturday from 9am to 5:30pm. When large liners are in port, stores often open in the evening or even on Sunday.

**FINDING AN ADDRESS**   Some Front Street stores post numbers on their buildings; *others do not.* Sometimes the number posted or used is the "historic" number of the building, having nothing to do with the modern number. But somehow it all works out: you can always ask for directions, as most Bermudians are willing to help. Outside of Hamilton, don't count on finding numbers on buildings at all, or even street names in some cases.

**SALES TAX & DUTY**   There is no sales tax in Bermuda. Bermuda is not a "duty-free" island. Depending on which country you're returning to, you may have to pay duty (see "Information, Entry Requirements & Money," in Chapter 2, "Before You Go").

**"IN-BOND" [DUTY-FREE] SHOPPING**   Goods such as liquor and cigarettes can be purchased at in-bond, or duty-free, prices—often at a savings of around 35%—and should be ordered several days in advance of your departure. You cannot consume these items in Bermuda; you pick them up at the airport at departure. They must be declared on your country's custom declarations. Liquor purchases should be made at one of the island stores, as the airport doesn't have an in-bond liquor store.

*Note:* Like many other nations, including several in the Caribbean, Bermuda falls under U.S. law regarding "Generalized System of Preferences" status. That means that items crafted at least 35% in Bermuda can be brought back duty free, regardless of how much you spent. If you've gone beyond your $400 allotment, make a separate list for goods made in Bermuda. That will make it easier for Customs and ultimately for yourself.

# 2. HAMILTON SHOPPING A TO Z

## ANTIQUES

**HERITAGE HOUSE, 2 Front St. West. Tel. 809/295-2615.**

The Heritage House sells nautical prints, English antiques, old maps, modern porcelain, and the largest collection of fine art on the island. There's also a collection of greeting cards designed by local artists and printed in Bermuda, plus top-of-the-line gifts.

**PEGASUS, 63 Pitts Bay Rd. (Front St. West). Tel. 809/295-2900.**

Pegasus has a wide range of antique prints, engravings, and magazine illustrations. You'll find no better anywhere in Bermuda. The inventory is varied, with old maps of many different regions of the world, and more than 1,000 literary, sporting, medical, and legal caricatures from *Vanity Fair.* These cost $20 to $200, depending on the subject. The hand-colored engravings of birds, fruits, and flowers are worth framing and sometimes cost as little as $40 each. Owner Robert Lee and his wife, Barbara, scour the print shops of the British Isles to stock this unusual store. Most prints range from the late 1700s to the late 1800s and are carefully grouped according to subject. The authenticity of whatever you buy is guaranteed in writing. They also offer ceramic house signs, costing $95 and up each, made at a small pottery in England. Each is unique, since the buyer chooses the design, after which the "house" and the house name or a number and street are hand-painted to his specifications. The shop also has a wide range of English greeting cards, many with botanical designs. All maps, lithographs, and engravings are duty free and will not affect your take-home quota. The shop is across the street from the Princess Hotel in Hamilton.

**TIMELESS ANTIQUES, 26 Church St. Tel. 809/295-5008**

Terra-cotta tile steps lead you down to spacious display rooms where you can look over carved early English oak tables, chests, and chairs, clocks of all types and ages, icons, candelabra, pictures, what have you. The shop also provides expert clock repair and restoration services. Packing and shipping of larger items are arranged for you. The shop is opposite the bus terminal.

## ART

**WINDJAMMER GALLERY, corner of Reid and King Sts. Tel. 809/292-7861.**

Housed in a charming yellow cottage, this gallery exhibits paintings and bronze sculptures by local and international artists. It also has an extensive selection of cards, prints, and limited editions, including photographs and signed silk-screen prints. The gallery has the last private garden in Hamilton, adjacent to the gallery and used for the display of life-size sculpture.

**TOLARAM'S, 101 Front St. East. Tel. 809/292-5469.**

For Asian art Tolaram's truly is, as it claims, the "treasure house of the East." It has carved jade, soapstone, Chinese cloisonné, gold and silver jewelry, Chinese porcelain, Indian brassware, and a host of other objects. You can also purchase Seiko and Pulsar watches here at considerable savings. Another Tolaram shop is in St. George's on Duke of York Street.

## BEACHWARE

**CALYPSO, 45 Front St. Tel. 809/295-2112.**

Calypso has the largest and most comprehensive selection of beachwear in Bermuda. The shop is the exclusive island retailer of Louis Vuitton luggage and accessories, and the only store in Bermuda that manufactures its own fashions. Exclusive and exotic designs by Polly Hornburg are available in a variety of internationally collected fabrics. There are branches at both Princess hotels and the Coral Beach and Tennis Club.

## BOUTIQUES

**BANANAS, Front St. West, opposite the Bank of Bermuda. Tel. 809/295-8241.**

Bananas offers "Bermuda signature" items that are of good quality and colorful. You'll find T-shirts, jackets, beach bags, and beach umbrellas that will let your friends know where you've been. The store has several branches.

**27TH CENTURY BOUTIQUE, Chancery Lane, between Front St. and Reid Sts. Tel. 809/292-2628.**

Long known as a stylish and trend-setting boutique, and on one of the most charming shopping streets in Hamilton, it offers a fashionable selection of designer clothing, as well as shoes and accessories, for both women and men.

## CASUAL WEAR & SUNGLASSES

**SAIL ON BERMUDA, Old Cellar, Front St. Tel. 809/295-0808.**

This shop offers everything in casual wear from bright bathing suits to accessories and children's wear. It also has the best T-shirts in Bermuda. A small addition, called Shades of Bermuda, has the finest collection of sunglasses on the island.

## CHINA & GLASSWARE

### A. S. COOPER & SONS, 59 Front St. Tel. 809/295-3961.

Bermuda's oldest and largest china and glassware store, family-owned since 1897, offers a broad range of fine bone china, earthenware, oven-to-table cookware, and jewelry. Among the famous names represented are Coalport, Minton, Royal Doulton, Belleek, Aynsley, Wedgwood, and Royal Copenhagen. The Crystal Room contains Orrefors, Waterford, Royal Brierley, and Kosta Boda among other selections. The Collector's Gallery is known for its limited editions of Bing & Grøndahl, Beswick, and Lladró. A perfume department has selections from the world's greatest perfumeries.

### BLUCK'S, 4 Front St. Tel. 809/295-5367.

Established in 1844, Bluck's is well known for some of the finest names in china and crystal, including Royal Worcester, Spode, Anysley, Royal Doulton, and Herend porcelain from Hungary. The choice in crystal is equally impressive: Waterford, Baccarat, Daum, and of course, Lalique, exclusive with Bluck's. Upstairs, you'll find a superb Antiques Room filled with fine English furniture, antique Bermuda maps, and an impressive array of old English silver. Bluck's has branch shops on Water Street in St. George's and in the Southampton Princess and Sonesta Beach hotels. There's another at the Royal Naval Dockyard.

## DEPARTMENT STORES

### H. A. & E. SMITH LTD., 35 Front St. Tel. 809/295-2288.

This store has been selling top-quality merchandise since 1889, at substantial savings over U.S. prices. Smith's comprehensive stock includes sweaters for men and women in cotton and in cashmere, lambswool, and Shetland, as well as superb British sportswear. Lladró porcelain and English bone china from Royal Crown Derby, Royal Doulton, Royal Worcester, and Aynsley are featured, along with sparkling crystal from Waterford, Thomas Webb, Baccarat, and Swarovski. The perfume room features cosmetics and an outstanding collection from the top French *parfumeurs*. Smith's is noted for an excellent selection of handbags, gloves, fabrics by the yard, and children's clothing. It also carries such exclusive merchandise as Fendi handbags from Italy, Burberrys rainwear from London, and Rosenthal china.

### TRIMINGHAM'S, 37 Front St. Tel. 809/295-1183.

Family-owned since 1842, Trimingham's specializes in fine European imports at savings of up to 40% and more over U.S. prices. Spode, Aynsley, and Royal Worcester china are featured along with Waterford and Galway crystal. The cashmere, lambswool, and specialty knitwear collection is unrivaled in Bermuda, and Trimingham's own lines of men's and women's wear are famous for their quality. French perfumes and European accessories are best buys here, as are fine jewelry, paintings, and gifts. Trimingham's Hamilton store is open daily. Branch shops are found throughout the island and at major hotels.

## FASHIONS

### CECILE, 15 Front St. West. Tel. 809/295-1311.

Cecile lies near the Visitors Service Bureau and the Ferry Terminal. It's well stocked (with prices up to 35% less than in the United States) and is a center for high fashion in Bermuda. Cecile's claims that a visit to the shop is like a visit to the fashion capitals of the world—from France, Tiktiner; from Germany, Mondi; from Hong Kong, Ciao and Ciaosport; from Israel, Gottex swimwear. Its sweater and accessory boutique is outstanding as well, with many hand-detailed and hand-embroidered styles. Cecile has branches at the Southampton Princess, Marriott's Castle Harbour, and Sonesta Beach hotels.

### ST. MICHAEL (BERMUDA) LTD., 7 Reid St. Tel. 809/295-0031.

St. Michael (Bermuda) Ltd., the brand name of Marks & Spencer, brings you reliable quality merchandise from Marks & Spencer in England. You'll find men's, women's, and children's fashions in everything from resortwear to sleepwear, including lingerie. There are also well-tailored dresses and suits, dress shirts, blazers, and British-tailored trousers, as well as swimwear, toiletries, and English sweets and biscuits.

## FOOTWEAR

### W. J. BOYLE & SON, Queen and Church Sts. Tel. 809/295-1887.

In business since 1884, this shop specializes in selling brand-name footwear made in England, Spain, Brazil, and the United States, including Clarks of England, Bally, and Loake Brothers. Footwear for men, women, and children is offered.

## GIFTS

### VERA P. CARD, 11 Front St. Tel. 809/295-1729.

Vera P. Card is known for its superb offerings of "gifts from around the world." These include the island's largest collection of ship's clocks, mantle clocks, and table clocks. Famous-name watches include Nivada, Girard Perregaux, and Michel Herbelin. The dinnerware collection features such famous names as Rosenthal, and the crystal department offers works also by Rosenthal among others. Hummel and Lladró figurines are on sale, too. Look for Coalport English bone china, and for a collection of jewelry in exquisite designs. Other branches are found at 103 Front Street in Hamilton; 13 York Street and 7 Water Street in St. George's, and at the Sonesta Beach and Marriott Castle Harbour hotels.

## JEWELRY

### ASTWOOD DICKINSON JEWELLERS, 83–85 Front St. Tel. 809/292-5805.

Here you'll find a treasure trove of famous-name watches, including Patek Philippe, Concord, Tissot, Omega, Chopard, and Movado, plus designer jewelry, all at prices generally below U.S. retail. From its original Bermuda collection, you can select a gold memento of the island. Other Astwood Dickinson shops are in the Walker Arcade and at the Sonesta Beach, Hamilton Princess, and Southampton Princess hotels.

### BERMUDA JEWELLERY CENTRE, 12 Church St. Tel. 809/292-4199.

Opposite City Hall, this shop carries a good selection of gold and silver jewelry, and it's the authorized dealer for Citizen watches. The Ana-Digi-Temp watch will even tell you the temperature.

### CRISSON JEWELLERS, 55 and 71 Front St. Tel. 809/295-2351.

Crisson sells, in addition to others, such top-name Swiss watches as Ebel, Rolex, and Vacheron & Constantin. You'll also be able to purchase gold and silver jewelry for men or women, as well as Bermuda charms.

**E. R. AUBREY, JEWELER, 19 Front St. West. Tel. 809/295-3826.**
Opposite the Ferry Terminal, this shop has a rich collection of gold chains, rings with precious and semiprecious stones, and charms, including the Bermuda longtail.

## LEATHER ITEMS

**THE HARBOURMASTER, Washington Mall. Tel. 809/295-5333.**
This is your best bet for luggage and leather goods. Items in its leather collection, many often sold at prices 30% less than in the United States, include leather handbags from Italy, briefcases and luggage from Colombia, leather manicure sets, an extensive collection of wallets, and a large selection of nylon and canvas tote bags. The shop also sells a number of travel accessories, including luggage carts and many other items. Also in Hamilton is a branch store at the corner of Reid and Queen Streets (tel. 809/295-4210), carrying essentially the same merchandise.

## LINENS

**IRISH LINEN SHOP, 31 Front St. (corner of Queen St.). Tel. 809/295-4089.**
At Heyl's Corner, near the "Birdcage" policeman (or -woman), this shop stocks not only table fabrics of pure linen from Ireland, but also a wide-ranging selection of other merchandise from Europe—everything from quilted placemats to men's shirts in French cotton from Souleiado of Provence. European linens purchased in Bermuda can often save you as much as 50% over American prices. The owners go over to Europe twice a year to bring back imports, including Madeira hand embroidery and Belgian lace. The shop has other branches at Somers Wharf in St. George's and on Cambridge Road, Mangrove Bay, in Somerset.

## LIQUORS & LIQUEURS

**BURROWS, LIGHTBOURN LTD., 87 Front St. Tel. 809/295-0176.**
Burrows, Lightbourn Ltd., which is recommended for liquor purchases, has been in business since 1808. You can make your own combination-pack of liquors by asking for a "Select-a-Pac" consisting of any five fifths or two half gallons. Orders must be placed 24 hours prior to departure, except on Sunday, when 48 hours before departure is required. The store will deliver your liquor packages to the airport or else aboard ship. There are three stores in Hamilton, one in St. George's, one in Flatts Village, yet another in Paget, and one in Somerset. Of course, you can also buy liquor to drink while in Bermuda.

**GOSLING BROTHERS, LTD., corner of Front and Queen Sts. Tel. 809/295-1123.**
This large competitor of Burrows, Lightbourn has been selling liquor in Bermuda since 1806. Here's where you can buy Gosling's Black Seal dark rum, perhaps a bottle to sample on the island and another as an "in-bond" purchase to take back with you. The bottle you drink on the island is likely to cost 50% more than the "in-bond" bottle. If you want to purchase liquor to take home with you, you can make arrangements to have it sent to the airport, using your duty-free liquor allowance.

## MUSIC

**THE MUSIC BOX, 58 Reid St. Tel. 809/295-4839.**
By anyone's estimate, this is the largest and most complete record store in Bermuda, with an especially strong selection of music by local musicians whose live

performances you might have heard in some of the island's hotels. Owned by Eddy de Mello, one of Bermuda's most influential music agents, this store stocks albums of the music we recommended earlier, as well as an impressive array of classical and popular music from other idioms. Especially visible are recordings by musical stars from The Bahamas and such Caribbean islands as Jamaica and Trinidad.

## NEEDLEPOINT PATTERNS

**KNIT SHOP, 48 Reid St. Tel. 809/295-6722.**

The Knit Shop is the place to go if you knit, embroider, or sew. There is a good choice of needlepoint and cross-stitch patterns with Bermudian themes, all of which are also available in kits.

## PERFUMES

**PENISTON-BROWN CO., 23 Front St. West. Tel. 809/295-0570.**

Opposite the Ferry Terminal, this shop carries almost all of the world's most popular perfumes, and you can learn something about the art of choosing and wearing perfume, from the shop's helpful "fragrance specialists." Branches of the store are found at Queen Street in Hamilton and at King's Square in St. George's.

## SILVER

**OTTO WURZ CO., 2 Vallis Building, 3 Front St. Tel. 809/295-1247.**

Otto Wurz lies at the western end of Front Street past the Ferry Terminal and the Bank of Bermuda between Par-la-ville and Bermudiana Roads. It specializes in articles made of silver, including jewelry, charms, and bracelets. It also has a large selection of pewter tankards and flasks from England.

## STAMPS & COINS

**BERMUDA COIN & STAMP CO. LTD., Walker Arcade, Front St. Tel. 809/295-5503.**

Philatelists and numismatists will enjoy this shop, where they can browse among a wide selection of stamps and coins, some of which are real treasures. Commemorative groupings are also offered.

## WOOLEN GOODS

**ARCHIE BROWN & SON, 49 Front St. Tel. 809/295-2928.**

Archie Brown & Son, in business for more than half a century, features sweaters for men and women in cashmere, cotton, lambswool, and Shetland; for women, there are matching skirts. Colors range from neutral to spectacular.

**CONSTABLE'S OF BERMUDA, Emporium, 69 Front St. Tel. 809/295-8060.**

Stepping into this spacious and well-carpeted store has induced culture shock in the hardiest travelers. Everything inside has been hand-woven or hand-knitted in Iceland. The inventory ranges from thick woolly blankets to patterned sweaters (cardigans and pullovers) for men and women. You'll also find mittens and wool caps.

**ENGLISH SPORTS SHOP, 95 Front St. Tel. 809/295-2672.**

This shop was established in 1918 and is credited with being one of the island's leading retailers of quality classic and British woolen items for men, women, and children. It has branch shops in the major hotels.

**SCOTTISH WOOL SHOP, 7 Queen St. Tel. 809/295-0967.**
The Scottish Wool Shop carries a wide range of tartans for men, women, and children—all imported from Great Britain. It also has a wide selection of woolens and cottons made especially for this shop. Merchandise includes an array of women's accessories; children's toys; and Shetland, cashmere, lambswool, and cotton sweaters.

# 3. SHOPS AROUND THE ISLAND

As you leave Hamilton and tour the island, you may want to continue your shopping expedition—especially for typical Bermudian items—at one of the following addresses.

For other shopping suggestions, consider the **Bermuda Craft Market** and the **Bermuda Arts Centre** (see "Ireland Island," in Chapter 6, "What to See & Do in Bermuda"). Those interested in Bermudian art might also want to pay a visit to the **Birdsey Studio** in Paget Parish (see "Paget Parish," in Chapter 6, "What to See & Do in Bermuda").

**THE OLD MARKET, Main Rd., Mangrove Bay, in the village of Somerset. Tel. 809/234-0744.**
The Old Market occupies premises dating from 1827, when it was built as a private home. This unusual shop offers everything from old coins, brass, and crystal, to costume jewelry and casual clothes.

**GLOBE GIFT SHOP, King's Square, St. George's. Tel. 809/297-1670.**
This gift shop in a historic old building offers a good selection of souvenir and gift items. You'll find T-shirts, charms, Bermuda cedar objects, and straw bags. The shop, which also sells stamps, bus tokens, cigarettes, ice cream, sodas, and candy, is open daily from 9am to 11pm.

**BRIDGE HOUSE STRAW MARKET, King's Square, St. George's. Tel. 809/297-1853.**
Here you'll find a wide array of straw products such as hats, bags, and calypso dolls. Bermuda pottery and cedar items, T-shirts, charms, and other costume jewelry are also offered.

**ART HOUSE, 80 South Shore Rd., Paget. Tel. 809/236-6746.**
The Art House specializes in original paintings and hand-signed lithographs by artist Joan Forbes. Ms. Forbes is a Bermuda-born artist who studied in Massachusetts and Canada before returning home to pursue a living creating watercolors and lithographs of Bermudian landscapes. Prices range from $10 to $50 for lithographs, and from $75 to $3,000 for original watercolors. She also sells an array of craft and gift items made on the island.

**ISLAND POTTERY, Royal Naval Dockyard, Ireland Island. Tel. 809/234-3361.**
At this popular attraction, visitors go inside a workshop occupied by Bermudian craftspeople. The spacious stone-built warehouse has a gift shop in one section and the workshop in the other. Artisans in traditional aprons toil over potter's wheels, turning out their wares. Since the pottery is made in Bermuda, it is duty free.

# CHAPTER 10

# BERMUDA NIGHTS

**1. CULTURAL ENTERTAINMENT**
**2. THE CLUB & MUSIC SCENE**

The nightlife in Bermuda may not be the primary reason that visitors flock here. Yet there's a lot of it, although it seems to float from hotel to hotel. For this reason, it's hard to predict which pub or nightspot will have, say, the best steel-drum band or calypso. Many of the local pubs feature sing-alongs at the piano bar, a popular form of entertainment in Bermuda. Most of the big hotels offer shows after dinner, with combos filling in between shows for couples who like to dance.

The tourist office and most hotels distribute free copies of such "what's happening" publications as *Preview Bermuda, Bermuda Weekly,* and *This Weekly in Bermuda.* A calendar of events also appears in *The Bermudian,* which sells for $4 at most newsstands.

You might also listen to the local TV station, which constantly broadcasts information for visitors, including not only cultural events but various other nightlife offerings around the island. Also, tune in to an AM radio station, 1160 (VSB), from 7am to 12:30pm daily; this broadcasts news of any cultural or entertainment events on the island. Discount tickets are almost never offered; students and senior citizens sometimes are granted discounts.

# 1. CULTURAL ENTERTAINMENT

## BERMUDA FESTIVAL

Bermuda's major cultural season is the **Bermuda Festival,** staged for a two-month period in January and February. Outstanding artists, including classical and jazz, perform on the island along with major theatrical entertainments. During the festival, performances are given every night but Sunday. Tickets for these events range in price from $18 to $25, and most of the performances are at City Hall Theater, City Hall, Church Street, Hamilton. For more information and reservations, you can write to: Bermuda Festival & Point Pleasant Rd., P.O. Box 297, Hamilton HM AX, Bermuda (tel. 809/295-1291).

## MAJOR PERFORMING ARTS COMPANIES

The **Bermuda Philharmonic Society,** conducted by Graham Garton, presents four regular concerts during the season. In addition, special outdoor "Classical Pops" concerts are presented at the end of May in St. George's and the Royal Naval Dockyard. Concerts usually feature both the Bermuda Philharmonic orchestra and choir with guest soloists. Tickets and concert schedules may be obtained from the Harbourmaster, Washington Mall (tel. 809/295-5333). Tickets cost $18.

Ask at the tourist office if the **Gombey Dancers** will be appearing at any time during your stay. This local dance troupe of highly talented men and women often performs in winter. This is the island's single most important cultural event with African influences, a tradition dating from the mid-1700s and once considered part of the "slave culture." On all holidays, you'll see the "gombeys" dancing through the streets of Hamilton in their colorful costumes.

In addition, the **Bermuda Civic Ballet** presents classical ballets at different venues on the island. Again, ask at the tourist office if any performances are scheduled at the time of your visit.

The **Gilbert & Sullivan Society of Bermuda** keeps alive the musical legacy of these English favorites, staging a production every year, most often in October. Sometimes this group will stage a popular Broadway musical. The events are highly advertised.

## MOVIES

The **Little Theater** in Hamilton is a good choice if you want to take temporary leave of all that gorgeous sun, or if you have nothing else planned of an evening, and would like to see a recent Hollywood or foreign movie that you may have missed back home. The 173-seat theater, located at 30 Queens St. (tel. 809/292-2135), is open seven days a week and shows films at 2:15, 7:15, and 9:30 pm. Prices are between $5 and $7. You can reach the theater by taking bus no. 1, 2, 10, or 11.

# 2. THE CLUB & MUSIC SCENE

**CLAY HOUSE INN, 77 North Shore Rd., Devonshire Parish. Tel. 809/ 292-3193 for reservations.**

For the most authentic show on the island, I recommend the Clay House Inn. It's well worth the cover charge, as you're likely to be entertained by folkloric dancers, a "real-thing" steel band, limbo dancers, and calypso artists. In all, it's a package of real island entertainment. The show starts daily at 10:15pm.

**Admission:** $22.50, including two drinks. **Bus:** No. 10 or 11

**THE CLUB, Bermudiana Rd. Tel. 809/295-6693.**

The club is the most sophisticated place in Hamilton for late-night viewing of the island's nighttime elite. It's above the Little Venice restaurant, which has a discreetly understated mirrored entrance that reflects the two stone lions at its portals. Dress is "smart casual." There is dancing, and drinks cost extra. Complimentary admission is granted after you dine at the Little Venice, the New Harborfront, or La Trattoria restaurants. Open daily from 10pm to 3am.

**Admission:** Nonmembers $10. **Bus:** No. 1, 2, 10, or 11

**EMPIRE ROOM, in the lower lobby of the Southampton Princess, 101 South Shore Rd. Tel. 809/238-8000.**

For sheer glitz and glamour, the Empire Room offers the only Las Vegas–style revue in Bermuda. The carefully choreographed revues are presented on a revolving stage in an amphitheater. The predominant color here is red and the shows are tastefully provocative.

The Empire Room is open from April to October on Monday through Saturday. A dinner and show package is offered at 7pm. Then, at 9pm, the doors reopen for a Broadway-style show that begins at 9:30pm.

**Admission:** Dinner/show package at 7pm $59 per person; Broadway-style show and two drinks at 9:30pm $36 per person. **Transportation:** Private hotel ferryboat from Hamilton.

**GAZEBO LOUNGE, in the Princess, 76 Pitts Bay Rd., Hamilton. Tel. 809/295-3000.**

The Gazebo Lounge is one of the most stylish nightclubs in the capital. This beautiful hotel lounge with a magnificent view of the harbor presents acts of international and local renown. Doors open at 9:30pm for an all-star steel-band performance that lasts one hour. A cabaret developed by Bermuda's most famous choreographer, Greg Thompson, begins at 10:45pm and lasts until just before midnight. For clients wanting a full evening celebration, the hotel offers a dinner/cabaret package for $55 per person, reasonably priced by Bermudian standards. It includes a four-course meal at either of its most upscale restaurants (Harley's or the Tiara Room—your choice), followed by admission to the cabaret. Open from April to October, Monday through Saturday from 9:30pm until the end of the show.

**Admission:** Cabaret including two drinks $32; dinner and cabaret $55. **Bus:** No. 7 or 8.

**THE OASIS NIGHTCLUB AND KARAOKE BAR, in the Emporium building, 69 Front St., Hamilton. Tel. 809/292-3379.**

Acknowledged as the leading disco on the island, the Oasis Club is reached by riding a glass-cased elevator to the second floor of a stylish commercial building in the center of Hamilton. Drinks are served at a black-lacquer bar placed within a high-tech decor. The place is thoughtfully designed to permit normal conversation in one area while a high-volume acoustical system emits some of the best sounds in Bermuda in another. The club is divided into two sections: the Lounge and the Disco. One admission entitles guests to enter both areas. Drinks cost $4.95. Open daily from 9pm to 3am.

**Admission:** $5–$10. **Bus:** No. 3, 7, or 11.

**PROSPERO'S, in the Grotto Bay Beach Hotel, 11 Blue Hole, Hamilton Parish. Tel. 809/293-8333.**

Few guests are really prepared for what they find once they pass the ancient calabash tree that flanks the entrance to Prospero's. If you brought your couture silks to Bermuda, don't wear them here, since dripping water might dampen your outfit more than your spirits. The entrance leads you down a flight of narrow stone steps to a dimly illuminated, concrete walkway that carries you over Bermuda's version of the River Styx, out of which rises a single enormous stalagmite whose base was formed before the grotto was flooded with seawater. The cave is said to be 500,000 years old, but the rhythms reverberating around the rock formations are unmistakably 20th century. Musical styles run the gamut from the 1940s to today.

You can chat on the bridge and eye newcomers looking furtively for Cerberus; or you can stand at the bar, dance under stalactite spears, or select one of several table groupings spread under a plastic Napoleonic tent. The occasional dripping from the ceiling is hardly noticed by the crowd, which can become pretty rowdy during College Weeks. If you're transported to the point where you want to jump into the deep subterranean lake, you won't be the first to do so; and if the waters haven't been disturbed for a while, you'll find that there's a layer of freshwater about five inches thick floating on top of a saltwater base. Drinks cost from $5 and up; there's no minimum. Prospero's is open daily from 7:30pm to 1am.

**Admission:** Free. **Bus:** No. 3, 10, or 11.

## SCANDAL, 119 Front St. Tel. 809/292-4040.

Located within one of the largest drinking emporiums in Bermuda, directly on the waterfront, this nightclub prides itself on its low prices, its plush banquettes, and the vibrant color scheme of black and hot pink. Patronized by local residents, with a broad-based clientele aged between 18 and 40, it plays music that ranges from the 1960s to the most recent releases of the 1990s. Two bars punctuate the echoing spaces of this single-story disco. It is open Tuesday through Saturday from 9pm to 3am. Drinks cost from $3.75.

**Admission:** Women free; men $5. **Bus:** No. 1, 2, 10, or 11.

## A. METRIC MEASURES

### LENGTH

| | | |
|---|---|---|
| 1 millimeter (mm) | = | .04 inches (*or* less than 1/16 in.) |
| 1 centimeter (cm) | = | .39 inches (*or* just under ½ in.) |
| 1 meter (m) | = | 39 inches (*or* about 1.1 yards) |
| 1 kilometer (km) | = | .62 miles (*or* about ⅔ of a mile) |

**To convert kilometers to miles,** multiply the number of kilometers by .62. Also use to convert kilometers per hour (kmph) to miles per hour (m.p.h.).
**To convert miles to kilometers,** multiply the number of miles by 1.61. Also use to convert from m.p.h. to kmph.

### CAPACITY

| | | | | | | |
|---|---|---|---|---|---|---|
| 1 liter (l) | = | 33.92 fluid ounces | = | 2.1 pints | = | 1.06 quarts |
| | = | .26 U.S. gallons | | | | |
| 1 Imperial gallon | = | 1.2 U.S. gallons | | | | |

**To convert liters to U.S. gallons,** multiply the number of liters by .26.
**To convert U.S. gallons to liters,** multiply the number of gallons by 3.79.
**To convert Imperial gallons to U.S. gallons,** multiply the number of Imperial gallons by 1.2.
**To convert U.S. gallons to Imperial gallons,** multiply the number of U.S. gallons by .83.

### WEIGHT

| | | |
|---|---|---|
| 1 gram (g) | = | .035 ounces (*or* about a paperclip's weight) |
| 1 kilogram (kg) | = | 35.2 ounces |
| | = | 2.2 pounds |
| 1 metric ton | = | 2,205 pounds (1.1 short ton) |

**To convert kilograms to pounds,** multiply the number of kilograms by 2.2.
**To convert pounds to kilograms,** multiply the number of pounds by .45.

### AREA

| | | | | |
|---|---|---|---|---|
| 1 hectare (ha) | = | 2.47 acres | | |
| 1 square kilometer (km²) | = | 247 acres | = | .39 square miles |

**To convert hectares to acres,** multiply the number of hectares by 2.47.
**To convert acres to hectares,** multiply the number of acres by .41.
**To convert square kilometers to square miles,** multiply the number of square kilometers by .39.
**To convert square miles to square kilometers,** multiply the number of square miles by 2.6.

# TEMPERATURE

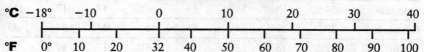

**To convert degrees Celsius to degrees Fahrenheit,** multiply °C by 9, divide by 5, and add 32 (example: 20°C × 9/5 +32 = 68°F).

**To convert degrees Fahrenheit to degrees Celsius,** subtract 32 from °F, multiply by 5, then divide by 9 (example: 85°F − 32× 5/9 = 29.4°C).

# B. SIZE CONVERSIONS

The following charts should help you to choose the correct clothing sizes in Bermuda. However, sizes can vary, so the best guide is simply to try things on.

### WOMEN'S DRESSES, COATS & SKIRTS

| American | 3 | 5 | 7 | 9 | 11 | 12 | 13 | 14 | 15 | 16 | 18 |
|---|---|---|---|---|---|---|---|---|---|---|---|
| Continental | 36 | 38 | 38 | 40 | 40 | 42 | 42 | 44 | 44 | 46 | 48 |
| British | 8 | 10 | 11 | 12 | 13 | 14 | 15 | 16 | 17 | 18 | 20 |

### WOMEN'S BLOUSES & SWEATERS

| American | 10 | 12 | 14 | 16 | 18 | 20 |
|---|---|---|---|---|---|---|
| Continental | 38 | 40 | 42 | 44 | 46 | 48 |
| British | 32 | 34 | 36 | 38 | 40 | 42 |

### WOMEN'S STOCKINGS

| American | 8 | 8½ | 9 | 9½ | 10 | 10½ |
|---|---|---|---|---|---|---|
| Continental | 1 | 2 | 3 | 4 | 5 | 6 |
| British | 8 | 8½ | 9 | 9½ | 10 | 10½ |

### WOMEN'S SHOES

| American | 5 | 6 | 7 | 8 | 9 | 10 |
|---|---|---|---|---|---|---|
| Continental | 36 | 37 | 38 | 39 | 40 | 41 |
| British | 3½ | 4½ | 5½ | 6½ | 7½ | 8½ |

### MEN'S SUITS

| American | 34 | 36 | 38 | 40 | 42 | 44 | 46 | 48 |
|---|---|---|---|---|---|---|---|---|
| Continental | 44 | 46 | 48 | 50 | 52 | 54 | 56 | 58 |
| British | 34 | 36 | 38 | 40 | 42 | 44 | 46 | 48 |

## MEN'S SHIRTS

| American | 14½ | 15 | 15½ | 16 | 16½ | 17 | 17½ | 18 |
|---|---|---|---|---|---|---|---|---|
| Continental | 37 | 38 | 39 | 41 | 42 | 43 | 44 | 45 |
| British | 14½ | 15 | 15½ | 16 | 16½ | 17 | 17½ | 18 |

## MEN'S SHOES

| American | 7 | 8 | 9 | 10 | 11 | 12 | 13 |
|---|---|---|---|---|---|---|---|
| Continental | 39½ | 41 | 42 | 43 | 44½ | 46 | 47 |
| British | 6 | 7 | 8 | 9 | 10 | 11 | 12 |

## MEN'S HATS

| American | 6⅞ | 7⅛ | 7¼ | 7⅜ | 7½ | 7⅝ |
|---|---|---|---|---|---|---|
| Continental | 55 | 56 | 58 | 59 | 60 | 61 |
| British | 6¼ | 6⅞ | 7⅛ | 7¼ | 7⅜ | 7½ |

## CHILDREN'S CLOTHING

| American | 3 | 4 | 5 | 6 | 6X |
|---|---|---|---|---|---|
| Continental | 98 | 104 | 110 | 116 | 122 |
| British | 18 | 20 | 22 | 24 | 26 |

## CHILDREN'S SHOES

| American | 8 | 9 | 10 | 11 | 12 | 13 | 1 | 2 | 3 |
|---|---|---|---|---|---|---|---|---|---|
| Continental | 24 | 25 | 27 | 28 | 29 | 30 | 32 | 33 | 34 |
| British | 7 | 8 | 9 | 10 | 11 | 12 | 13 | 1 | 2 |

# INDEX

## GENERAL INFORMATION

# SIGHTS & ATTRACTIONS

**NOTE:** An asterisk * indicates one of author's favorite.

# ACCOMMODATIONS

**KEY TO ABBREVIATIONS:** B = Budget; CC = Cottage colonies; E = Expensive; GH = Guesthouses; HU = Housekeeping units; M = Moderate; R = Resort hotels; $ = Super-value choice; VE = Very expensive; * = Author's favorite.

# RESTAURANTS

## BY CUISINE

**KEY TO ABBREVIATIONS:** B = Budget; E = Expensive; I = Inexpensive; M = Moderate; $ = Super-value choice; VE = Very expensive; * = Author's favorite.

# BY LOCATION

*AC1*

## Please Send Me the Books Checked Below:

### FROMMER'S COMPREHENSIVE GUIDES
(Guides listing facilities from budget to deluxe,
with emphasis on the medium-priced)

| | Retail Price | Code | | Retail Price | Code |
|---|---|---|---|---|---|
| ☐ Acapulco/Ixtapa/Taxco 1993–94 | $15.00 | C120 | ☐ Jamaica/Barbados 1993–94 | $15.00 | C105 |
| ☐ Alaska 1994–95 | $17.00 | C130 | ☐ Japan 1992–93 | $19.00 | C020 |
| ☐ Arizona 1993–94 | $18.00 | C101 | ☐ Morocco 1992–93 | $18.00 | C021 |
| ☐ Australia 1992–93 | $18.00 | C002 | ☐ Nepal 1994–95 | $18.00 | C126 |
| ☐ Austria 1993–94 | $19.00 | C119 | ☐ New England 1993 | $17.00 | C114 |
| ☐ Belgium/Holland/ Luxembourg 1993–94 | $18.00 | C106 | ☐ New Mexico 1993–94 | $15.00 | C117 |
| ☐ Bahamas 1994–95 | $17.00 | C121 | ☐ New York State 1994–95 | $19.00 | C132 |
| ☐ Bermuda 1994–95 | $15.00 | C122 | ☐ Northwest 1991–92 | $17.00 | C026 |
| ☐ Brazil 1993–94 | $20.00 | C111 | ☐ Portugal 1992–93 | $16.00 | C027 |
| ☐ California 1993 | $18.00 | C112 | ☐ Puerto Rico 1993–94 | $15.00 | C103 |
| ☐ Canada 1992–93 | $18.00 | C009 | ☐ Puerto Vallarta/Manzanillo/ Guadalajara 1992–93 | $14.00 | C028 |
| ☐ Caribbean 1994 | $18.00 | C123 | ☐ Scandinavia 1993–94 | $19.00 | C118 |
| ☐ Carolinas/Georgia 1994–95 | $17.00 | C128 | ☐ Scotland 1992–93 | $16.00 | C040 |
| ☐ Colorado 1993–94 | $16.00 | C100 | ☐ Skiing Europe 1989–90 | $15.00 | C030 |
| ☐ Cruises 1993–94 | $19.00 | C107 | ☐ South Pacific 1992–93 | $20.00 | C031 |
| ☐ DE/MD/PA & NJ Shore 1992–93 | $19.00 | C012 | ☐ Spain 1993–94 | $19.00 | C115 |
| ☐ Egypt 1990–91 | $17.00 | C013 | ☐ Switzerland/Liechtenstein 1992–93 | $19.00 | C032 |
| ☐ England 1994 | $18.00 | C129 | ☐ Thailand 1992–93 | $20.00 | C033 |
| ☐ Florida 1994 | $18.00 | C124 | ☐ U.S.A. 1993–94 | $19.00 | C116 |
| ☐ France 1994–95 | $20.00 | C131 | ☐ Virgin Islands 1994–95 | $13.00 | C127 |
| ☐ Germany 1994 | $19.00 | C125 | ☐ Virginia 1992–93 | $14.00 | C037 |
| ☐ Italy 1994 | $19.00 | C130 | ☐ Yucatán 1993–94 | $18.00 | C110 |

### FROMMER'S $-A-DAY GUIDES
(Guides to low-cost tourist accommodations and facilities)

| | Retail Price | Code | | Retail Price | Code |
|---|---|---|---|---|---|
| ☐ Australia on $45  1993–94 | $18.00 | D102 | ☐ Mexico on $45  1994 | $19.00 | D116 |
| ☐ Costa Rica/Guatemala/ Belize on $35  1993–94 | $17.00 | D108 | ☐ New York on $70  1992–93 | $16.00 | D016 |
| ☐ Eastern Europe on $30  1993–94 | $18.00 | D110 | ☐ New Zealand on $45  1993–94 | $18.00 | D103 |
| ☐ England on $60  1994 | $18.00 | D112 | ☐ Scotland/Wales on $50  1992–93 | $18.00 | D019 |
| ☐ Europe on $50  1994 | $19.00 | D115 | ☐ South America on $40  1993–94 | $19.00 | D109 |
| ☐ Greece on $45  1993–94 | $19.00 | D100 | | | |
| ☐ Hawaii on $75  1994 | $19.00 | D113 | ☐ Turkey on $40  1992–93 | $22.00 | D023 |
| ☐ India on $40  1992–93 | $20.00 | D010 | ☐ Washington, D.C. on $40  1992–93 | $17.00 | D024 |
| ☐ Ireland on $40  1992–93 | $17.00 | D011 | | | |
| ☐ Israel on $45  1993–94 | $18.00 | D101 | | | |

### FROMMER'S CITY $-A-DAY GUIDES
(Pocket-size guides with an emphasis on low-cost tourist accommodations and facilities)

| | Retail Price | Code | | Retail Price | Code |
|---|---|---|---|---|---|
| ☐ Berlin on $40  1994–95 | $12.00 | D111 | ☐ Madrid on $50  1992–93 | $13.00 | D014 |
| ☐ Copenhagen on $50  1992–93 | $12.00 | D003 | ☐ Paris on $45  1994–95 | $12.00 | D117 |
| ☐ London on $45  1994–95 | $12.00 | D114 | ☐ Stockholm on $50  1992–93 | $13.00 | D022 |

## FROMMER'S WALKING TOURS
(With routes and detailed maps, these companion guides point out
the places and pleasures that make a city unique)

| | Retail Price | Code | | Retail Price | Code |
|---|---|---|---|---|---|
| ☐ Berlin | $12.00 | W100 | ☐ Paris | $12.00 | W103 |
| ☐ London | $12.00 | W101 | ☐ San Francisco | $12.00 | W104 |
| ☐ New York | $12.00 | W102 | ☐ Washington, D.C. | $12.00 | W105 |

## FROMMER'S TOURING GUIDES
(Color-illustrated guides that include walking tours, cultural and historic
sites, and practical information)

| | Retail Price | Code | | Retail Price | Code |
|---|---|---|---|---|---|
| ☐ Amsterdam | $11.00 | T001 | ☐ New York | $11.00 | T008 |
| ☐ Barcelona | $14.00 | T015 | ☐ Rome | $11.00 | T010 |
| ☐ Brazil | $11.00 | T003 | ☐ Scotland | $10.00 | T011 |
| ☐ Florence | $ 9.00 | T005 | ☐ Sicily | $15.00 | T017 |
| ☐ Hong Kong/Singapore/ | | | ☐ Tokyo | $15.00 | T016 |
| Macau | $11.00 | T006 | ☐ Turkey | $11.00 | T013 |
| ☐ Kenya | $14.00 | T018 | ☐ Venice | $ 9.00 | T014 |
| ☐ London | $13.00 | T007 | | | |

## FROMMER'S FAMILY GUIDES

| | Retail Price | Code | | Retail Price | Code |
|---|---|---|---|---|---|
| ☐ California with Kids | $18.00 | F100 | ☐ San Francisco with Kids | $17.00 | F004 |
| ☐ Los Angeles with Kids | $17.00 | F002 | ☐ Washington, D.C. with Kids | $17.00 | F005 |
| ☐ New York City with Kids | $18.00 | F003 | | | |

## FROMMER'S CITY GUIDES
(Pocket-size guides to sightseeing and tourist accommodations and
facilities in all price ranges)

| | Retail Price | Code | | Retail Price | Code |
|---|---|---|---|---|---|
| ☐ Amsterdam  1993–94 | $13.00 | S110 | ☐ Montreál/Québec | | |
| ☐ Athens  1993–94 | $13.00 | S114 | City  1993–94 | $13.00 | S125 |
| ☐ Atlanta  1993–94 | $13.00 | S112 | ☐ New Orleans  1993–94 | $13.00 | S103 |
| ☐ Atlantic City/Cape | | | ☐ New York  1993 | $13.00 | S120 |
| May  1993–94 | $13.00 | S130 | ☐ Orlando  1994 | $13.00 | S135 |
| ☐ Bangkok  1992–93 | $13.00 | S005 | ☐ Paris  1993–94 | $13.00 | S109 |
| ☐ Barcelona/Majorca/ | | | ☐ Philadelphia  1993–94 | $13.00 | S113 |
| Minorca/Ibiza  1993–94 | $13.00 | S115 | ☐ Rio  1991–92 | $ 9.00 | S029 |
| ☐ Berlin  1993–94 | $13.00 | S116 | ☐ Rome  1993–94 | $13.00 | S111 |
| ☐ Boston  1993–94 | $13.00 | S117 | ☐ Salt Lake City  1991–92 | $ 9.00 | S031 |
| ☐ Cancún/Cozumel  1991– | | | ☐ San Diego  1993–94 | $13.00 | S107 |
| 92 | $ 9.00 | S010 | ☐ San Francisco  1994 | $13.00 | S133 |
| ☐ Chicago  1993–94 | $13.00 | S122 | ☐ Santa Fe/Taos/ | | |
| ☐ Denver/Boulder/Colorado | | | Albuquerque  1993–94 | $13.00 | S108 |
| Springs  1993–94 | $13.00 | S131 | ☐ Seattle/Portland  1992–93 | $12.00 | S035 |
| ☐ Dublin  1993–94 | $13.00 | S128 | ☐ St. Louis/Kansas | | |
| ☐ Hawaii  1992 | $12.00 | S014 | City  1993–94 | $13.00 | S127 |
| ☐ Hong Kong  1992–93 | $12.00 | S015 | ☐ Sydney  1993–94 | $13.00 | S129 |
| ☐ Honolulu/Oahu  1994 | $13.00 | S134 | ☐ Tampa/St. | | |
| ☐ Las Vegas  1993–94 | $13.00 | S121 | Petersburg  1993–94 | $13.00 | S105 |
| ☐ London  1994 | $13.00 | S132 | ☐ Tokyo  1992–93 | $13.00 | S039 |
| ☐ Los Angeles  1993–94 | $13.00 | S123 | ☐ Toronto  1993–94 | $13.00 | S126 |
| ☐ Madrid/Costa del | | | ☐ Vancouver/Victoria  1990– | | |
| Sol  1993–94 | $13.00 | S124 | 91 | $ 8.00 | S041 |
| ☐ Miami  1993–94 | $13.00 | S118 | ☐ Washington, D.C.  1993 | $13.00 | S102 |
| ☐ Minneapolis/St. | | | | | |
| Paul  1993–94 | $13.00 | S119 | | | |

## *Other Titles Available at Membership Prices*

### SPECIAL EDITIONS

| | Retail Price | Code | | Retail Price | Code |
|---|---|---|---|---|---|
| ☐ Bed & Breakfast North America | $15.00 | P002 | ☐ Marilyn Wood's Wonderful Weekends (within a 250-mile radius of NYC) | $12.00 | P017 |
| ☐ Bed & Breakfast Southwest | $16.00 | P100 | ☐ National Park Guide 1993 | $15.00 | P101 |
| ☐ Caribbean Hideaways | $16.00 | P103 | ☐ Where to Stay U.S.A. | $15.00 | P102 |

### GAULT MILLAU'S "BEST OF" GUIDES
(The only guides that distinguish the truly superlative from the merely overrated)

| | Retail Price | Code | | Retail Price | Code |
|---|---|---|---|---|---|
| ☐ Chicago | $16.00 | G002 | ☐ New England | $16.00 | G010 |
| ☐ Florida | $17.00 | G003 | ☐ New Orleans | $17.00 | G011 |
| ☐ France | $17.00 | G004 | ☐ New York | $17.00 | G012 |
| ☐ Germany | $18.00 | G018 | ☐ Paris | $17.00 | G013 |
| ☐ Hawaii | $17.00 | G006 | ☐ San Francisco | $17.00 | G014 |
| ☐ Hong Kong | $17.00 | G007 | ☐ Thailand | $18.00 | G019 |
| ☐ London | $17.00 | G009 | ☐ Toronto | $17.00 | G020 |
| ☐ Los Angeles | $17.00 | G005 | ☐ Washington, D.C. | $17.00 | G017 |

### THE REAL GUIDES
(Opinionated, politically aware guides for youthful budget-minded travelers)

| | Retail Price | Code | | Retail Price | Code |
|---|---|---|---|---|---|
| ☐ Able to Travel | $20.00 | R112 | ☐ Kenya | $12.95 | R015 |
| ☐ Amsterdam | $13.00 | R100 | ☐ Mexico | $11.95 | R128 |
| ☐ Barcelona | $13.00 | R101 | ☐ Morocco | $14.00 | R129 |
| ☐ Belgium/Holland/ Luxembourg | $16.00 | R031 | ☐ Nepal | $14.00 | R018 |
| ☐ Berlin | $13.00 | R123 | ☐ New York | $13.00 | R019 |
| ☐ Brazil | $13.95 | R003 | ☐ Paris | $13.00 | R130 |
| ☐ California & the West Coast | $17.00 | R121 | ☐ Peru | $12.95 | R021 |
| ☐ Canada | $15.00 | R103 | ☐ Poland | $13.95 | R131 |
| ☐ Czechoslovakia | $15.00 | R124 | ☐ Portugal | $16.00 | R126 |
| ☐ Egypt | $19.00 | R105 | ☐ Prague | $15.00 | R113 |
| ☐ Europe | $18.00 | R122 | ☐ San Francisco & the Bay Area | $11.95 | R024 |
| ☐ Florida | $14.00 | R006 | ☐ Scandinavia | $14.95 | R025 |
| ☐ France | $18.00 | R106 | ☐ Spain | $16.00 | R026 |
| ☐ Germany | $18.00 | R107 | ☐ Thailand | $17.00 | R119 |
| ☐ Greece | $18.00 | R108 | ☐ Tunisia | $17.00 | R115 |
| ☐ Guatemala/Belize | $14.00 | R127 | ☐ Turkey | $13.95 | R027 |
| ☐ Hong Kong/Macau | $11.95 | R011 | ☐ U.S.A. | $18.00 | R117 |
| ☐ Hungary | $14.95 | R118 | ☐ Venice | $11.95 | R028 |
| ☐ Ireland | $17.00 | R120 | ☐ Women Travel | $12.95 | R029 |
| ☐ Italy | $18.00 | R125 | ☐ Yugoslavia | $12.95 | R030 |